BILLION DOLLAR LOSER

BILLION DOLLAR LOSER

The Epic Rise and Spectacular Fall
of Adam Neumann and WeWork

REEVES WIEDEMAN

HODDER &
STOUGHTON

First published in Great Britain in 2020 by Hodder & Stoughton
An Hachette UK company

1

A CIP catalogue record for this title is available from the British Library

Hardback ISBN 9781529385069
Trade Paperback ISBN 9781529385076

Printed and bound in Great Britain by Clays Ltd, Elcograf S.p.A.

Hodder & Stoughton policy is to use papers that are natural, renewable
and recyclable products and made from wood grown in sustainable
forests. The logging and manufacturing processes are expected to conform
to the environmental regulations of the country of origin.

Hodder & Stoughton Ltd
Carmelite House
50 Victoria Embankment
London EC4Y 0DZ

www.hodder.co.uk

For Mom and Dad

CONTENTS

CONTENTS

"Either Adam will end up in jail, or he'll become a millionaire."
—Adam Neumann's high school driving instructor

BILLION DOLLAR LOSER

PROLOGUE

ON THE MORNING of April 12, 2019, Adam Neumann welcomed me into his office for one of the final interviews he would give as the cofounder and CEO of WeWork. Visitors to Adam's office over the years, as WeWork moved from one headquarters to another, were often struck by the fact that as his company got better at squeezing workers into ever-smaller spaces, Neumann's personal office kept getting bigger and bigger. He no longer had the punching bag, the gong, or the bar that occupied his previous suite, but this version had a private bathroom with a sauna and a cold-plunge tub. As we sat down at a round table so large it wouldn't fit inside many of the glass-walled cubicles for which WeWork had become known, Neumann apologized for the fact that his time was limited. "It's hard in a short time to get to know someone," he told me. "And to authentically describe truth."

Neumann had been running late, as he often was, which gave me time to survey the main floor of WeWork's headquarters, a workday playland at the top of a six-story building in New York City. It was late morning, and a barista was serving a second helping of caffeine to WeWork employees and their smiling visitors — refugees from stale offices elsewhere in the city. A large foyer was filled with couches and low-slung lounge chairs upholstered in bright primary colors, foosball and bumper-pool tables, and three flat-top arcade machines where pairs of employees were taking meetings.

Beneath a kitchen canopy draped with hanging plants, several water coolers were stuffed with a rotating orchard of fruit—watermelon, pine-apple, cantaloupe—and a dozen taps serving beer, cider, cold brew, seltzer, Merlot, Pinot Grigio, and kombuchas, plural. A placard helpfully explained to the company's fresh-faced workforce, where thirty-year-olds felt like senior citizens, that tilting your glass while dispensing a beer would lead to a smoother pour. The kitchen was flanked on one side by a series of restaurant-style booths, for casual meetings, and on the other by several long tables with no assigned seats. Each position had a sensor allowing any WeWorker to digitally mark that territory as his or hers for the day.

This was a version of the offices WeWork operated in more than four hundred locations around the world. People seemed to be getting work done, but it was hard to tell. The whole floor was crowded and noisy. The speaker system loudly played Lenny Kravitz's "Fly Away." A sign adver-tised a happy hour celebrating the final season of *Game of Thrones*.

When Neumann appeared, he strode into the room from the back of the sixth floor past the long tables where a few dozen of his employees worked on laptops. At six feet five inches, he towered over the trio of businessmen he was escorting to the exit, along with everyone else in the room. Neumann was intimidating to many of the WeWork executives who worked most closely with him, and induced caution among those wary of his ambition. But to many others—the employees inspired by his motivational speeches, the landlords who happily fed his insatiable appe-tite for real estate, the investors eager to latch themselves onto the next rocket ship—Neumann had become a millennial prophet for a new way of working and living, brushing back his flowing dark hair as he dispensed koans and made bombastic proclamations that somehow came true.

WeWork's core business was simple. It leased space, cut it up, and rented out each slice with an upcharge for hip design, flexibility, and regular happy hours. Other companies had risen, and in many cases fallen, by offering more or less the same service, which amounted to a straightforward arbitrage: lease long, rent short, and collect the margin. What separated Neumann's company was not only the impressive amount of physical space it occupied, with locations across thirty countries and counting, but also the grandeur of Neumann's vision for what the company would become. He had long resisted the obvious—that WeWork was a real estate leasing company—insisting that it was anything but: it was a tech start-up, a social network, a "community company," an organization bent on reshaping society. "We are here in order to change the world," Neumann once said. "Nothing less than that interests me."

* * *

IN THE NINE YEARS since WeWork's founding, practically every New York landlord, investor, and industry titan could tell a personal story about Neumann punctuating a business meeting with tequila shots. When we met, Neumann was wearing sneakers, black jeans, and a gray T-shirt—a study in nonchalance—and asked one of his assistants for hot water with lemon and ginger. He was still five months from the swift and sudden events that would find him walking the streets of New York barefoot, trying to maintain control of his company in the middle of the most humiliating attempt at a public offering in American business history, followed by his ouster with what appeared to be a billion-dollar exit package that fell apart once the world became a place where the last thing anyone wanted was high-density office space.

If Neumann sensed that the seeds of his demise had already been planted and were beginning to sprout, he showed no fear. "Our trajectory looks like Amazon's," Neumann told me, with a Magic 8 Ball resting behind him on his desk. "Except our market is larger and our growth is faster."

The boast was one Neumann had repeated many times, but he had a way of delivering canned lines with an enthusiasm that made each one feel handcrafted for its recipient. By 2019, every hyperambitious start-up founder—was there now any other kind?—presented his or her business as having the makings of a world-changing global behemoth. But it took a special kind of hubris to claim you would one day stare down Jeff Bezos in the rearview mirror. "Think of the stage that we're in as the books for Amazon," he said. "They used books to enter into the Every-thing Store. We used the work mission to enter into a larger category." What category was that? "The larger category of *life*." WeWork had just announced a new location in Johannesburg, putting the company on its sixth continent. "We're not going to Africa because we think that's a huge growth opportunity," Neumann told me. He described the decision to open in South Africa as a duty, given what he says he knew about "how we affect the GDP, how we affect employment."

Claiming an ability to bend entire economies to his will was a bold declaration for an entrepreneur just shy of his fortieth birthday. But Neumann had reason to feel confident. WeWork had become the largest office tenant in New York City, and second in London only to Her Majesty's Government. The company had tapped into a desire, especially strong among young workers, for an in-office experience more fulfilling than the one their parents' cubicles offered. The company's revenue had more or less doubled every year for a decade, and Neumann had raised more than $11 billion of investment capital. The vast majority came from Masayoshi Son, the founder of SoftBank, a Japanese technology conglomerate, and one of the few executives in the world whose am-bition exceeded Neumann's. Son had first invested in WeWork in 2017, partly through the Vision Fund, a $100 billion venture capital bazooka funded primarily by the Saudi Arabian government. He spent the final years of the 2010s investing previously unimaginable amounts of venture capital in an attempt to reshape a range of industries around the globe: $7.7 billion for Uber, $300 million for a dog-walking app, $375 million for pizza-making robots. Son had judged WeWork, and in particular Neumann, as uniquely capable of disrupting the roughly $200 trillion global real estate market. In January 2019, a few months before I sat down with Neumann, SoftBank had invested again, boosting WeWork's theoretical value to $47 billion and making it the second most valuable private start-up in America. WeWork bought Lord & Taylor's flagship Manhattan department store with plans to make it the company's next headquarters—a metaphor for the economic shifts of the 2010s: an old-world institution gobbled up by a fresh-faced newcomer fueled by Middle Eastern oil money, a sheen of technological disruption, and an impulse toward empire.

In his office, Neumann pulled out the pitch deck that he and his We-Work cofounder, Miguel McKelvey, had made in 2009, before WeWork opened its first space. The document imagined a variety of We-branded business lines: WeBank, WeSail, and so on. "This is clarity," Neumann said of his early vision. A few months before we spoke, WeWork had rebranded as the We Company, with three separate business lines—WeWork, WeLive, and WeGrow—under the banner of a new mission statement: "To elevate the world's consciousness." I told Neumann that when I shared the slogan with others, their first reaction was often to ask, *What does that even mean?* "That's a good thing," he said. "If they say, 'What does that mean?' it's a conversation topic. We're already there!" He said that each branch of the company aimed to make the world a better place—while making plenty of money in the process. WeWork's mission was to help people "make a life and not just a living." He believed that WeLive, which rented out microapartments with large communal spaces, could mitigate increases in loneliness and suicide so that "no one ever feels alone." WeGrow, the newest venture, was an elementary school run by his wife, Rebekah, with an annual tuition of up to $42,000 and a goal of "unleashing every person's superpower."

I asked Neumann what his superpower was. "Change," he said. "It's the best superpower to have." He said that this ability gave him "access to all superpowers," and asked if I had seen the TV show *Heroes*, which aired its final season on NBC in 2010, just as WeWork was launching.

The show featured a cast of ordinary people who found themselves suddenly endowed with various powers: telepathy, precognition, the ability to fly. Neumann self-identified with one character in particular. "There was one that was very strong," he said. "He had the ability to have all superpowers." The show in fact had two characters with this particular gift. Sylar, a serial killer, takes on the powers of people he murders. Peter Petrelli, the show's protagonist, absorbs the powers of those around him, becoming so strong at one point that the energy building inside him nearly blows up New York City.

* * *

"WHAT'S YOUR INTENTION when you came here today?" Neumann asked me toward the end of our interview. "Are you looking for good? Bad?" I had spent the latter half of the 2010s as a staff writer at *New York* magazine, exploring the increasingly warped start-up economy. I wrote about a rap lyrics website aspiring to "annotate the internet"; about *Vice*, a punk magazine looking to become "the new CNN"; and about Uber, the ride-sharing company that insisted it was much more than that. I visited Uber's headquarters in the spring of 2017, just as Travis Kalanick was being chastened for recklessness in the rabid pursuit of global domination. It felt as if most start-ups could think of no other worthy goal, and now an office-management company in New York City was deploying the same bravado as the new class of world-altering tech companies emerging from Silicon Valley.

WeWork seemed to capture both the early hope of the 2010s and the fractures forming as it came to a close. The company promised community to post-recession millennials entering the workforce with Obama-era ideals—Yes, *we* can. Neumann himself had been a college dropout, an immigrant on the verge of being forced to leave the country, and a failed entrepreneur. Yet through a mix of grit, luck, charm, ruthlessness, impeccable timing, and chutzpah, he had become, on paper, one of the world's wealthiest people—a bipartisan American hero. He mixed spirituality and business more intimately than any other entrepreneur, at a time when the line separating the two became especially blurry, and the world was embracing a new generation of messianic start-up founders who emerged in the wake of Steve Jobs's death, in 2011. "The past ten years was the decade of 'I,'" Neumann said then, passing the torch to himself. "This decade is the decade of 'We.'"

As the Obama era faded, Neumann watched his friend Jared Kushner, whom he met as a boyish New York landlord, follow his father-in-law to the White House. Hyperbole, autocratic leadership, and a disconnect from reality were suddenly assets on the path to power. Neumann attached himself and his company to the fire hose of cheap capital that washed over entrepreneurs willing to take giant risks, enabling new fortunes to be made on little more than ambition and an insistence that your company was harnessing the power of technology—no need to say exactly which one—to disrupt a new industry. Elizabeth Holmes, another once-lauded start-up founder, was accused of being a fraudster for promising something her company, Theranos, hadn't been able to deliver. Spreadsheets were out; megalomania was in.

For all of WeWork's success, its employees had followed the Theranos story with a growing sense of unease as cracks began to appear in We-Work's ever-optimistic narrative. SoftBank's investment was gargantuan by any measure, but Masayoshi Son, Neumann's chief advocate and business mentor, had backed out of an even larger deal at the end of 2018, as the blistering economy of the previous decade showed signs of quavering. Neumann's company spent so much money expanding around the world in 2018 that it lost nearly $2 billion, and even his employees didn't know exactly what it meant to say that they were now trying to elevate the world's consciousness. Neumann had been racing against time for the past decade, riding the longest economic expansion in American history while telling anyone who questioned his risky growth strategy that he wasn't playing by traditional business rules: he had launched WeWork on the heels of the Great Recession, and his goal was to become the kind of institution deemed Too Big to Fail before the next one arrived.

Now, in the decade's final turn, he was racing to the finish line. WeWork was running out of money. Neumann had tapped out the world of private capital and racked up hundreds of millions of dollars in debt. He was preparing to take WeWork public: the only viable path to continue its growth, as well as an opportunity to cash in on what he and others at WeWork had built. Neumann had played the post-recession economy to perfection. The challenge, as his company's stock market debut loomed, was whether he could get out in time.

"Before you ask, let's set an intention," Neumann told me in his office, when I started to pose a final question. "Ask a question that has an opportunity to give something to your readers that could make them grow. And maybe take a second to think." I paused and thought about something that had been bothering me. As WeWork snatched up real estate and expanded into various categories of life, the community Neumann was building seemed to be an insular one that excluded rather than embraced the rest of the world. He liked to call WeWork a "physical social network," in homage to the tech companies he hoped to emulate, but those companies had begun the decade as paragons of a new era only to reveal themselves to be doing as much harm as good. I asked Neumann if he worried that he was building a dystopian WeWorld separate from everything around it, benefiting a few, like him, to the detriment of everyone else. "It's a good question, so you did very well under pressure," Neumann said. He believed that his company was positioned to bring about positive change. "Instead of thinking of it as a WeWorld, let's just think of Powered by We," he said. "Think of it as what we call internally a WeOS. An operating system that makes work better, living better." He wanted to share a new company ethos that he said would define the year ahead: "We are captivated by the limitless potential of We."

Neumann got up to walk me to the door. "I saw you change as we were talking, just so you know," he said, standing over me. "You took in what I said about the fact that you could set an intention. It doesn't mean you're not going to find things that are problematic." He said that if I had any other questions as I spent more time looking into his company, he would happily talk with me again. "We're getting to know each other, and I hope we have a long relationship," Neumann said. "I'm planning to be here for some time."

CHAPTER ONE

Capitalist Kibbutz

WHEN ADAM NEUMANN was a teenager and still living with his mother and sister in Israel, he started taking lessons from a driving instructor. The Neumanns had bounced around for much of Adam's childhood—he lived in thirteen different places before he got to New York, at age twenty-two—and like any teenager longing for some sense of control over his fate, a car offered as much ownership as one could hope for. His mother, Avivit, spent some time teaching Adam the basics on quiet desert roads just east of the Gaza Strip. But toward the end of high school, Adam enrolled in classes with Arie Eigenfeld, who taught driver's ed in Kfar Saba, a town just north of Tel Aviv where the Neumanns had settled.

Eigenfeld didn't need long to recognize that Adam stood out among his peers. He had transferred to the school in eleventh grade, and his classmates remember him as being shy on the first day but never again after that. He wore his hair long, made casual conversation with teachers, and dated older students. More than twenty years later, one of his classmates can still remember Adam walking down the hallway past a group of girls who turned their heads in unison to follow his trail. Arie Eigenfeld liked Adam, too, but worried that he might be too charming for his own good. After watching Adam, with his hands at the wheel of a fast-moving vehicle, Eigenfeld declared at the time that he saw only two paths for

Neumann. "Either Adam will end up in jail," Eigenfeld said, "or he'll become a millionaire."

Adam was not born with his high school confidence. He was the child of two doctors, Avivit and Doron Neumann, who met in medical school at Ben-Gurion University. Avivit became an oncologist, while Doron went into ophthalmology. They married in 1978, and a year later, when Avivit was twenty-two, she gave birth to Adam in the desert city of Beersheba. Adam found his hometown so unremarkable that, years later, when WeWork employees suggested the company open one of its offices there, he objected. Beersheba, Adam said, was "a dump."

Adam endured what he often described as a difficult upbringing. (His great-grandfather emigrated from Poland to Israel in 1934 but failed to persuade his ten brothers and sisters to join him before it was too late.) The Neumanns moved from one small desert town to another, then to the suburbs of Tel Aviv, a nomadic life that forced Adam to break into strange communities as the new kid again and again. He was an indifferent student, and no one noticed that he was dyslexic until second grade, when his grandmother took him to lunch and realized he couldn't read the menu. He had become skilled at fooling his teachers and coaxing others to do what he needed. His parents, meanwhile, were distracted by struggles in their marriage, and Adam had a strained relationship with both of them. Avivit often brought Adam and his younger sister, Adi, to the cancer ward where she worked. "He always saw people suffering," Avivit later told an Israeli publication. "I didn't conceal suffering from them." The long hours at the hospital could be exhausting, and one night after work, Avivit was reading the tale of Snow White as a bedtime story to her daughter when she blurted out, "Snow White had growth in her liver and went to hospice."

Two weeks before their tenth wedding anniversary, Avivit and Doron got divorced. Adam later described this as the hardest moment of his life. He grew bitter toward his mother as she dragged Adam and Adi to more new homes. Soon after the divorce, the three Neumanns moved to

Indianapolis, where Avivit finished her medical residency. Adam struggled to adapt again, this time to a new country where he didn't speak the language—the American government chopped off the last n from the family surname—at an already difficult juncture. "He fell apart," Avivit said of her son.

In Indianapolis, Avivit took Adam to see a child psychiatrist, who handed him a glittery wand. Adam had been asking his mother when she would reconcile with Doron. "Wave it around your parents three times, and they'll get back together," the doctor said. Adam told him that he didn't believe in magic. If that was the case, the psychiatrist said, why was he still clinging to a fantasy? "We went for eight sessions, and I got a brand-new kid—no drugs required," Avivit said later. But the Neumanns were unhappy in Indianapolis, living on Avivit's meager salary. Adam started working a newspaper route and insisted on giving half his earnings to his mother, to cover his share of the rent.

After two years in Indiana, the Neumanns moved back to Israel in 1990, settling in a small town called Nir Am, a mile from the Gaza Strip, in a rocky desert lined with date palms and pomegranate trees. Nir Am is a kibbutz, one of the utopian communities that had sprung up in Israel over the preceding decades, initially defining themselves through a mixture of socialism and Zionism as part of an effort to build self-sustaining communities across the country. Kibbutzniks share both child-rearing duties and professional responsibilities, working different jobs for the same salary.

Even in a more egalitarian setting, Adam struggled to make friends. Most kids on the kibbutz had lived there since birth, and Adam was an outsider when he first arrived. One early attempt at fitting in was foiled when he invited several kids to watch a movie on the Neumanns' VCR only to arrive home and find that his mother had taken the device to the hospital to entertain one of her cancer patients.

Adam would eventually look back fondly at his time on the kibbutz. He made friends and grew into the kind of teenager residents recall wearing his hair in a ponytail and breaking into the kibbutz swimming pool to go skinny dipping. But he would also claim to recognize something rotten at the core of Nir Am's utopian idealism. There were crops to till, citrus groves to pick, and dairy cows to milk, but the primary industry was a silverware factory. Adam observed that one man worked grueling sixteen-hour days running the factory that kept the kibbutz afloat while another man only had to spend half as much time taking care of the kibbutz garden. "I knew that they both made the same amount of money," Adam said later. "And it never made sense." Having lived a disjointed life, marked by divorce, displacement, and a perpetual sense of feeling left out, he had finally discovered a community that filled some of those gaps only to find it lacking. The Neumanns spent just a few years at Nir Am, but when Adam began building WeWork, he said that he had learned some foundational lessons from his time there. WeWork would be "a capitalist kibbutz," he said. "On the one hand, community. On the other hand, you eat what you kill."

* * *

AFTER HIGH SCHOOL, Adam surprised his classmates by enrolling in the Israeli Naval Academy, an officer training program that typically requires at least six years of military service rather than the usual three. Adam's fellow cadets remember him as a talented sailor who seemed to treat officer school as a game, bucking protocol to do whatever he wanted. One of them recalled Adam being reprimanded after giving an unauthorized TV interview with his sister, who had won a national modeling competition that made her famous and turned Adam into a mini-celebrity by proxy. "Every system should have an Adam," one of Neumann's fellow officers said. "It makes life more interesting."

Adam graduated officer school and served on a missile boat stationed in Haifa, but he left before his full term of service was up. He later described his navy career in varying terms depending on his audience, telling early WeWork employees he was a flunky who applied for submarine duty despite his height, while boasting to a friend, over drinks at a chic bar in the West Village, that he had been in command of a warship in the Persian Gulf.

Among the virtues of moving to New York: you can tell your story however you want. Adi had moved to the city to pursue modeling and called every now and then to implore Adam to join her. He arrived in Manhattan shortly after 9/11, with little idea what he wanted to do. Adi had already built a successful career as a model, appearing on the cover of Russian *Vogue* and *Elle* Spain. She rented a fifteenth-floor apartment at the top of a building in Tribeca, ten blocks north of Ground Zero, and let her older brother move in rent-free. Adam's grandmother covered his tuition at Baruch College, in Manhattan, where he enrolled as a twenty-two-year-old freshman.

Adam arrived in New York eager to build a new life while adjusting to a different culture yet again. One New York friend didn't know what to think when Adam walked barefoot down St. Marks Place, the bohemian strip in the East Village, to buy a marijuana pipe from a hookah shop. Adam hated the fact that no one made conversation on the elevator in the Neumann's apartment building; an Israeli wouldn't hesitate to simply knock on his neighbor's door if he needed something, but Adam hardly knew any of his new neighbors. "Is this an American thing, or do people really not want to talk?" he asked his sister. Adi tried to explain that sometimes people just want a little peace and quiet at the end of the day, but Adam wouldn't have it. He persuaded his sister to take part in a competition. For a month, they would try to befriend as many neighbors as they could, as measured by their ability to comfortably knock on someone's door for a cup of coffee or something stronger. Adi won—"She was a supermodel," Adam said, explaining her advantage—but her brother claimed victory. The building became friendlier. Tenants threw welcome parties for new neighbors and sent people off with gifts when they left.

The contest gave Adam an idea. At Baruch, he was part of the first class of undergraduates to be offered courses in a newly popular field: entrepreneurship. Adam decided to enter a start-up competition at school, pitching the idea of a real estate company that would operate communal apartment buildings designed to bring people out of their units and into shared common spaces. He lost in the first round when a professor deemed the idea impractical: even if Adam could figure out how to coax people into giving up their personal space, the professor said, he could never get enough money to disrupt the residential real estate market in New York City.

Adam still wasn't much for schoolwork, but he embraced New York as a living classroom for practicing the art of negotiation on bouncers and by "hitting on every girl in the city," as he later put it. (Much of his course work, Adam said, focused on "women's studies.") The Neumanns made for an attractive duo in the bars and clubs of New York, where Adi's modeling success earned them entry into fashion shows and appearances in society-page photographs. Religion had never been a big part of the Neumanns' life in Israel, but Adam and his sister joined SoHo Synagogue, a religiously inclined social club that aimed to become "the world's first-ever lounge-themed sanctuary" by catering to a young and hip crowd. (Its contact form offered an age range from twenty-one to thirty-eight.) The Neumanns' Tribeca apartment became a gathering point for a clique of young Israelis on the make, with attractive people coming and going on their way to and from a good night out.

But the apartment and the reputation were largely Adi's, and Adam was still figuring out how to establish a presence apart from his younger sister. He told some acquaintances that he might try modeling, but what he cultivated most was an image as someone always there at the end of the night, boasting about how he intended to fulfill his driving instructor's prophecy and get rich—or despairing about how broke he was and would always be.

Over time, the partying grew old. Adam started to wake up after a night out with a sick feeling in his stomach that was different from a hangover.

18

Two years after Adam moved to New York, a friend visiting from Israel surveyed Adam's life and asked whether it was enjoyable enough to compensate for leaving his family and country behind. Adam woke up the next morning and decided to make a change. He decided to start his first business.

* * *

IN THE MID-2000S, a new economy was emerging from the wreckage of both 9/11 and the dot-com crash that scarred the beginning of the decade. YouTube was beginning to stream videos, and Baruch College students were being invited to sign up for Facebook. In this environment, Adam decided that the most promising business he could start would be manufacturing high-heeled women's shoes that transformed into flats. The idea was to allow someone like his sister, and the subjects of his women's studies fieldwork, to walk to and from auditions without stumbling across the cobblestone streets of Tribeca. He later described the concept as *"Hunger Games* meets *Sex and the City,"* but the actual shoe leaned more toward the former. When the first sample arrived, its collapsible mechanism kicked in so sharply that it nearly sliced a finger off one of his employees.

Adam spent a month stewing and thinking about what had gone wrong with his "very dangerous shoes." During a night out with friends, one of them jokingly asked why baby clothes didn't have knee pads. Wasn't it painful to crawl across hardwood floors? The next morning, Adam registered a trademark for a new company called Krawlers, replacing the *c* with a *k*, "for extra coolness," he later said. He came up with a tagline: "Just because they don't tell you, doesn't mean they don't hurt."

Adam threw himself into Krawlers, working out of Adi's Tribeca apartment, with a seed investment of $100,000 from his grandmother. (Adi herself invested several thousand more.) His Baruch classmates were skeptical, but he persuaded one of his professors to fly to China and help source a supply chain. They found a willing manufacturer, but the samples arrived in disarray. The buttons were sharp and had a tendency to stab; the legs were long and baggy, with knee pads the size of oven mitts. As he pitched the product, experienced retailers, not to mention anyone who had ever cared for a child, weren't certain that knee pads were necessary to service the few months that babies spent crawling. But Adam already had a reputation at Baruch as a skilled presenter, and he was something of a unicorn in his chosen industry—a single, childless twenty-something man with a table at the baby clothes trade show, where people lined up to hear his pitch: "My generation will *not* accept our babies crawling on the floor with their knees hurting!"

Adam later made narrative hay out of his Krawlers experience—a charming story about a young entrepreneur with a harebrained idea. But he took the business seriously, pivoting from knee pads to a wider range of baby clothes. As he finished up his final semester at Baruch, Krawlers was large enough to have several employees. But for all his charisma, Adam struggled to close deals, not to mention make payroll. "I was doing about $2 million in sales," he said later. "And $3 million in expenses." The stress had him smoking two packs of cigarettes a day. Ravenously competitive and fearful of another failure, he decided that Krawlers needed his full attention. It was time to double down. Adam dropped out of Baruch just a few credits short of graduating, upsetting his grandmother, and prompting his own employees to tell him he was being a fool.

* * *

ONE DAY IN 2007, Stella Templo was sitting in her office at Spar & Bernstein, a Manhattan law firm that specialized in immigration work, when a co-worker stormed in. Templo and her colleagues were used to dealing with people in their most desperate moments, but a potential client who had come in that morning was talking so frantically that Templo's coworker could barely understand what he was saying. She offered to buy Templo lunch if she would take the client off her hands.

"You can't smoke inside, can you?" Adam said to Templo as he settled into her office. Templo tried to keep up as Adam explained his situation. He had come to New York on a student visa hoping to get rich in America, then go back home to Israel, but he hadn't done the former and wasn't prepared to do the latter. He had dropped out of college to run his baby clothes business, and his visa was expiring. He had already consulted several other immigration attorneys in the city, none of whom offered much hope. If he couldn't figure out a solution, and fast, he would have to leave the country.

Templo found the conversation exhausting and difficult to follow, but there was also something appealing about Neumann's manic energy. He was fun to talk to, even if she wasn't sure what to take seriously. When Templo asked what Adam wanted to do, he replied instantly that he hoped to leave a positive impact on the world.

Templo laughed. Didn't Adam just say that he ran a baby clothes company?

Adam admitted that his current occupation wasn't the most likely path to making a difference, but he thought it might be the start of something. "Would I want to be prime minister of Israel?" Adam said. "Maybe."

Templo ran Adam through his options. He wasn't an ambassador, and he wasn't going back to school. He had recently started dating an American, but they weren't rushing into a green card situation. Eventually, Templo arrived at the O-1A, a visa reserved for "individuals with an extraordinary ability in the sciences, education, business, or athletics." It was meant for people in the top 1 percent of their fields, Templo explained; the paraplegic race-car driver she had recently helped could claim to be the world's best paraplegic race-car driver because he was the only one. As Templo put it, "A Nobel Prize gets you in." Adam, meanwhile, was a dropout selling onesies.

"I don't even know if *you* believe you're extraordinary," Templo told

Adam as he fidgeted in her office, still desperate to get outside for a cigarette.

"Right now," Adam said, "I'm not sure, either."

Templo got to work on the application. (She gave several pairs of Krawlers to her sister, who had recently given birth, and received an unhelpful review: "A baby could never even fit into this.") When she asked Adam to drum up letters of support, he sent recommendations from his Baruch professors, the operator of a baby clothes trade show, and Susan Lazar, his new business partner. Lazar was a fashion designer who had shut down her successful clothing line in 2000. (Lauryn Hill, the R&B singer, was such a fan that she bought out the denim from Lazar's warehouse when it closed.) A year later, Lazar launched Egg, a high-end baby clothes brand that sold a cashmere onesie and matching hat for $195. Neumann met Lazar through a mutual rabbi at SoHo Synagogue, and while Krawlers and Egg covered different markets, they started talking about how they could work together. Celebrities bought Lazar's clothes from Manhattan boutiques, but she didn't know how to expand the brand; Adam's product left much to be desired, but he knew how to make a pitch. They decided to combine Krawlers and Egg under a parent company called Big Tent.

To save money, Adam moved the company to Dumbo, a gentrifying neighborhood just across the bridge from Manhattan. The rent was cheap, and it afforded Adam a private office while his employees handled the merchandise in another room. At the time, he didn't talk much with his staff about making an impact on the world; he seemed more focused on establishing his place in it, and boosting his company's bottom line. Adam liked to walk into the room where his employees stuffed boxes and tally up the dollar value of every shipment going out the door. When one employee asked him what parent would pay $400 for a baby-size leather jacket, Adam replied that moms and dads weren't the audience. "These are 'Granny Grabbers,'" he said. "No parent would buy this, but every grandparent will spoil their grandchild."

To keep the business growing, Adam needed to raise money. Adi had recently started dating Nathaniel Rothschild, an heir to his family's fortune who was also a partner at a hedge fund. Adam eventually scored a meeting with Rothschild, who didn't typically invest in baby clothes companies, but agreed to throw in several hundred thousand dollars.

By early 2008, Templo's application had worked. Adam could stay. His clothes were available in hundreds of stores, mostly mom-and-pop boutiques, all around the country. But as the recession hit, even grandparents reined in their spending. "We are already noticing the tough economic times," Adam told *Women's Wear Daily* in early 2008. (The company got a brief bump later that year when Sarah Palin appeared at the Republican National Convention with her youngest son, Trig, wearing a $60 blue-striped Egg romper.) Adam had burned through the initial investments from his family and was making his way through the Rothschild money. His hands shook constantly from all the cigarettes. Desperate for cash, Adam decided to rent part of his Brooklyn office space to another company, becoming a landlord for the very first time.

* * *

ON A HOT New York evening, while still puzzling over what to do with his baby clothes business, Adam arrived at Rebekah Paltrow's apartment in the East Village, sweating from a bike ride across Manhattan. He was there to pick Rebekah up for their first date. The pair had been set up by Andrew Finkelstein, a college friend of Rebekah's who had met Adam at a party. Adam was twenty-eight with a reputation as a playboy; Rebekah was a year older and hadn't seriously dated anyone in six years. After attempting to make it in Hollywood like her cousin Gwyneth Paltrow, the actress, Rebekah had moved back east and spent a month at Omega, a retreat center outside New York, to become certified as a Jivamukti yoga instructor. "My intention when I met him," she said later of Adam, "was just, 'How do we expand this good vibration to the planet?'"

The couple's first moments were tense. "You, my friend, are full of shit," Rebekah told Adam on their first date. "Every single word that comes out of your mouth is fake." Adam was brimming with confidence yet couldn't afford to pick her up in a taxi and didn't offer to pay for their meals. He talked constantly about money, a sure sign that he didn't have any.

"You're obviously broke," Rebekah told him.

"I'm not broke," Adam said. "I'm an entrepreneur."

Rebekah responded that her father had been an entrepreneur but still managed to make sure she ate. Adam clearly didn't care about baby clothes and wasn't all that good at selling them. Maybe he was just in the wrong business.

Adam would later refer to meeting Rebekah as a transformational event. "Rebekah and I are cofounders in life," he told me. No one had ever held Adam to account in the way Rebekah had, and he started to think she might be right. He was a big talker with little to show for it. Rebekah, meanwhile, saw a potential in Adam she couldn't easily describe. "There was an energy between us that felt like it was larger than just the two of us," she said later. Adam might be full of shit, but their first date seemed like a moment when time stopped, and she could see into their future together. After just a few months of dating, they got engaged. Adam later cited Rebekah as his inspiration to leave baby clothes behind in search of something more. "I knew that there was no ceiling on his potential—or on our potential together," Rebekah said. "I just knew that he was going to be the man that was going to, hopefully, help save the world."

CHAPTER TWO
Green Desk

"I'VE BEEN THINKING a lot about the future," Miguel McKelvey wrote to his mother in a postcard from Greece. It was 1999, and he was on a post-college trip around the world, having just graduated from the University of Oregon with an architecture degree. "I'm sort of losing the idealistic dream of being a 110% architect because it seems like an incredibly hard way to have a good relationship and have kids and all that," he wrote. He was thinking of going back to school or maybe starting a business with a childhood friend. But his friend wanted to stay in the Pacific Northwest, and Miguel couldn't shake a lingering ambition for more. "I still know I want to move to New York," he wrote. "I still have the need to build something great."

Like his WeWork cofounder, Miguel was raised in unusual circumstances. His mother, Lucia, was living in Taos, New Mexico, in the 1960s when she and three friends became mothers in quick succession. The dads left, one by one, and the newly single moms came together in what Miguel described as a matriarchal collective. They lived separately while raising their children communally and found ways to support themselves outside of ordinary social structures and expectations—an American kibbutz.

The group lived a "gypsy-like" existence, as one of Miguel's fraternal "siblings" put it, and ultimately settled in Eugene, Oregon. The mothers objected to the word *hippie*, but if someone insisted on using the term, they preferred "country intellectual hippie." Miguel was "a weird name for a white kid," McKelvey admitted, but it wasn't any stranger than his middle name: Angel. The family ate tofu and tempeh before doing so was fashionable and often sat around in a circle analyzing one another's dreams. Miguel remembers losing sight of his mother at a music festival when he was seven, and instead of growing anxious, he simply lay down in the grass and fell asleep. One of his siblings said it felt like the ad hoc family had created its "own religion."

As in most collectivist efforts, money was hard to come by. The mothers were community organizers and activists, dragging their kids to antiwar protests; when they had to get jobs, Lucia explained to Miguel, "We were all smart enough to fake our résumés." (Much later, Miguel would cite *What's Happening*, the local events newspaper his mother started, as a foundational example of how to engage your community in an entrepreneurial way.) They went dumpster diving behind grocery stores and otherwise subsisted largely on food stamps, splurging for an annual trip to King's Table Buffet, where Miguel ate bowls of soft-serve until he felt sick. For entertainment, he made a game out of dropping bouncy balls through the holes in the rusted floor of the family Volvo and watching them bound down the road.

Miguel rebelled against his upbringing. "I wanted to eat McDonald's, not co-op tempeh," he said. He told other kids that he couldn't talk about his dad because he was an undercover cop. Miguel was tall, and sensitive about both his height and the fact that he was overweight; he tried to hide in the background whenever he could. He played on the South Eugene High School basketball team, where the coach had strict rules—no jump shots from outside the key, never dribble with your left hand—that Miguel found refreshing in their rigidity. He spent the summer after high school working twelve-hour days at a fish processing plant in Alaska, often taking on six extra hours of overtime to make more money.

When Miguel arrived at Colorado College, a private liberal arts school that recruited him to play basketball, he had a vision for his life that bore little resemblance to the one he had lived. He planned to major in business, but quickly found himself hating economics and having a great time in art. During a sculpture class, his professor, Carl Reed, identified something "architectural" in Miguel's work, as if he were trying to solve spatial problems through art. Reed suggested that architecture might offer a happy medium between his interests and ambitions.

Miguel left Colorado College and spent a year busing tables while reading any architecture book he could get his hands on. When he arrived at the University of Oregon, back home in Eugene, he stood out even among the odd coterie in the school's architecture program. (One of his classmates built a shed around his desk, took off all his clothes, and started living inside it.) He was six feet eight inches tall, and landed a spot on the Oregon basketball team, but he was quiet for a jock. Miguel often spent fourteen-hour days in the architecture studio with his headphones on, listening to the same song over and over. He went into what he described as a state of "suspended unconsciousness," only to snap out of it hours later, bewildered by his own myopia. His quiet intensity could be intimidating. One day, a classmate walked up and asked if she could talk to him for a moment. "You know everyone thinks you're a total asshole, right?" she said. "I just want to tell you, you're actually really nice."

* * *

MIGUEL GRADUATED IN 1999 with a 4.0 GPA but no clarity about his future. He had planned to move to New York but instead followed a friend named John Hayden to Tokyo, where they went to clubs and found themselves being asked to translate the vernacular of American pop lyrics into Japanese. (There were a lot of questions about TLC's "No Scrubs.") Over sushi one night, Hayden and McKelvey came up with an idea for a website to help people learn colloquial English. They called it *English, baby!* and gave it a tagline: "Learn English. Find friends. It's cool."

English, baby! didn't have anything to do with architecture, but Miguel had graduated into the peak of the first dot-com bubble. Young entrepreneurs who didn't seem any smarter than he was were suddenly becoming unfathomably rich. "There were so many people getting so much investment money for what seemed like such trivial ideas," he said later. Miguel went back to Eugene and became the chief creative officer of *English, baby!* By 2000, the site had three thousand users in sixty countries with hopes for much more. Miguel figured that within a year *English, baby!* would raise a chunk of venture capital, scale up to a hundred employees, and hit the stock market at a nine-figure valuation.

The frothiness of the start-up economy was so extreme that Miguel's projection wasn't entirely unreasonable. The value of the S&P 500 tripled in the latter half of the '90s, with new companies appearing each week and claiming to harness the nascent power of the internet to disrupt one industry after another. In 2000, a few well-placed tech bets allowed Masayoshi Son, from SoftBank, to rise from relative obscurity and briefly become the world's richest man.

Even as the internet bubble began to burst, Hayden and McKelvey believed they were well positioned compared to other upstarts. "Unlike online bookstores, *English, baby!* can't be easily duplicated by merely walking down the street to the nearest book vendor," an Oregon newspaper wrote about the start-up in 2000. They adopted the hyperbole that was endemic to every tech company: *English, baby!* was "reshaping the way people around the world learn."

But Hayden and McKelvey made a critical error: by 2003, *English, baby!* was profitable. They had downsized their goals, pivoting the business to cater to American universities that might pay for the service to help foreign students. The spoils of the boom, meanwhile, were going to companies that pursued the most ambitious version of themselves. "In retrospect, it didn't go far enough into becoming a social network, and we missed out," McKelvey said later. His vision for the company simply hadn't been large enough.

As Miguel approached his thirtieth birthday, he wondered what he was doing. *English, baby!* wasn't his passion, and if he wasn't going to get rich, why was he still there? He missed architecture, and the itch to get to New York remained. In 2004, he applied for architecture jobs in the city. When a firm in Brooklyn got back to him, asking if he could come for an interview the next day, he lied about his whereabouts, bought a plane ticket, and showed up the next morning. He'd never been to Brooklyn before, but he got off the F train in Dumbo and walked into a beaten-up building where he found JORDAN PARNASS DIGITAL ARCHITECTURE on a company directory that had been scrawled in black Sharpie on the wall.

The two architects at JPDA didn't seem to care that Miguel had been out of the field for half a decade. (He'd followed his mother's example and puffed up his résumé.) They were desperate for help meeting the demands of a new client: American Apparel, the clothing company, had hired JPDA to open its first New York locations. Could Miguel start the next day? It was a Thursday, and he persuaded them to give him until Monday. He flew home, packed up his stuff, and arrived back in New York with only a duffel bag. Miguel's birthday was July 4, and not long after arriving in New York for good he celebrated turning thirty by watching fireworks along the East River from a Brooklyn rooftop. *This is it*, he figured. *I did it.*

Miguel was prepared to begin the long career journey facing every young architect—he was the firm's junior draftsman at $10 an hour—but he found himself on an unexpected rocket ship. American Apparel was taking off, and Dov Charney, the firm's founder, asked JPDA to help open stores all over the country. Miguel was suddenly working less as an architect than as the manager of a national rollout. In four years, he helped open more than a hundred American Apparel locations. He enjoyed the work and liked the fact that American Apparel professed to be doing good by making its clothes in the United States. "We can create jobs in the U.S., and we can treat workers well, and we can use immigrant labor in a positive way," Miguel told a newspaper in 2006.

But cranking out one more or less identical white box after the other grew old, and the company's culture, beneath the surface, was taxing. Charney was a demanding and volatile boss with ambitions to turn his boutique into an empire. "This is the most important moment of your life," he yelled at Miguel when it appeared that a new store in Denver might not open in time for Black Friday, threatening him with serious consequences if it didn't. Miguel held on while Charney pressed everyone forward, and the pace gave him a firsthand look at the pitfalls of unrestrained growth. "We've decided to slow down slightly in order to focus on organization and management," Miguel told a newspaper in South Carolina, explaining why American Apparel was postponing a store opening there.

New York had begun to wear on McKelvey, too. Everything was expensive, and his apartment was tiny. As Miguel surveyed the work he had done, he realized that his greatest sense of achievement had come when he stayed up late to solve a rat problem at JPDA's office in Dumbo. He had watched a rat enter and exit the room by flattening itself like a pancake to squeeze beneath the door; he googled "Can rats flatten themselves?" discovered that they could, and devised a solution to close the gap. But Miguel had not come to New York to score minor victories. One day he decided to take a walk and ended up wandering the city for hours. He thought about where his New York dream had taken him and found the results disappointing. He decided to open himself to whatever opportunity wandered in through the door.

* * *

A FEW WEEKS LATER, Miguel took the train from Brooklyn to Tribeca to hang out with Gil Haklay, an Israeli architect who also worked at JPDA. At Haklay's building, Miguel was followed into the elevator by a man who announced his presence in multiple ways: his height, the volume of his voice, his lack of a shirt or shoes. It was a sweaty summer day in New York, but even so, this was odd. On the ride up, the man chatted with the other passengers, holding the door open to continue the conversation as they exited. *This dude is crazy,* Miguel thought. The man introduced himself to Miguel as Haklay's roommate, Adam Neumann.

Miguel wasn't quite sure what attracted him to Neumann. They were both children of single mothers from atypical upbringings who could talk to each other more or less at eye level: at six feet eight, Miguel was one of the few people Adam had to look up to. In most every other way, they were opposites. Adam's hair flowed neatly down to his shoulders, while Miguel wore his short with a trim, loosely maintained beard—the aesthetic divide between Manhattan and Brooklyn personified. Miguel was shy and methodical, shrinking his personality to rightsize himself; Adam was brash and kinetic, growing taller as he spoke. He was the kind of person you found a reason to keep talking to, and when Adam moved his baby clothes company into 68 Jay Street, the same Dumbo building where JPDA had its office, the two quickly became friends. Miguel's stability and even-keeled nature seemed to serve as a balm for Neumann, while Miguel saw in Adam "a brashness, which I think is cool, but which I don't have," he said. "I like to be *next* to the center of attention."

In Brooklyn, Adam was still struggling to get his business on course. He was pacing constantly around the office, which he did whenever he needed to think, and started wandering around Dumbo, often with Miguel. Both men were angsty about their careers and shared similar feelings about New Yorkers—Miguel couldn't understand why he knew almost none of the other residents in his Brooklyn apartment building. Adam mentioned his old idea from Baruch about building more communal living situations, and the pair spent a few months looking for a residential building to convert.

Eventually they noticed that their landlord was renovating 68 Jay Street. Adam knew from experience that managing real estate was among the most trying aspects of running a young company and told Miguel about an acquaintance of his who ran a business that sliced up a big office space into smaller units and rented out the individual parts to small companies. Miguel had been thinking about office design since his days in Oregon. His walk to the *English, baby!* office went past a building with a ground-level window that let hardly any light into a basement filled with drab cubicles. There had to be something better.

On a whim, Adam decided to ask Joshua Guttman, their landlord, if Guttman would let him turn one of the empty floors he was renovating into a version of the office suite business he had seen. "You know nothing about real estate," Guttman said.

"Your building is empty," Adam replied. "What do *you* know about real estate?"

Adam knew this was a bluff. Guttman owned buildings throughout Brooklyn, while Adam sometimes struggled to pay his rent on time. But he kept asking until Guttman decided to show him another building he had purchased nearby. It was a century-old coffee factory, with exposed brick, wooden beams across the ceiling, and views of the East River. Guttman asked Neumann what he would do with the space. Instead of putting up a bunch of walls, Adam said he would divide up the floor into semiprivate offices with a single receptionist handling everything. He and Guttman would split the profits. Guttman told him to come back with a formal business plan.

Adam found Miguel and told him what had happened. "What are we gonna do?" Miguel said.

"I don't know," Adam replied. He didn't have a name for the business or much more than an outline of how they might operate it. Adam had talked his way in the door but needed someone to build the thing he imagined.

"Okay," Miguel said. "I'll figure it out."

*   *   *

THAT NIGHT, Miguel pulled an all-nighter to craft a business plan. He decided the new space would be called Green Desk, to target eco-conscious consumers. Adam and Miguel weren't climate warriors; they simply thought the branding would attract the kind of customers they wanted. Miguel designed a logo, wrote a mission statement, and went to Kinko's to print business cards and flyers. The next morning, Miguel came in with a rough floor plan and a one-page spreadsheet laying out a basic business model, hoping that if he got everything done overnight, Guttman would presume they had been planning for months.

The pitch worked. Guttman agreed to renovate the space, while the partners each put in $5,000 to start building it out. Adam kept running his baby clothes business but Miguel threw himself into Green Desk full-time, designing the space along with Haklay, who joined as a third partner. They bought butcher blocks at Ikea to serve as desks and put up glass walls between each of them. Miguel posted ads on Craigslist and started giving tours to interested tenants with nothing more than masking tape on the floor to mark where the offices would be.

As they prepared to open in the spring of 2008, the timing seemed as if it couldn't be worse. The global economy was in free fall. Guttman warned them that people don't rent new offices in a down market: big companies consolidate, small businesses collapse, and freelancers work from home.

But when Green Desk opened in May, it was an instant hit. "Everyone who had been fired from their jobs came," Adam said. "Everyone who didn't want to be at home because they were depressed." Green Desk leased offices to a fashion designer, a private equity firm, a calligrapher, and the website Gothamist, among others. "I distinctly remember Adam and Miguel building all the Ikea furniture for the office," Jen Chung, Gothamist's cofounder, said. The space developed into a mini community, with happy hours and chats around the coffeepot; disagreements emerged, but a certain civility prevailed. When Gothamist fought with Green Desk over who should pay for a conference room setup, they came to a compromise. Miguel bought the table; Gothamist bought the chairs.

Green Desk grew quickly, adding floor after floor in Guttman's building, and Adam and Miguel started thinking about what made the business work. The sustainability pitch was all well and good—fair-trade coffee, Seventh Generation cleaning supplies—but they weren't going to solve climate change. As a business proposition, environmentalism didn't offer much more than a marketing gimmick. What people seemed most attracted to was the flexibility of a month-to-month lease and the feeling of camaraderie. When Adam and Miguel filled up the entire building, they threw a party on the ground floor to celebrate and had everyone participate in an icebreaker. Much as Neumann's competition with his sister had opened up their apartment complex, Green Desk became a friendlier place.

Guttman wanted to expand Green Desk into the rest of his Brooklyn real estate portfolio. But Adam and Miguel had begun to think bigger. "We're not gonna change the world with 'green,'" Adam said. They had already run businesses they didn't really care about. Bringing people together sounded exciting and potentially lucrative. Workers were increasingly disillusioned by corporate America and looking for physical connection in a digital era. With the recession lifting, there was money to be made for those willing to take a risk. This could go national, they thought—maybe even all over the world.

In 2009, Neumann, McKelvey, and Haklay sold their Green Desk stakes to Guttman, who set about growing the business in his other buildings. The three cofounders each netted roughly half a million dollars, paid out over the next several years. Haklay decided his share was more than enough and flew home to Israel—the dream Adam had laid out for himself when he first came to the United States. But after years of barely getting by, he had turned a small investment into a lucrative payout in just over a year. Adam wasn't ready to go home. He wanted more.

CHAPTER THREE

154 Grand Street

ADAM TOLD MIGUEL not to deposit his share of their Green Desk payout into his checking account. "You know I'll spend it," Adam told him. They agreed to pour the money into their new venture, which they would enter as equals in the same collaborative spirit they hoped to foster in their new office spaces. The partners were different people, with different priorities, but their company's founding documents would include language declaring that if the cofounders couldn't agree on something, they would stay in a room with each other until the situation was resolved.

Among the first decisions to make was choosing a name—something to signal a communitarian spirit without, as Miguel put it, being "too hippie dippie." Miguel would later say that the defining part of his childhood, when it came to running his business, wasn't growing up in a matriarchal collective but living in the town that birthed Nike and seeing up close how powerful branding could be. This was a business, after all, not an invitation to sit in a circle and analyze each other's dreams. Adam and Miguel were already thinking beyond offices to other kinds of spaces that could be ripe for reimagining—apartments, hotels, restaurants, banks, coffee shops. They wanted a name to capture that ambition.

After months of fruitless brainstorming, Andrew Finkelstein, who had introduced Adam to his now-wife Rebekah, threw out an idea one night. (Finkelstein was a Hollywood agent and later represented Denzel Washington and Lin-Manuel Miranda.) "It's WeWork," Finkelstein said. "It's WeLive, it's WeSleep, it's WeEat."

Now they needed space. Adam and Miguel's separation from Green Desk included a noncompete agreement prohibiting them from operating in Brooklyn for several years, so they started looking at buildings in Manhattan, where real estate prices were still depressed from the financial crisis, as well as San Francisco, where the tech world was rushing to replace Wall Street as the heart of American business ambition. Co-working spaces were popping up all over both cities, with laptop-enabled freelancers renting desks in shared spaces with a DIY aesthetic. Adam and Miguel's hope was to thread a needle between that openness and the cloistered world of traditional offices.

But landlords were resistant to the idea. Companies that had tried to serve as office middlemen before had struggled in recessionary economies. Landlords preferred tenants likely to be around for the length of a fifteen-year lease; an untested company renting space to other untested companies felt like the opposite of that. "Three-quarters of the landlords that we met in the beginning were like, Why don't I just do it myself and then I'll make the money that you think you're going to make?" Miguel said later. "We didn't have a great answer to that question."

On the other hand, even Lehman Brothers wasn't a solvent tenant anymore, and landlords needed to fill space somehow. Plus, Adam was relentless. He went back to landlords over and over again, just as he had with Guttman. In the fall of 2009, Adam and Miguel met the owner of a building on Canal Street that they hoped might work primarily for the residential idea they had in mind. The landlord wasn't interested in leasing to them but said that he had a friend they should meet—in fact, he was on his way over.

Joel Schreiber didn't shake anyone's hand as he walked into the room wearing a dark suit and traditional Hasidic sideburns. Schreiber was a young real estate developer—he was still in his twenties, younger than Adam and Miguel—who had spent the first half of the 2000s building a residential portfolio in Brooklyn and New Jersey before pushing into commercial real estate in lower Manhattan. Miguel didn't know what to make of Schreiber, but Adam was happy to step into the role of dealmaker. He and Schreiber got into a car and talked about the idea for hours. Schreiber came away impressed most of all with Adam's charisma and energy.

The conversation ended with the original sin of WeWork's runaway valuation. While Schreiber didn't have a building to offer, he said that he had money, and he wanted to invest. How much did Adam and Miguel think their hypothetical company was worth? The cofounders weren't necessarily looking to add a third partner but figured there wasn't much harm in throwing out an outrageous number. The next day, they told Schreiber that WeWork, which didn't have a single location, was worth $45 million. Without asking questions or pushing back, Schreiber agreed to commit $15 million to fund the idea in exchange for a third of a company that did not yet exist.

* * *

SCHREIBER WAS A KNOWN quantity in New York real estate, and his involvement gave Adam and Miguel credibility. He made introductions to landlords and personally guaranteed the company's leases. When I spoke to Schreiber years later, he said that he considered himself the company's third founding partner; others told me WeWork would not have happened without him.

That fall, a friend suggested that Adam look at a building at 154 Grand Street, in SoHo. Commercial real estate is rated on a scale from Class A, which includes the world's premier skyscrapers, to Class D—fixer-uppers like the narrow brick building on the corner of Grand and Lafayette that

Neumann was touring. An illegal Craigslist hotel was operating out of the building's north wing, and the entire thing was in desperate need of a gut renovation that would cost millions. It sat across from a vacant lot and had a single cramped elevator that took fifty-six seconds to get to the top floor. There were only six floors.

Even the owner of such a run-down building wasn't eager to turn it over to Adam and Miguel. "We had no business taking out a forty-thousand-square-foot lease," Miguel admitted. The negotiations grew tense with the building's landlord, as Adam and Miguel pushed to keep the rent low while asking for generous construction allowances to renovate the space—a crucial component of the company's future expansion. The landlord, meanwhile, wanted WeWork to hire his brother to handle the remodeling. Miguel would never be the hardened negotiator between the two cofounders, and even years later, he found it painful to walk by the building and think about the tension at WeWork's founding. Adam caused further angst when he declined to pay the full finder's fee to the friend who told him about the building.

But by November, the deal was done. Construction began immediately, with a plan to open one floor at a time. In the absence of anything real to show off on tours, Adam's ambitions filled the void. He told prospective tenants that he intended to put a gym in the basement, and that he was in talks with the city about building a park in the empty lot across the street. (A decade later, the basement still has no gym, and the empty lot remains empty.)

While Adam unfurled his vision, Miguel took on the grubby task of making it real. After evicting the residents in the north half of the building, they discovered an S&M dungeon in one of the rooms. Each floor was roughly the size of one of the American Apparel stores McKelvey had been opening, but American Apparel had a well-oiled formula. WeWork was starting more or less from scratch, and costs had to stay low to make the business feasible. Miguel balked when a contractor's estimate to wire the space for internet came in at $100,000—a number that was suspiciously round and upsettingly high—and figured he could do the work for $8,000 in materials and fifty hours of trial and error. He left the wires exposed, snaking through the halls in colorful bundles; it wasn't refined, but it worked. Miguel wanted to return the painted brick walls to their natural state, so he drove to New Jersey, loaded his trunk with fifty-pound bags of baking soda, and brought them back through the Holland Tunnel as the weighted-down chassis of his car rubbed against his tires. A cloud billowed out of 154 Grand while he soda blasted the paint off the walls. "It was awesome," Miguel said later.

Miguel wanted to make WeWork feel less like an office and more like one of the boutique hotels popping up around the city. He outfitted the space with residential furniture and incandescent lighting, and left the windows at 154 Grand untinted, to let in more light. The individual offices would consist of glass cubes held together by aluminum supports. In theory, the cubes made each office feel bigger, allowing light to filter into every space while offering a modicum of privacy—like the new Standard hotel, straddling the High Line and making voyeurs of guests and passersby alike. The transparency conveyed a sense that everyone with a WeWork office was in this together.

WeWork opened for business in February of 2010 with seventeen tenants—musicians, tech start-ups, an architect. The conditions turned off some office-seekers. People who walked in wearing wingtips were less likely to sign up than those wearing sneakers. But the exposed brick and creaky hundred-year-old floorboards were aesthetic kitty litter for a newly displaced workforce skeptical of artifice and craving authenticity. WeWork wasn't the cheapest office in New York, but people were willing to pay for the thoughtful design, the flexible lease terms, and a sense of community. *Need a lawyer? There's one five glass cubes down the hall.* Adam and Miguel began referring to tenants as "members," which had the dual benefit of obscuring the fact that WeWork was essentially an office landlord while also making people feel as if they were part of a club.

Being more than an office was core to how Adam and Miguel wanted to position their company. WeWork would present an alternative to the American dream, which no longer meant decades spent climbing a corporate ladder. The post-recession path to riches involved founding a start-up and disrupting the way things had been done. WeWork would provide a haven for those making this shift: it was a start-up begetting start-ups, a place where young entrepreneurs could build a collapsible-heel prototype, then move on if it failed without a long-term lease weighing them down. Who knew how much space a company would need in five months, let alone five years? The new economy was too precarious for that. "I'm competing against 'work,'" Adam liked to say. "I'm competing against the old notion that the way things were done is the way things need to be done today...Why do I need to pursue my parents' dreams? They're not mine." Miguel designed the company's first logo: a stick figure taking a sledgehammer to a desktop computer.

* * *

AS 154 GRAND FILLED UP, they needed a second location. Adam and Miguel had friends scouting potential spots in Toronto and San Francisco, and Joel Schreiber sent them to a building in Midtown, across from the Empire State Building on Fifth Avenue. It had been previously occupied by a branch of JPMorgan Chase's lending and mortgage division, which didn't have much work in a post–housing crisis world. The space had been on the market for months, and Schreiber knew the owners; the Zars were an Iranian-American family who ran a conservative business averse to speculative risks. Schreiber told Adam that if he could charm David Zar, the youngest family member, a deal might happen.

Adam met Zar at 349 Fifth Avenue wearing a bomber jacket over a white T-shirt. Zar wanted to find six different companies to occupy each of the six floors. After fifteen minutes of walking around, Adam told Zar that he wanted the entire building.

"Who are you again?" Zar said.

Adam invited Zar to visit 154 Grand. They took a tour and spent several hours talking in a ground-floor lounge late into the night, hashing out terms over a bottle of Johnnie Walker Black. When Zar shared the late-night deal with his family, they were hesitant; the Zars preferred to bet on tenants with long-term viability. Adam later recalled that when Zar came back to explain his family's reservations, Adam dismissed them. "I understood that Persians were men of their word," he told Zar.

The Grand Street lease had been a test run, with a five-year term. At 349 Fifth, Adam agreed to take out a more traditional fifteen-year lease. The Zars put up close to $1 million for the renovations and gave WeWork the right to use four large ad spaces on the side of the building, which WeWork would eventually call its Empire State location. Before construction had even begun, Adam put up large WeWork banners so that tourists waiting in line to enter the Empire State Building would see the name of his new company. A few months later, Zar saw Neumann at an event. Adam pulled him in for a hug and thanked him—less for the space itself than the publicity that came with it. "You put us on the map," he told Zar. "You made us real."

CHAPTER FOUR

"I Am WeWork"

"THE '90S AND EARLY 2000S were the 'I' decade—iPhone, the iPod,"
Adam told the New York *Daily News* in 2011, as WeWork opened its
third location, in Manhattan's Meatpacking District. "Everything was
about me."

Like many entrepreneurs, Adam admired Steve Jobs and all that he
stood for—wild ambition, ruthless drive. But he warned that some aspects
of Jobs's revolution had come with a price. "Look where that got us: in a
terrible recession," Adam said. "The future is community." America was
preparing to reelect a former community organizer as president. Occupy
Wall Street took over a park in lower Manhattan, and a sense persisted
that the old world order no longer served humanity's needs. WeWork
was premised on the idea that even the most iconoclastic entrepreneurs
couldn't build a business without help. With Jobs having left Apple to deal
with pancreatic cancer, Adam seemed eager to position his company as a
rising star of the new economy and himself as a candidate for America's
next entrepreneur in chief. "The next decade is the 'We' decade," he told
the *Daily News*. "If you look closely, we're already in a revolution."

Many of WeWork's first employees were bewildered by Adam's bombast.
WeWork's offices were nice—but a revolution? And yet the community-
building mission Adam preached was also what attracted many of them

to leave decent but boring jobs elsewhere. WeWork wasn't offering big salaries, nor was it handing out stock options like most tech start-ups, so Adam and Miguel's promise that WeWork was helping to build a better way of working was their primary recruiting tool.

Danny Orenstein, WeWork's third employee, came from JPDA, Miguel's old architecture firm, where the same economic forces that had hurt Krawlers—Neumann still owned the brand, but had handed over the day-to-day operations—had forced American Apparel to put its expansion plans on hold. Jordan Parnass laid off most of its twenty-five employees. Orenstein survived the culling, but he was ready to move on to something new, and spotted a listing for a job at WeWork on Craigslist. A few days later, he was driving a carful of televisions from an electronics store in lower Manhattan to 154 Grand with Miguel and Kyle O'Keefe-Sally, one of Miguel's fraternal "siblings" from Oregon, who had flown to New York from California to help his brother out. Orenstein was a foot shorter than McKelvey, but they quickly connected, architect to architect. If nothing else, it felt good to do something other than crank out new spaces for a hard-charging CEO.

A few days after joining WeWork, O'Keefe-Sally pulled Orenstein aside and told him that he needed to meet Adam. "Take everything he says with a grain of salt," O'Keefe-Sally cautioned. Whereas Miguel was relatively pragmatic, Adam tended to live in the clouds. Their conversation was brief, but Orenstein found himself immediately overwhelmed by Adam's intensity and ambition. He was eager to get back to the work of actually building 154 Grand.

Even early on, Adam was imagining a company with a hundred locations and telling friends that he was building a $100 billion business. No one in the New York real estate world knew what to make of Adam's T-shirt and jeans—then mayor Michael Bloomberg met Adam and told him he should cut his hair—or the confidence he was already displaying. At a real estate conference on Park Avenue, Adam asked one attendee what company leased the most office space in New York. The answer was

JPMorgan, which occupied three million square feet. Adam had only a few spaces, but said that he intended to surpass the bank.

One night, Orenstein was working late at the office when Adam asked him what his girlfriend thought about the long hours he was putting in along with everyone else. Orenstein said that she understood—WeWork was a start-up, and for now it needed his attention. Adam nodded, then asked what would happen when the company expanded and Orenstein was opening WeWorks around the globe. He and Miguel had sketched out a map on a piece of paper showing where they wanted to go next: San Francisco, Los Angeles, Toronto—"cities that speak to the rest of the world"—with lines vectoring onward to Montreal, Boston, Chicago, Israel, and London.

Orenstein told Adam that, if it came down to it, he and his girlfriend would break up, of course. Orenstein thought his voice was heavy with sarcasm, but Adam seemed to miss it. His English was still far from perfect, and some things got lost in translation. He shot Orenstein a serious look. "Your girlfriend needs to understand this would be very bad for her," Adam said of the potential breakup. "She's dating someone who is working at the next Google."

* * *

ORENSTEIN WAS ONE member of a motley crew. A friend of Miguel's from high school who practiced law back in Oregon served as the company's general counsel, so they could use his "Esq." on their letterhead. Kyle O'Keefe-Sally's sister Chia joined, too, helping WeWork open a space in San Francisco, its first outside New York. Marga Snyder, a former concierge at the Iroquois hotel, agreed to run the company's events. Its first IT director was a high school student who went by the nickname Joey Cables. Devin Vermeulen, WeWork's first creative director, came from Brooklyn Industries, a clothing company that helped pioneer the hipster-professional aesthetic, and was told that he had the job so long as he had a laptop, because they weren't going to buy him one. Like most young companies of the 2010s, WeWork made use of several unpaid interns, who were tasked with googling "how to fix a pinball machine" when Adam and Miguel didn't want to pay a professional, and figuring out how to acquire a 212 area code, a rare New York treasure. A tenant at 154 Grand offered to sell one for more than $10,000, but Adam dispatched an intern to find another for less.

Every early WeWork employee joined the company in amorphous roles that invariably required more construction work than their job titles suggested. "Am I gonna have to keep doing this much physical labor?" Vermeulen grumbled to Orenstein a few days in. Building each floor of 154 Grand required so much shuttling of supplies that they began filling the elevator to the brim, then stacking more items on top of the elevator so they could make fewer trips. When a new floor was set to open, everyone was expected to spend a long night painting walls, picking up trash, attaching sconces, plugging in lightbulbs, and drilling a seemingly endless supply of Ikea table legs into butcher's block slabs the company was offering for desks. Adam rejected calls to delay openings rather than force employees to work weekends—as long as the Wi-Fi was functional, he said, tenants would happily pay rent on an office with a few sloppily painted walls.

The pace was frenetic. "Half day?" one manager asked an early employee who started packing up at 6:00 p.m. WeWork finished renovating its first floor at Empire State in just twenty-nine days, and was working on the others when Adam closed a deal for a third location, in the Meatpacking District, near the southern end of the High Line. Adam wanted to get started on the new space immediately. One morning, he conducted a walkthrough of a new floor at the Meatpacking location and proceeded to point out a number of minor blemishes. Several employees had pulled an all-nighter to get the space to this point, which Adam neglected to acknowledge.

The team tried pushing back on Adam's timelines, but he was so

persuasive that by the end of many conversations they would often find themselves apologizing for expressing any doubt in the first place. But they were nearing a breaking point, and the team deputized Orenstein and Vermeulen to press the founders on the issue. Everyone was exhausted, they said, and making mistakes that might come back to burn the company. Adam's terse reply was expected—he pointed out that the employees had agreed to his expedited timelines—but Miguel's equally cold response surprised them. "Come to me with solutions," he said. "Not problems."

One day, Orenstein, O'Keefe-Sally, and Vermeulen went up to the roof of Empire State with Miguel. It was snowing in New York, but it was a relief to get some fresh air, away from the perpetual construction zone that was their lives. They had all been at WeWork for less than a year, and for the most part, they loved the messy fun of building a company with colleagues who had become close friends. The product was a hit, with a waiting list for new offices, but some employees worried that the company was showing early signs of losing its way. They had joined WeWork in part because it promised an escape from the rat race—a solution, even. But the focus on building a community, and creating a better way of working, seemed to be taking a back seat to conversations about efficiency, growth, and the company's valuation, never mind that it was only a number made up between Adam, Miguel, and Joel Schreiber.

On the roof, Orenstein asked Miguel whether he thought all the time and the stress was worth it. Miguel's experience processing fish for eighteen hours a day and enduring Dov Charney's wrath numbed him slightly to the grinding demands Adam was putting on the company and its employees. Plus, Miguel wanted to grow quickly, too. At the same time, his wife had given birth to their first child just before WeWork opened, and he was struggling to balance fatherhood with work—the very concern he had expressed to his mother in a postcard a decade earlier. Miguel told the group on the roof that he did think it would all be worth it while admitting that the company was already moving at such a speed that staying true to its mission was going to require constant vigilance.

* * *

ADAM AND MIGUEL took on different roles at WeWork. Miguel's official title was chief creative officer, responsible for the design of each space and managing the construction process. But when he stopped working at the end of each day, sometimes after midnight, he would often look back and marvel at everything start-up life had required him to do since waking up that morning: billing, sales, accounting, a splash of computer programming, buying a hundred coffee mugs from Ikea.

Adam, meanwhile, kept his hand in every part of WeWork's operation, insisting on approving the layouts of each new space, but he spent much of his time stepping into the role of CEO, spooling out a vision for the company and wooing potential partners. He was already developing a reputation around New York for pouring shots during meetings—vodka in the early days, until he developed a preference for tequila. Adam was the dreamer and dealmaker; Miguel kept WeWork grounded. When Adam wanted to advertise WeWork as a "community" in its marketing materials, Miguel pushed back. Calling yourself a community was a distinction that had to be earned, he said, and WeWork hadn't done enough to claim that yet.

With Miguel managing WeWork's build-out, Adam began to form a back office staffed in large part by his friends and family. His cousin-in-law, Chris Hill, came from wholesale produce distribution to become WeWork's chief operating officer. When Stella Templo, Adam's immigration attorney, stopped by 154 Grand Street in 2010 to help Adam renew his visa, she looked around WeWork and saw everyone smiling. Immigration work was a grind, and she decided to quit her job and take a pay cut to serve as Adam's assistant and help Miguel's friend in Oregon with the company's growing legal needs. Adam flew friends from Israel to New York ostensibly for a friendly visit only to give them hammers and put them to work. When Hill asked for help managing the company's rapidly expanding operations, Adam hired Zvika Shachar, a high school

friend from Kfar Saba who worked at a Sushi Samba in Israel and spent six months helping Hill via Skype before joining the company in New York. Ariel Tiger, a friend from the navy, became WeWork's first CFO. Tiger had graduated at the top of Adam's class at the Israeli Naval Academy, though Adam bragged to a group of WeWork employees that he had bested Tiger in a sailing course.

"I beat you in everything else," Tiger said.

"You beat *everyone* in everything else," Adam replied.

When a group of WeWork employees watched a video of Neumann and Tiger's graduation from officer school, they instantly spotted Tiger at the front of the line. It took longer to find Adam, who was in the middle of the pack but also stood out—taller than everyone else, marching slightly out of step.

Adam liked to maintain a close circle of confidants. One night at Empire State, Orenstein was chatting with a colleague who was complaining about Adam when Orenstein noticed a man he didn't recognize sitting nearby, seeming to pay them no attention. A few weeks later, Orenstein was walking with Adam from the Neumanns' loft in Tribeca, where they often held meetings before and after work, to the new Meatpacking District location. Adam told Orenstein that he had heard about the complaining. The mystery man, he said, was another friend of his. Adam was irked by the complaints and disappointed in Orenstein. The next time someone spoke out against him, Adam expected Orenstein to stand up for his boss.

A hierarchy was already emerging within WeWork's kibbutz. After seeing several employees walking around the office in shorts and worn-out T-shirts—they had been up late the previous night building out a new floor—Adam gathered his employees and said that they were ambassadors of WeWork's "premium" brand and needed to dress accordingly. When Kyle O'Keefe-Sally pointed out that Adam wore a T-shirt and jeans most days, as he was at that moment, Adam replied that his shirts were from James Perse and cost $200. "This is different than the T-shirts you wear," Adam said. "I look like someone people want to be." In 2011, WeWork required employees to sign a noncompete agreement restricting them from opening a related business for eighteen months after leaving the company. Similar office spaces were cropping up around the country, and Adam and Miguel didn't want any additional competition.

Lisa Skye, WeWork's second employee, was the only person who refused to sign the document. Skye had joined WeWork a few weeks before 154 Grand opened, when Adam met her at a networking event she was running and asked her to become WeWork's first "community manager"—an all-purpose job encompassing sales, customer service, light janitorial work, and any other tasks that emerged while operating an entire building more or less by oneself.

Skye liked her job, and the company. When Joel Schreiber failed to come through with a chunk of his promised $15 million investment, Skye gave WeWork a $200,000 emergency loan. She barely blinked when Adam recommended, as he did to many of his employees, that Skye meet with Eitan Yardeni, his rabbi at the Kabbalah Centre. Yardeni told Skye what she already knew: she served as a balance for Adam, allowing him to go forth and make deals, expanding his territory, knowing that Skye and others were holding down the fort behind him.

But Skye was working herself to the bone. She had just spent her Sunday installing translucent frosting on the glass walls between each office. (It turned out that WeWork members only wanted so much connection to their neighbors.) The company was growing quickly, yet the benefits didn't seem to be accruing to those doing much of the building. Adam and Miguel told employees they would receive equity in the company soon, but kept pushing off the actual date that might happen. When Skye and several other employees asked for raises, Adam complained that he didn't think he was getting what he paid for as it stood. He told one employee he could save money by getting a roommate.

Adam and Miguel called Skye into a conference room to ask why she wasn't signing the noncompete. Skye said that she had come to realize that she would never have a real voice at the company despite having helped build it from the beginning. She was thirty-three, and if Adam was intent on growing as fast as they were, she might be happier opening a space or two of her own, just as Adam and Miguel had originally done.

"Why would you want to do that?" Miguel said. "It's a ton of work."

The implication that the company's founders were working so much harder than everyone else was galling, but after Adam left the meeting, Miguel stayed behind to chat with Skye. It was clear that although the company was not even a year old, the cofounders were no longer equal partners. Miguel admitted to harboring doubts. Adam's ambitions were giving him flashbacks to his American Apparel experience. But Miguel also said that he didn't have the inclination to get in Adam's way. He had made a decision to fasten his seatbelt and see where WeWork could go.

* * *

IN THE MIDDLE OF 2011, Josh Simmons was referred for a job at WeWork by a friend who worked on a short film starring Rebekah Paltrow, Adam's wife. Simmons had been working the front desk at a hotel spa in New York, but when he met Adam for an interview, they spent much of the time talking about Simmons's previous experience in campus ministry at a college in South Carolina. Adam had become increasingly religious, at Rebekah's behest, and he called his wife into the office so they could talk more about the Neumanns' embrace of Kabbalah, the Jewish mystical tradition, and how spirituality had come to play a role at WeWork.

Simmons started working as a community manager at the Empire State location, where the sixth and final floor had just opened six months after the first. Empire State was a refined version of 154 Grand, and Simmons's job was to help the community develop a more professional feel, even though it had the company's first permanent beer keg and the tenants remained an eclectic group. (A team from SoftBank Capital, an investing arm of the Japanese conglomerate, considered a WeWork office in 2012, but decided that it didn't quite fit the firm's more refined needs.) One day, Simmons's colleague pulled out a drawer in the base of a couch and found it filled with clothes. Simmons had noticed one of the members looking increasingly disheveled. It turned out that the man's start-up was in the tank, and he couldn't pay the rent on his apartment, so he had chosen to move into his WeWork office instead.

Simmons found WeWork to be fun and challenging, even if the job wasn't exactly what he thought he was signing up for. "You can't let anything sit vacant," Adam told Simmons and the other community managers, who were tasked with handling sales along with their other duties. It wasn't the ministry, but Simmons liked making the lives of members a little better every day. "We were constantly told that it wasn't about the money," Simmons said. One day, Adam called Simmons and another employee over to meet a potential investor Adam was escorting through a WeWork location. When Adam asked the employees how old they were, Simmons and his colleague both replied that they were in their twenties.

"See?" Adam said. "I can hire a bunch of young people and pay them nothing."

The worst part, Simmons realized, was that Neumann was right. Many of WeWork's new hires were recent graduates happy to have a job of any kind on the heels of the recession and eager to join a company that promised to bring a social life to the workplace. But Simmons was married, with a baby on the way; it wasn't as much of a perk to hang out and drink free beer at work with his colleagues, as WeWork employees did many nights of every week. Adam had never worked for anyone, and as at many start-ups, employment basics sometimes fell by the wayside. WeWork had only just begun offering health insurance, and there was no parental leave policy beyond an understanding that men wouldn't be taking much time off; Adam barely stopped working when Rebekah gave birth to their first child, in 2011.

A year after joining WeWork, Simmons got a job offer that doubled his WeWork salary. When he told Chris Hill, the COO, Hill said the company couldn't match the offer, which had come not from a large corporation, but from a local church. "Inherent in that is that the church cared more about people," Simmons explained. Adam had talked to Simmons about how much spirituality influenced his approach to business, but the message had started to ring hollow. Adam had recently called Simmons into a room to administer what felt like a loyalty test: Adam had gotten into a dispute with another employee, and wanted to make sure he knew which side Simmons was on. In the meeting, Adam made a decree that lodged itself into Simmons's brain as he left Neumann's company to join the church. "I," Adam said, "*am* WeWork."

CHAPTER FIVE

Sex, Coworking, and Rock 'n' Roll

EVERY GENERATION REMAKES the office to suit its needs. The Industrial Revolution produced the factory, and the large manufacturing floors championed by the mechanical engineer Frederick Taylor were the original open-plan offices. When the first white-collar workspaces emerged in the twentieth century, they resembled an assembly line. In 1939, Frank Lloyd Wright's Johnson Wax Headquarters introduced brighter lighting and more humanity. Cubicles took off in the 1980s alongside the desktop computer, giving workers a bit more individual privacy and dominating the work landscape until Silicon Valley start-ups set about knocking down walls and recruiting laptop-enabled workers with beanbag chairs and foosball tables.

The emergence of "coworking" was an offshoot of that movement. Brad Neuberg, a software engineer in San Francisco, coined the term in 2005. He was trying to find a happy medium between the drudgery of office life and the solitude of freelancing. Starbucks wasn't offering free Wi-Fi, and the coffee shops that did, like Ritual Roasters on Valencia Street, were so crowded that working there meant waging a constant battle for a seat and access to an electrical outlet. Neuberg wanted something like the coffee-houses of the Enlightenment, where people met to exchange big ideas while also doing business. The modern version would have programmers swapping code and laughing at memes around the Chemex.

That year, Neuberg started inviting other freelancers to work out of a space that he rented from a feminist collective in the Mission for $300 a month, provided he set up and put away the tables and chairs himself. People started to trickle in after he handed out flyers in coffee shops. One of them was Chris Messina, a product designer who invented the Twitter hashtag. In 2006, Messina, Neuberg, and Tara Hunt, who worked in marketing, opened a more permanent space called Teh Hat Factory. (The misspelled article was an intentionally nerdy joke: "teh" is a common way for clumsy fingers to mistype "the.") Teh Hat Factory operated out of a loft apartment, with bedsheets hung from the ceiling as dividers. No one was trying to make any money. "The openness was important to us," Hunt said. "Plus, the coworking business model is shit. We didn't see it as a viable venture-backed business. Unless you nickel-and-dime people, you're never gonna be able to scale this."

Coworking spaces began to open all across the country: a few months before Green Desk opened, in 2008, the *New York Times* dedicated an article to dozens of spaces popping up in New York City and elsewhere. Miguel visited one aimed at programmers that reminded him of a nightclub in Berlin, with matte black walls, low light, and loud music. A mile from Green Desk in Brooklyn was Green Space, which had the same environmental focus. The amenities of coworking were already more or less standard: nap rooms, happy hours, good coffee.

Adam would later say he "never saw other coworking spaces" before opening Green Desk, but he knew about the business. Back when he was at Baruch, one of his classmates, Malka Yerushalmi, introduced him to her son, Cheni, an Israeli entrepreneur running an office-space company called Sunshine Suites. Cheni opened Sunshine Suites in 2001, the year Adam moved to New York, and now had several locations in Manhattan. According to Yerushalmi, he gave Adam a tour of his space near Washington Square Park and explained to him how the business worked.

Community was a key part of the operation—he referred to tenants as "Shiners" and fielded a very bad softball team—as was a bespoke licensing agreement he and a lawyer had drawn up that offered several advantages over a traditional lease. Yerushalmi says he didn't think too much of the fact that Adam visited Sunshine Suites for another tour in 2007, as a prospective tenant, without saying he was coming by.

A year later, when Neumann opened Green Desk, Yerushalmi was unbothered; Adam was across the river in Brooklyn, and no one was delusional enough to think the commercial office world could be dominated by a single person. Neumann and Yerushalmi occasionally chatted about the business, sharing tips on how to offer secure Wi-Fi and conduct background checks on potential tenants. In 2009, Adam asked Yerushalmi to lunch and told him he was leaving Green Desk behind to go out on his own. WeWork opened at 154 Grand Street, just south of the Sunshine Suites location Adam had toured, with a membership agreement that looked similar to the one Yerushalmi had shared with Adam.

As WeWork continued to grow, opening one location after another, Yerushalmi finally called Adam to remind him that they had been introduced by Yerushalmi's mother and to tell him that he was a "fucking piece of shit." When Stella Templo joined WeWork, one of her first tasks was to rewrite its member agreement.

What Yerushalmi and other coworking operators lacked was not only Adam's ambition but also his connection to capital. Joel Schreiber had only come through on a small portion of his promised investment—he never received his full 33 percent stake—but Adam had since been able to turn to the well-connected circle of friends he now had in the city. In the summer of 2011, Adam rented a house in the Hamptons, telling his employees that the place was a bit of a stretch budgetwise but that it was worth it to impress and make connections with wealthy New Yorkers. Sam Ben-Avraham, the founder of Kith, the hip clothing empire, invested several million dollars, along with other acquaintances of Adam's who put money into the company. Most coworking operators were lucky to cobble together six figures' worth of investment. By 2012, Adam had raised nearly $7 million from friends and family alone.

* * *

A CHUNK OF WEWORK'S EARLY money came from Rebekah, Adam's wife, who invested part of a $1 million nest egg into her husband—the man she believed would save the world—and his company. The money was a gift from her parents. Bobby and Evelyn Paltrow had Rebekah in 1978, more than a decade after her three older siblings were born. "She grew up very much like the gift of the family," her cousin Gwyneth said. "Like this beautiful surprise princess."

Rebekah is six years younger than Gwyneth, whose parents are Blythe Danner, the actress, and Bruce Paltrow, a Hollywood producer. (Steven Spielberg is her godfather.) Rebekah's father, Bobby, is Bruce's younger brother. The Paltrows are descended from Polish Jews—Paltrowicz was the family name—and Rebekah's great-great-great-grandfather was a rabbi who studied Kabbalah and was said to possess mystical powers. When a fire erupted outside his Polish town, he supposedly walked onto a balcony, waved a handkerchief, and extinguished the flames.

While her cousin bounced between Los Angeles and New York, Rebekah was born in Great Neck, the Long Island town that served as inspiration for F. Scott Fitzgerald's West Egg. The family eventually moved to Bedford, a wealthy enclave an hour north of Manhattan. Rebekah would later try to claim a humble upbringing in an interview with a fashion magazine—"I grew up off a dirt road, in, like, a treehouse"—but her cousin politely corrected the characterization. "They were well-off," Gwyneth said. "Her mom came from a lot of money and they had a huge piece of property. Her mother, Evelyn, has amazing taste—every linen perfect. They had a lot of help and every comfort."

While Bruce Paltrow made a name for himself in Hollywood, Bobby set about building North American Communications, a junk-mail business.

"For him, I don't think it mattered so much what it was," Rebekah said. "It was a love of the process of business." In 1986, when Rebekah was eight, two charities operated by Bobby—the American Cancer Research Fund and the American Heart Research Foundation—pleaded guilty to ten charges of mail fraud after raising around $2 million through fake charitable mailings. The government said Bobby had pulled off an "old-fashioned swindle," funneling charitable contributions back into his own coffers. North American Communications printed and assembled the mailers for the charities, which used their tax status to send the mailers out at a reduced rate; when the donations came in, the money never went to any medical research. The organizations were ordered to pay a $100,000 fine and donate $300,000 to legitimate charities. Two decades later, in 2014, Bobby pleaded guilty to that tax fraud.

For high school, Rebekah went to Horace Mann, an elite private school in the Bronx, where the pressure to succeed academically was matched only by the pressure to thrive socially. One of her high school classmates described Rebekah, who went by Rebbi, as bucking both trends. "Rebbi just did not give a shit," the classmate said. "She very much had that don't-give-a-fuck-pre-socialite energy, maybe more than anyone else in our class." Rebekah fell in with the wealthy and popular crowd and was well liked. She didn't seem all that ambitious and received two distinctions in her senior yearbook—"Contributes the Most to the New York State Liquor Tax" and "Most Points on License."

Gwyneth had always cast a long shadow over her cousin, and as Rebekah enrolled at Cornell University, in 1996, Gwyneth was starring in a film adaptation of *Emma* and dating Brad Pitt. (Gwyneth dedicated her Oscar win, for *Shakespeare in Love*, in part to Rebekah's brother, Keith, who had died of cancer in 1989.) Rebekah didn't shy away from drawing attention to the connection, introducing herself at Cornell as Rebbi Paltrow when a first name would have sufficed; *Bustle* later reported that she told a member of a sorority she was attempting to join that, yes, she would be invited to Brad and Gwyneth's wedding. Unlike her cousin, who started acting as a teenager, Rebekah didn't know what she wanted to do, but she came from a family of entrepreneurs. After graduating, she moved to New York to join a training program for stockbrokers at Salomon Smith Barney.

It didn't go well. Rebekah quit the job after just a few weeks. Her parents had divorced, after years of tension, and Rebekah's boyfriend left her for her best friend. "There was a lot of betrayal and pain," she said later. "But ultimately, thank God, that led me on a journey." Newly untethered, she flew to India at the age of twenty-three and took a fourteen-hour bus ride to Dharamsala, the mountain community where the Dalai Lama lived in exile from Tibet. She meditated several hours a day, studied yoga, met His Holiness, and drank a lot of chai tea.

Not long after Rebekah came back to the United States, still uncertain what to do, she went to see a performance by Michael Franti and Spearhead, the funk-rap group that inflected its music with themes of social justice. (They had recently released an album called *Stay Human.*) Rebekah followed the band to its next concert, where she managed to deliver them a letter. A few weeks later, Franti's manager called to say the note had inspired the band—did she want to come hang out with them in San Francisco? Rebekah lived and toured with the group for around a year, taking no specific role or salary. "It wasn't the point," she said. "I was on a journey of self-discovery and I knew these people were part of it." She eventually came to the same conclusion that many wandering twentysomethings do. "I saw how Michael was using art to make an impact," Rebekah said. "I decided I wanted to act."

Rebekah moved to Los Angeles, where she spent several years taking acting classes and going to auditions. Her cousin's career continued to thrive—*The Royal Tenenbaums*, an Austin Powers movie, the lead role in a Sylvia Plath biopic—but Rebekah struggled to gain traction. "The acting was too much effort, and I wasn't getting where I wanted to go," Rebekah said. "So I moved back to New York. And then I met Adam."

* * *

REBEKAH AGREED TO Adam's swift marriage proposal on the condition that he kick some bad habits. They ritually dumped artifacts of his cigarette smoking and soda drinking down the garbage chute of Rebekah's apartment building. She didn't drink much and often went home before Adam did, slowing down his frenetic energy. "I adore Adam, but he's a handful," Gwyneth said of her cousin-in-law, adding that without Rebekah around, it felt like Adam was liable to explode at any moment.

Rebekah wasn't a regular presence in the early days of WeWork, and didn't pitch in much to the late-night construction efforts. But she held significant sway over her husband. WeWork employees would sometimes go home at night thinking they had a plan, only to have Adam return the next morning to say that he had talked things over with Rebekah and come up with a new course of action. Rebekah helped Adam answer his emails and made him lunch—whatever he needed. "I became passionate about him achieving his maximum potential," Rebekah said, describing herself as "acting like a muse—which used to be a problem for me when I was younger because I wanted to be the main act."

While Adam set about building WeWork, Rebekah was still trying to make it as an actress. A few months after WeWork opened, the company cohosted a party at Milk Studios, the chic photography studio in Manhattan, along with *Corduroy*, a fashion magazine. The party served as a social coming out for WeWork, which set up one of its glass cubes in a corner, and for the Neumanns. Adam posed for party pictures in a black blazer and Converse sneakers, and Sean Lennon performed. (Pete Doherty, the British indie rocker, was supposed to play but got held up at customs.) Rebekah landed a short profile in the magazine that listed her as an actor. "This Paltrow," it read, "is noticeably grounded." Rebekah had been cast in a production of Chekhov's *Three Sisters* directed by the English actress Eve Best for the Old Vic New Voices theater troupe, a group made up of emerging actors. The production had no rehearsal space, so she offered up a wing of 154 Grand. The actors once spooked some of WeWork's members by doing an exercise in which they ran up and down the stairwells screaming as loudly as they could.

In the summer of 2010, Rebekah and Adam reached out to Hunter Richards, a young screenwriter whose script about two scientists exploring the depths of human consciousness the Neumanns were interested in buying. Richards met the Neumanns for dinner and absinthe at the Waverly Inn, a West Village hot spot. Adam told Richards he didn't totally understand a director's role in making a movie; Richards said it was sort of like being CEO. When Richards boasted that he had made his first million in his twenties, after selling a script, Adam promised to top him. "I'll make my first billion," he said.

Rebekah told Richards that she was launching a production company, Boheme Films, to make "spiritually progressive" movies. She had an idea for a short film. Would he consider directing? The Neumanns had money, and Richards wanted to try out a new camera, so he agreed, telling them he thought they could shoot the whole thing for $30,000. But Rebekah wanted to pull out every stop. They hired a star-studded cast— Rosario Dawson, Sean Lennon, and Lynn Cohen, fresh off her role as Miranda's housekeeper in *Sex and the City*—along with a twenty-person crew that included a cinematographer flown in from Canada and an assistant director who worked on *The Hurt Locker*, which had recently won the Oscar for best picture. Richards presumed that Dawson would play the lead—he said Dawson thought she would, too—but when they arrived on set, Rebekah made clear the role was hers. "I could have put my foot down, but they were paying the bill," Richards said.

The Neumanns ended up spending more than $100,000 to make the fifteen-minute movie. "It was, and probably still is, the most expensive short film I ever worked on," Atit Shah, the assistant director, said. The Neumanns splurged on the glitzy parts of the production, insisting on extra visual effects to accompany a moment when Rebekah's body is consumed in rays of light. But they skimped on some of the basics, chastising a producer for putting everyone in hotel rooms after a daylong shoot in Westchester County rather than having them drive back to their homes in New York.

Most of the crew never saw the final cut of *Awake*, but the Neumanns invited WeWork's staff to the film's premiere, at the Tribeca Grand hotel. The movie's plot seemed to reflect the Neumann's embrace of their spiritual side. Dawson plays Rebekah's friend, and finds her character surrounded by pills and booze in her apartment, drives her outside the city, and tells her to take a walk in the woods. There, Rebekah happens upon a tent, inside of which Sean Lennon is sitting cross-legged on a pillow, waiting for her. "Please, sit down," Lennon says. "You have been searching your entire life— from religion to relationship, from sex to substances, from psychoanalysis to reality television—but the answer has been residing in you all along."

"I don't mean to be rude, but I don't believe in God and spirituality and horoscopes," Rebekah says, tearing up. "I just want the pain to go away."

"Fear is a source of all pain and suffering in this world, from every act of violence to every war," Lennon says. "It's fear that is poisoning you now." He tells Rebekah to write down every thought and memory she has ever had.

Rebekah sits in front of a fireplace, cataloging memories while images from her real life—her childhood, her wedding to Adam—appear on-screen. When she hands them to Lennon, he tosses them into the fire. "Listen, darling, every thought carries its own vibration," Lennon says, encouraging her to join him in a chant, at which point rays of light shoot out of her body.

"Who are you?" Rebekah asks.

"I," Lennon says, before snapping his fingers and sending the screen to black, "am awake."

* * *

AS AN ADDITIONAL condition of their engagement, Rebekah insisted that Adam work on his spiritual life. He agreed to go to therapy for the first time, which helped him become less bitter about his difficult childhood. Rebekah also brought Adam to a meditation class led by Dechen Thurman, Uma Thurman's brother. After class, Rebekah and Adam went to Thurman's walk-up apartment in the Village. Adam asked Thurman, who also taught Jivamukti yoga, what kind of living Rebekah could expect to make if she opened a yoga studio of her own. Thurman described an inequitable system whereby young instructors work long hours for low pay, hoping for long-term financial and spiritual gain that mostly accrues to a select few at the top.

Rebekah also started taking Adam to classes at the Kabbalah Centre in Manhattan. Early devotees of Kabbalah, which dates back to the twelfth century, were almost exclusively rabbis like Rebekah's great-great-great-grandfather who sought a more personal and less doctrinal relationship with God. Kabbalah's modern version had a more American flavor. The Kabbalah Centre was founded by Philip Berg, an insurance salesman and rabbi from Brooklyn, and his wife, Karen, whom he married after leaving his first wife and their eight children. The Bergs opened the Kabbalah Centre in Los Angeles in 1984 and set about expanding their empire with the help of their two sons, Michael and Yehuda.

By the late '90s, the Bergs claimed thousands of adherents to a religion that spoke less about God than it did about "energy." The Bergs branded Kabbalah as "technology for the soul," and it manifested as a prosperity gospel rooted in a grab bag of Jewish teachings. During services, men wore white to attract positive energy, and everyone took part in primal, ecstatic singing. At a Kabbalah service in Los Angeles, a *Vanity Fair* reporter watched as the congregants yelped while pumping their hands in the air. "We're sending energy towards Chernobyl," one said. "We're transforming negative energy to light!"

The Bergs had also turned Kabbalah into a robust commercial operation. They sold books promising "total fulfillment" and "endless joy" through, among other things, "the ecstasy of chocolate." The center hawked candles with names like Sexual Energy and Dialing God as well as Kabbalah Mountain Spring Water, which the Bergs claimed could cure various ailments. (The water came from a treatment plant in Canada.) They were especially successful at attracting celebrities: Madonna, Demi Moore and Ashton Kutcher, Roseanne Barr, Lucy Liu, the fashion designer Donna Karan, and Marla Maples, Donald Trump's second wife. Kabbalists were encouraged to wear red string bracelets on their wrists—available for purchase on the center's website for $26—as protection from various negative energies. The bracelets became status symbols in the 2000s; Paris Hilton and Lindsay Lohan were spotted wearing them.

Rebekah had followed her cousin Gwyenth into Kabbalah during her time in Los Angeles. (Several of the acting roles Rebekah did land—appearances in two episodes of *Punk'd*, Ashton Kutcher's prank show, and a line of dialogue in a Lucy Liu movie—came alongside other Kabbalah Centre members.) By the end of the decade, both Neumanns had become regulars at the center in New York. It was a hierarchical institution, favoring celebrities and the wealthy, and during Friday dinners the Neumanns were often seated at a head table next to Eitan Yardeni, the rabbi, who devoted time to many of Kabbalah's VIPs. ("I felt I had a bigger responsibility," Yardeni once said, of working with Madonna.) While Rebekah came in with a pedigree, some Kabbalah Centre members were skeptical of Adam, who was eager to prove himself; a friend from the time said Adam didn't want to be known for having married a Paltrow. "Adam was Kabbalah to the nth degree," a WeWork executive who also knew Neumann from the center said. "He was the life of the party, but he also learned all this consciousness shit there."

Growing up in Israel, Adam had never felt much connection to religion; his parents didn't celebrate Jewish holidays or keep Shabbat, and he saw observant Judaism mostly as a nuisance that meant he couldn't go to the beach on Saturdays because the buses weren't running. But as his decade of unsuccessful striving in New York came to a close,

Kabbalah offered structure, meaning, and a way of seeing the world. The Neumanns were married at the Urban Zen Center, an event space in the West Village run by Donna Karan, and Adam started wearing a red string bracelet. Adam and Rebekah hung a painting over the bed in their Tribeca loft with warped text reading:

CHANGE THE
WAY YOU SEE
EVERYTHING

Kabbalah changed the way Adam saw his professional life. On a practical level, the Neumanns' involvement in the Kabbalah Centre elevated Adam and Rebekah into another caste of moneyed New Yorkers—in 2009, Rebekah sat next to Demi Moore at the premiere of one of Kutcher's movies—and produced many of WeWork's earliest financial backers. In 2012, Adam told a New York real estate publication that Kabbalah itself was the inspiration for WeWork. "I noticed that in the Kabbalah community, people were really helping each other," he said. "I wanted to translate that into business." WeWork employees noticed that the language and teaching of the Kabbalah Centre bled into day-to-day life at the company. Both Neumanns talked a lot about "energy," and Adam often told employees he had come to a decision after consulting with Yardeni. Adam pushed WeWork employees to take Kabbalah classes, and started holding regular meetings with Yardeni at WeWork headquarters that senior employees were encouraged to attend.

Kabbalah gave Neumann not only a sense of purpose but an instructive guide to running an organization with devoted adherents. The Kabbalah Centre became an all-consuming experience for many members. In Kabbalah, all people are said to possess a spark of God inside them, their talents representing divine energy spreading into the world. But the secret knowledge that Kabbalah rabbis are believed to have allows them to wield extraordinary influence over their followers.

"Adam was kind of a lost soul—incredibly outgoing, and willing to do whatever it took, but no core value system," the WeWork executive who knew Adam from the Kabbalah Centre said. "Through Kabbalah, Adam became like a prophet. It was like putting a basketball in Michael Jordan's hands."

* * *

TWO HUNDRED EUROPEANS listened raptly in November of 2011 as Adam appeared on a large projector screen wearing a white collared shirt that was rakishly unbuttoned. The crowd was in Berlin while Adam was in New York, videoconferencing his image into the second annual Coworking Europe conference.

A month earlier Adam's assistant had reached out to Jean-Yves Huwart, the conference's Belgian founder, to inform him that WeWork was the largest coworking operator in the United States. This was news to Huwart, who had never heard of WeWork and couldn't find many photos of its offices online. Coworking was a disaggregated industry made up almost entirely of small-time operators, so the idea that any company would become a country's dominant player was an idea Huwart had not even considered. Adam's assistant sent along a few Photoshopped images of how the spaces the company was building in New York and San Francisco would look, plus a biography explaining that her boss was working on multiple projects: namely, his continued ownership of a baby clothes company and "changing the way people work... with his company WeWork."

One of the few Americans in Berlin for Coworking Europe was Alex Hillman, who ran a coworking space in Philadelphia. Hillman had heard of WeWork and Neumann, and was eager for his talk: "Coworking, Enterprise 2.0, and Intrapreneurship: The next Google, Starbucks, or Facebook Will Start out of a Coworking Space." But Hillman grew concerned as he listened. Adam was using all the rhetoric about building community that had attracted Hillman to coworking in the first place, but to his ear, Adam's speech sounded less like a man addressing his comrades than someone fine-tuning an investor pitch. Hillman was already taken aback to see that Coworking Europe had attracted a surprising number of corporate real estate types—wingtips among the sneakers—and startled to find many of the conference's attendees fawning while Neumann spoke. "It felt very much like the big *1984* head was up on a screen with a bunch of people blindly ogling at this messianic message," Hillman said.

When he got home, Hillman wrote a blog post about what appeared to be a dawning era for a previously sleepy industry. He titled it "Sex, Coworking, and Rock 'n' Roll."

A few months later, Jean-Yves Huwart met Adam in New York at We-Work's newest location, on Varick Street. WeWork had never previously offered true coworking, preferring the semiprivacy of its glass cubicles, but the Varick location had several open spaces dedicated to various industries—WeCross, to mix architects with designers, and WeWork Labs for tech start-ups. This was coworking on a massive scale. The location had seven hundred desks and one of the largest open-plan offices Huwart had ever seen. When they met, Adam told Huwart he was planning a trip to Israel, where he hoped to open WeWork's first international location. Perhaps Adam could stop in Brussels, Huwart's hometown, and build one there along the way?

Both Neumann and Huwart were heading to Austin, Texas, for GCUC—the Global Coworking Unconference Conference. GCUC was a gathering that had blossomed along with the industry from a happy hour at South by Southwest in 2008 into a multiday event. Liz Elam, GCUC's founder, invited Adam to join her as her guest at a party at the W Hotel dubbed "A Celebration of American Start-ups." While a local band played, Adam's assistant told Elam that she had to go find some marijuana for her boss.

Adam was, by that point, a mini celebrity at GCUC, having recently expanded WeWork to the West Coast, with a new location in San Francisco. He had begun taking on many of WeWork's public speaking opportunities, a role Miguel didn't care for, and was speaking on a panel titled "Why Real Estate Can Make or Break You" alongside coworking CEOs based everywhere from Boston to Miami. Adam told the audience that the business was really two businesses: real estate and community. He liked to think less about ROI, or return on investment, than about ROC—return on community.

But he was also trying to be smart about the real estate side. With the market still emerging from the recession, Adam said he was signing leases at low prices for terms as long as thirty years. "If WeWork, God forbid, wouldn't work out, I'm holding leases that are worth tens of millions," he bragged, before lamenting that the state of affairs was already shifting. Rents were rising so quickly in San Francisco, he said, that the price of one WeWork deal had gone up 15 percent in the course of a single negotiation.

Adam was by far the most captivating presence onstage and got the panel's last word. He said that he had initially been uncertain about coming to GCUC. "I was asking myself, Why am I coming to a place where I'm gonna talk to all my potential competitors?" After thinking about it, Adam said, he realized that his company was "about 'We' and about collaboration" and that he should approach everyone in the room not as a rival but as a potential partner. "Every single person here who has a coworking space, or is thinking of doing a coworking space, contact WeWork," he said. "We're planning to be all over the country very, very soon. Instead of us opening all the locations, we would love to partner with some of you ... Together, we can build a community that can change the world."

* * *

TO NEUMANN'S POTENTIAL PARTNERS, this seemed less like an invitation than a warning. Neuberg, Hunt, and Messina, from Teh Hat Factory, didn't know what to think of Adam's growing company. Sticking people into glass boxes and hosting the occasional happy hour wasn't the kind of community they wanted to build, but WeWork clearly had its appeal. Neuberg had always figured there would be a Starbucks of coworking— he thought it might end up *being* Starbucks. The early anarchist impulse behind coworking was slowly being swallowed up. Neuberg himself took a job at Google.

Jesse Middleton, who cofounded WeWork Labs, invited Messina to talk to Adam about the early days of coworking. They met in Adam's office, on the top floor of WeWork's new headquarters, near City Hall. Adam told Messina that he was in the process of building "the Microsoft Office of workplaces," a universal platform on which all kinds of work could be done. The idea, as Messina received it, was "to build a cradle-to-grave experience for workers—to own their lives." Adam seemed less interested in picking Messina's brain than in figuring out whether he was planning anything that might stand in WeWork's path. "What's so funny to me, and perhaps tragic in this indirect way, is that people will see this community that we've built, and they will try to figure out how to sequester profit from it," Messina told me. Talking to Adam, he said, felt like living through *The Matrix*. "I am Neo, and I see you, Agent Smith," Messina said. "If you feel you need to, you will do whatever it takes to annihilate me right now."

At the time, Adam was winning a war of attrition. In 2011, General Assembly opened in Manhattan's Flatiron District as a gathering space for New York's tech scene, with a large coworking operation. GA was backed by big money—Jeff Bezos invested—and had no fear of WeWork. "Why are you worried?" Brad Hargreaves, one of its founders, told his partners. "They named the company *WeWork*."

But GA also had a robust business hosting computer programming classes, and coworking gave its founders pause. It was difficult to meaningfully differentiate their offering from anyone else's, and the previous two recessions had wiped out office middlemen as tenants vacated and left them stuck with long-term leases. Jake Schwartz, one of GA's cofounders, spent the 2000s in finance and watched hedge funds rise and fall on a similar premise: the carry trade, which involved borrowing money at low interest rates in order to invest in things that could produce a much higher return—before the bill came due, one hoped. If the returns were less robust than expected, your business could end up underwater.

Coworking seemed to require a risk-taking mindset that the GA founders couldn't stomach, and they decided to scrap the coworking side of their operation. "If you were thoughtful about it, the question was, When do you get to a profit?" Schwartz said. "We got out of coworking because the margins were so bad it didn't seem like you were going to ever get there." Later, Schwartz met Adam for lunch, during which he expressed his concern about Neumann's industry. "I don't have to worry about that," Adam said, explaining that so long as the economy was humming along, he had only one goal. "My job is to keep growing until I'm too big to fail." Adam wanted to become just as enmeshed in the real estate world as the big banks had become in the broader economy; if WeWork grew large enough, landlords would have to bend to its will.

Adam's focus on growth at the expense of profitability fit with an emerging business theory that it was best to acquire customers by any means necessary and then figure out how to make money later. In 2012, Adam outbid Juda Srour, another office operator in New York, for a space just off Bryant Park, paying a premium of more than 25 percent above Srour's bid. Srour couldn't understand how Adam expected to turn a profit while paying that much in rent. When they spoke on the phone, Adam told Srour he was missing the point. "What I see, you don't see," Adam said. "I'm not looking to make money right now. I'm just looking to add people."

* * *

A FEW WEEKS after GCUC, Liz Elam, the conference's founder, flew to New York and had breakfast with Adam. Elam couldn't help but be impressed with WeWork's scale, even if she thought the aesthetic was a little over the top and the glass cubes difficult to actually work in. The more pressing question, as they talked about WeWork's business model, was that Elam couldn't figure out how WeWork's numbers could bridge the gap between Adam's promise of massive profits and the realities of the coworking business she knew so well. The expansion he was talking about, without much concern for producing an immediate margin, didn't make any sense to her. Elam also pointed out that no one had successfully found a way to "scale" a feeling of community, which required time and effort and a personalized touch that defied the optimization necessary to grow as rapidly as Neumann seemed intent on doing.

"That's why I'm going to hire you," Adam told Elam. He said that he wanted to buy her company and her conference and didn't see Elam as having much choice in the matter. "If you don't join me, you will compete with me," Adam said. "And you will lose."

Elam wasn't interested. "If you can't explain your financial model to me, I can't go work for you," she said later. "Plus, it felt like I was doing a deal with the devil." But Elam had been around enough successful entrepreneurs to recognize that Adam had some of the ineffable qualities that enable some founders to convince employees, investors, and everyone around them that their companies can achieve the impossible. While Elam sat in Adam's office, he picked up the phone to work on a real estate negotiation he had been trying to nail down. "He was the best negotiator I've ever seen—brash, succinct, calculating big numbers in his head on the fly," Elam said. "It felt effortless."

The negotiation Elam watched Neumann handle was more audacious than any Adam had pulled off thus far. That spring, at a wedding, Adam was talking to Rebekah's cousin Mark Lapidus, who worked in real estate, about a deal he was trying to close. "I just went hard on a building,"

Adam told Lapidus. "You've probably heard about it—the Woolworth Building."

Lapidus knew the Woolworth Building, the iconic Manhattan tower that had once been the world's tallest. "What do you mean you're *buying* it?" Lapidus said.

"I'm buying the upper floors," Adam said. "It's complicated."

"What do you mean?" Lapidus said.

"Well, I have no equity," Adam went on. "I have no debt and I'm trying to negotiate these condo docs. I have no idea what I'm doing."

Joel Schreiber had suggested to Adam that the Woolworth Building could make a trophy WeWork location. Adam considered the idea but didn't think the building was quite right for WeWork. He did think, however, that it might work as high-end residential, a market he had begun to learn more about. That year, the Neumanns purchased a $1.7 million home in the Hamptons, with a heated pool and four bedrooms—no more need to rent access to New York's summertime elite. The Neumanns deputized Danny Orenstein and several other WeWork employees to manage the renovation of their five-thousand-square-foot loft in Tribeca, a project that involved painting most of the space black, including the floors.

Adam didn't have the financial heft to take over the entire Woolworth Building, but he was ensconced enough in the world of New York money to have people to turn to. He brought in Marc Schimmel, a real estate developer he knew from the Kabbalah Centre who had invested in WeWork, as well as Alchemy, another developer. The group teamed together to pay $68 million for the top thirty floors in the building, with the investors putting up the cash, while Adam, who brought the deal together, would receive a minority stake in exchange for his continued marketing and branding expertise. "I don't know what possessed him to think he could do it, but he did it," Kenneth Horn, a partner at Alchemy, said. Horn came away impressed with Adam's negotiation skills, calling him "a bulldog." One of the Woolworth owners later admitted that Adam had probably persuaded him to sell for less than he should have.

Late one Friday night after the deal closed, Adam brought several WeWork employees to the fifty-seventh floor of the Woolworth Building, which once held an observatory with a view across all of Manhattan. Adam liked to impress people by showing off the property and telling them that he was going to market the topmost condos as "suites in the clouds." The space was empty at the time, so Adam and his employees wandered around, chucking empty beer bottles down an elevator shaft and listening to them clink and crash all the way down. Adam picked up a beer bottle that was sitting on the ground and told his employees to take a swig. He then had everyone follow him to a ledge, where there weren't any guardrails. There was a chance of falling, but in that moment, Adam was at the top of his world, gazing over the skyline of New York City.

CHAPTER SIX

The Physical Social Network

ON MARCH 1, 2012, WeWork rented out the Box, a nightclub on the Lower East Side. It was the company's second anniversary, and they were throwing a party: WeSoirée. Evening wear was encouraged, and guests were given WeWork-branded caution tape to drape across their shoulders at the photo booth—a nod to the company's constant state of construction. The entertainment for the night, sponsored by four different beer and liquor companies, included several magicians. One of them accompanied Adam on stage, stood next to him, and pulled out a wallet that suddenly burst into flames.

Adam dressed up for the occasion in a dark blazer and red scarf. The party was filled with some of the new investors he had been courting as he cast about for more funding to keep up with WeWork's growth: it was opening its fourth location in New York, and its first in Los Angeles. In addition to celebrating a birthday, WeWork was debuting a new slogan, with a video to accompany the rebrand. The clip depicted animated humans walking between buildings tagged with WeWork's name. "Ben had Jerry," the video's narration began. "Jobs had Wozniak. The Beatles had each other." The idea was that world-spanning partnerships could be formed only when people got in a room together. The word *me* appeared on the screen, then flipped upside down: *we*. A map of the United States showed beams of light emanating not from WeWork headquarters in New York, but from its recently opened location in San Francisco, the heart of the networked world.

Onstage at the Box, Adam told the crowd that his company was not a real estate business but instead one connected to the dominant companies emerging from Silicon Valley. "Until today, we were a boutique office space," Adam said. "Starting tomorrow, we're going to be the world's first 'physical social network.'"

WeWork's business didn't seem to share much with the tech companies taking off in the Mission or Menlo Park. The empires of the 2010s— Facebook, Twitter, Uber, Airbnb—were being built on "platforms" with "network effects" that made them more and more valuable with each user that signed up; WeWork leased office space in half a dozen buildings to people who paid rent. But Miguel and Adam had been talking about the networking aspect of WeWork since the beginning, a decade after Miguel had missed the social revolution with *English, baby!* When Lisa Skye woke up on her first day at WeWork back in 2010, she found a two-sentence email from Adam in her inbox: "Good morning. Let's build the largest networking community on the planet." The idea was to connect WeWork's buildings and members so that belonging to the WeWork community would become as valuable as the space itself. "We happen to need buildings just like Uber happens to need cars," Adam would say. "Just like Airbnb happens to need apartments."

The 2010s offered plenty of incentives for Adam to present WeWork as a social network. While he had no trouble finding wealthy friends in New York willing to invest a few million dollars into a steadily growing real estate firm, the global expansion he and Miguel had in mind would require the kind of investment capital flowing most freely to companies that claimed to use technology to disrupt staid industries. A successful real estate mogul might convince investors that his company was worth five times its revenue, while tech founders who promised exponential growth from the networks they were building could suddenly command valuations that were ten or even twenty times the amount of money they were bringing in. David Fincher's film *The Social Network*, about Facebook's rise, had offered an unflattering portrayal of Mark Zuckerberg while still feeding the notion that Silicon Valley cowboys were a new breed of celebrity—a billion was the new million.

Adam had begun trying to work his way into that world. "He liked sitting at the big kids' table," Aber Whitcomb, one of the cofounders of MySpace, who made an early $100,000 investment in WeWork, said. "Adam was focused on building a billion dollar company, and being a billionaire." He started hanging around the edges of a social circle in New York that orbited Sean Parker, the Napster founder and Facebook president who was played by Justin Timberlake in *The Social Network*. Parker was becoming known for throwing lavish parties at a town house in the West Village, and Neumann kept pestering a mutual friend to get him in the door. "Adam just wanted in so bad," the friend said. "He knew that the billionaire founder was the next rock star." When Adam eventually met Parker, he gave him an informal WeWork pitch: "I'm doing *The Social Network*, but the *physical* social network." Parker never invested.

* * *

THE IDEA OF ADAM as a tech entrepreneur was a stretch. He didn't know how to code; in fact, he barely used a computer at all. Adam let Rebekah and his assistants handle most of his email, given his dyslexia, and his text messages often arrived resembling a form of Morse code. One day in late 2011, Stella Templo told Adam he had just received an email from Michael Eisenberg, a partner at Benchmark. "Is that supposed to mean something to me?" Adam said. Templo told him that Benchmark was among Silicon Valley's premier venture capital firms, having backed eBay, Instagram, and Uber, among others. Miguel remembered them well from his experience in the first dot-com boom. Adam took the meeting.

Eisenberg was based in Israel, and after meeting Adam in New York, he pitched the company to his Benchmark partners in the Bay Area. Bruce Dunlevie, who cofounded Benchmark in 1995 and quickly turned a $6.7 million investment in eBay into a $5 billion stake, was initially uninterested. Benchmark was known for its selectivity, investing in fewer companies than other top VC firms. Dunlevie saw WeWork as a real estate business, which Benchmark knew nothing about. The firm looked for businesses that scaled; WeWork had to build new spaces to get more customers, which was a lot more expensive than signing up new users on an app, or convincing people to use their own cars to serve as your taxi drivers.

But Benchmark was also in the business of unearthing macroeconomic shifts, not minor competitive advantages. Both Benchmark's partners and the companies in its portfolio were trying to discern the demands and desires of a growing millennial workforce. The firm was also beginning to invest in companies, like Uber, that were trying to transform the physical world as much as the digital one. Benchmark might not know much about real estate, but it seemed like an industry ripe for some kind of disruption: the firm had several portfolio companies in New York with WeWork offices. Dunlevie decided to give Neumann a call. On the phone, Adam said the only way Dunlevie could understand what made WeWork different was to visit New York and see for himself. Dunlevie didn't usually fly to meet start-ups; they came to him. But he told Adam he would be there in three weeks and not to take money from anyone else in the meantime.

Dunlevie met Adam at Empire State. They walked downtown, to the Meatpacking District, and on to Varick Street, where WeWork Labs was located. Dunlevie was drawn to Adam's enthusiasm as they walked and talked, the conversation veering from the minutiae of the office-leasing business at one moment to Maslow's hierarchy the next: if the foundational need for having a job was resolved—getting paid—were there higher-order desires WeWork could fulfill? Dunlevie was twenty years Adam's senior, and the youthful vibe in WeWork's spaces jumped out at him as he thought back to his investment in eBay. At the time, it wasn't obvious where eBay's revenue would come from, but it was clear that the company had a devoted community that must count for something.

Dunlevie asked Adam how much he thought WeWork was worth. Adam and Miguel wanted Benchmark on board, knowing the prestige its imprimatur could offer in the tech world. Benchmark-backed Uber had recently been valued at $346 million. Adam's early gambit with Joel Schreiber had taught him the value of going big, and he threw out a number that made Dunlevie blanch.

Dunlevie was intrigued but Benchmark's partners made decisions collectively, and he said that Adam and Miguel needed to meet the rest of the firm, including Bill Gurley. Before joining Benchmark, in 1999, Gurley made a name for himself as one of Wall Street's top tech analysts. If Dunlevie sometimes invested based on energy, Gurley lived by data. He maintained a blog called *Above the Crowd*, in reference to his height—at six feet nine, he could look down on both Adam and Miguel—where he had recently published a post titled "All Revenue Is Not Created Equal," expressing concerns that shares of LinkedIn were trading at fifteen times the company's revenue. This was the kind of valuation that had emerged before the last dot-com bust, and Gurley worried that other fast-growing companies couldn't meet such lofty expectations. "Growth all by itself can be misleading," Gurley wrote. Businesses with such valuations, he said, needed network effects that allowed them to easily acquire customers. They also needed a "moat," as Warren Buffett put it, to prevent competitors from pillaging their castle. The last internet bubble had given rise to a rash of companies that generated what he called "profitless prosperity" as they sold goods and services for less than they were worth to build market share. Some, like Amazon, had pulled off the trick; many more had burned millions of dollars only to be long forgotten.

No one had yet tried to claim that real estate might be subject to network effects or that you could build a moat in a business where even the largest players control only a fraction of a percentage of the market. But Adam and Miguel flew to San Francisco armed with their new slogan and a pitch deck to make their case at Benchmark headquarters on Sand Hill Road, the heart of Silicon Valley's venture capital world. This was a more intimidating experience than pitching Joel Schreiber. Adam and Miguel stood at the head of a conference room table watching nervously as Gurley sat at the opposite end, flipping through the business model they had been working off of for the past year. "We had looked at it a thousand times," Adam said later. A few minutes into the presentation, Gurley pointed out a mistake.

Benchmark's partners were skeptical, but Dunlevie remained curious. The "unit economics"—how much money the company made on a single user—were much stronger than that of most tech companies, which could go years without deriving revenue from their users. WeWork was bringing in millions, and by the end of 2012, it made a tidy $1.7 million profit—the last profitable year in the company's history, according to the *Wall Street Journal*. There was no meaningful technology underpinning WeWork's business, but Adam and Miguel said they were eager to build some: for every rent-paying member, the founders thought they might be able to add ten digital members to their network.

Dunlevie admitted that he was interested less in the underlying numbers than he was in the way he felt at WeWork—the fact that there was something happening "that you couldn't quite put your finger on." Conventional venture capital wisdom dictated that you bet on entrepreneurs as much as on their companies. Benchmark decided to give Adam a shot. "Let's give him some money," Dunlevie said. "He'll figure it out."

* * *

ADAM WAS HESITANT about the deal. He didn't like the fact that Benchmark had pushed back on his proposed valuation and insisted on a lower one. Miguel thought they should forget about the number and focus on the validation Benchmark would give to their business. Both partners' stakes would be worth tens of millions of dollars, and considering where they had come from—and how big they believed the company could become—why jeopardize a game-changing deal to squeeze out a couple extra million dollars?

To break the stalemate, Miguel decided to make Adam an offer. If he agreed to Benchmark's terms, Miguel would turn over some of his WeWork stake to his partner. They would remain equals until the company's valuation increased to a point where Miguel's shares were worth $100 million. He would then begin transferring more and more of his stake in the company to his partner, so that the fifty-fifty split they started with would become heavily weighted toward Adam. Benchmark's offer pushed Miguel's theoretical wealth into territory he had barely imagined, and all he wanted was to continue growing the company. If Adam was so concerned about WeWork's valuation, transferring some of his equity to motivate his cofounder was a trade Miguel was willing to make.

Stella Templo emailed WeWork's staff on Adam's behalf: "A New Benchmark," she wrote in the subject line. The firm was investing $16.5 million in WeWork's Series A round of venture capital funding alongside $1 million from Rhône, a private equity firm run by Steven Langman, whom Adam knew through the Kabbalah Centre. The investment valued the company at $100 million. WeWork's several dozen employees celebrated with cheap champagne; Adam had drilled into them the importance of keeping costs low, so Dom Pérignon felt like an extravagance. Miguel went out to dinner with a friend who asked him if he was going to retire. "Why?" he said. "This is so much fun."

But the new money came with increased expectations. Dunlevie and Langman joined Adam on WeWork's first board of directors and brought with them a new level of business sophistication. At one point, after reading an email from Dunlevie critiquing an aspect of WeWork's model, Templo turned to Ariel Tiger, the CFO, and said, "You've never been called stupid so eloquently." Benchmark's involvement also meant that Adam needed to make good on his promise to build WeWork into a social network. At one point during the negotiations between Benchmark and WeWork, Facebook bought Instagram—a Benchmark company—for $1 billion.

WeWork had a long way to go to become a tech company. For starters, its IT department had been run up to this point by Joseph Fasone, a high school student from Queens who went by Joey Cables. In 2010, Fasone rented an office in the original WeWork for a tech-support business he ran. When his day ended at Hunter College High School, on the Upper East Side, Fasone took the 6 train downtown to spend a few hours at 154 Grand before going home to his parents' house. Beyond what Miguel had picked up through his early wiring efforts, WeWork had no one with any technological expertise, and the internet was occasionally spotty. A few weeks after Fasone moved in, he knocked on Miguel's office door to explain that it was difficult to operate a tech-support company without functioning internet. Miguel apologized, then asked a favor: Could Fasone take a look at the problem? Miguel opened WeWork's IT closet and handed him a list of passwords.

A month later, Adam and Miguel offered Fasone a job as WeWork's director of IT. He was sixteen. "Something would break, and I couldn't call my IT director because he was in algebra," Lisa Skye said.

By the end of 2010, when he was a junior in high school, Fasone had dropped out to join WeWork full-time. He kept odd hours and could often be found playing PlayStation in the IT closet he occupied as an office at Empire State. But he was good at his job and not that much younger than the company's increasingly youthful workforce. A year after joining WeWork, Fasone started dating a WeWork community manager.

But functional Wi-Fi was a basic office requirement, not a valuation multiplier. That's where the physical social network came in. Adam and Miguel's pitch deck from 2009 had listed WeConnect as a café offering "unlimited internet" and "high end coffee," but the name had since been reattached to a piece of software that WeWork hoped would not only make it easier to print documents and book a conference room, but also offer a proprietary LinkedIn that would connect the company's scattered buildings. WeWork claimed that a third of its members already did business together: an accountant on the fifth floor of 154 Grand might hire a graphic designer on the third floor, and vice versa. WeConnect was meant to allow that accountant to connect with a graphic designer at WeWork's new location in West Hollywood or with any of the 3,000 other WeWork members.

Building WeConnect was more difficult than talking about it. Miguel used his basic programming skills from *English, baby!* and worked with his brother Kyle and a team of developers in India to build an early prototype. On launch day for a new feature, they looked on in horror when it took minutes for a single profile page to load. Another designer who worked on the project left after a few months, saying she couldn't "fully wrap my head around the scalability and sustainability of it all." By 2013, hardly any WeWork members were using the network in a meaningful way. It was nice to walk down the hall and meet other entrepreneurs, but the benefit of knowing every WeWork member wasn't clear, and there was no shortage of other ways to connect digitally.

On a conference call with Bruce Dunlevie and Michael Eisenberg, the Benchmark partners told Adam and Miguel they had done good work getting the company this far, but that WeWork needed to become more tech-forward and bring in the talent to get there. Specifically, Benchmark recommended hiring a chief product officer to take over for Miguel, who had performed the role without having the title. Miguel would manage the design of WeWork's physical spaces, while Adam oversaw the digital side. Adam tried to hire Aber Whitcomb, from MySpace, to run WeWork's tech team, but he turned down the job. Through a search firm, WeWork found Mike Sommers, a former vice president of product development at AOL.

"I'm here to build the killer app," Sommers told Miguel after taking the job.

Miguel took Benchmark's suggestion as a mild affront. He knew his technical skills were lacking, but he also knew the ins and outs of WeWork better than anyone. It wasn't obvious that the company could or should produce a killer app. Why not let him hire a head of engineering to handle the coding while he thought up ideas that made sense alongside WeWork's business?

Sommers lasted eight months—the first in a long line of executives brought in to push the company's technological capabilities. He was replaced by Roee Adler, the chief product officer at a start-up based in Tel Aviv, who came recommended by one of Michael Eisenberg's partners. Adler and a team of half a dozen engineers were tasked with figuring out how to fulfill WeWork's tech promise.

But the team found itself spending much of its time simply making sure the company's back end could keep up with its growth. "The member network was held up with chewing gum and prayers," a software engineer who joined the company in 2013 said. WeWork's operations depended on a hodgepodge of Google Docs and disorganized spreadsheets, and Adler's team built a pair of programs to streamline operations: Space Man would handle billing, while Space Station would help community managers keep track of their locations—everything from reports about broken toilets to notes about what kind of dessert each member liked so that community managers could hand out personalized gifts. Some employees questioned the value of building these systems at all. Why not buy software from Salesforce or another tech giant instead of leaning on the company's small team of developers and engineers to patch together its own system?

But Adam maintained a sense that he and his company could do the impossible, and everyone from Miguel on down found it easier to find a way to make things happen rather than question the wisdom of his ambitions. In this case, building software internally was crucial to presenting WeWork as a tech company, and finding new ways to make money. They hoped that the member network would allow them to sell various goods and services to members—from health-care plans to discounted software subscriptions—of which WeWork could take a cut. One employee looked into how the company might launch its own cryptocurrency. Data collection was becoming the cornerstone of every fast-growing tech company, and Adam walked in one day to tell the engineers that he wanted to see when and for how long members were using different parts of each WeWork by tracking their phones as they moved through the building.

"I don't think the technology is quite there yet," one WeWork engineer said.

"I think it is," Adam replied.

WeWork's engineers grew to live by what they called the BASS rule— Because Adam Said So. The team had a tradition of loudly clapping after an engineer presented a new product for his colleagues, but the applause became so regular that Adam walked out of his office one day to inquire: Why all the fuss if they weren't producing any results? (The team started booing one another instead, which Neumann liked better.) The engineers were working twelve-hour days, sometimes more, plus the weekend construction duty expected of every employee; one night, Joey Cables found himself installing a toilet in a new WeWork location. It wasn't totally clear to the tech team that their work could produce what Neumann wanted. "Adam used to say, 'We're on a rocket ship,'" the WeWork engineer said. "The joke was, 'A rocket ship to where?'"

CHAPTER SEVEN

Reality Distortion Field

A FEW WEEKS into 2014, Benjamin Dyett organized a meeting of what he called the Five Families of Coworking. Dyett was the owner of Grind, an upmarket coworking space that he opened in 2011. Landlords had begun to shift their attitude toward the new operators, thanks in part to the growing attention lavished upon WeWork, but the industry remained at a precarious moment: small fish swimming alongside much bigger sharks. The meeting of the Five Families was meant to build a community of communities. "We'll be enjoying some chit-chat, future talk, and best practices sharing, all fueled by some beer and wine," Dyett wrote in his invitation. "Leave all agendas and judgments at home."

There were now many more than five coworking families—the Neumanns and Dyetts as well as the Bacigalupos, the Levys, the Hodaris, the Lancasters, and so on—a dozen of whom showed up on a Monday night at a furniture showroom in the Time Warner Center, just off Central Park. "You had a lot of people who were bitter competitors, but there was a sense of camaraderie," said Tony Bacigalupo, who ran New Work City, a few blocks from 154 Grand. Dyett had gotten to know Adam over the years as someone eager to chat about the business, if a bit eccentric; Adam wasn't wearing any shoes when Dyett met him at WeWork's Varick location. Dyett and Neumann both had the same number of offices back in 2012; since then, Adam had raised far more money than any of his competitors, and his capital-boosted ambitions had left his rivals behind. "Everyone else had to make a profit," Dyett said. "Adam didn't."

Neumann showed up late to the meeting of the Five Families, flanked by two assistants. He walked past several rows of chairs occupied by other coworking operators who were listening to a presentation about the ins and outs of selecting office furniture. Adam settled into a bright orange couch at the side of the room, crossed his arms, and waited for a chance to speak. When the time came for Q&A, he lifted himself up onto the back of the couch, raised his hand, and proceeded to talk for the next twenty minutes. Adam didn't have urgent thoughts to share on the ergonomics of desk chairs; he wanted to deliver a warning. Everyone in the room had been building their businesses in boom times, with the market only going up in the half decade since the recession. There would be a correction, Adam said, and no one could say what that might do to their businesses. Would tenants abandon their month-to-month leases, leaving the Five Families to find a way to pay rent on their buildings without as much money coming in? He urged caution.

Adam then pivoted to laying out his plan for WeWork. His company was opening a new space every eighteen days, he said, and his aim was to make WeWork as big as he could as fast as he could—the same goal he expressed to Juda Srour and Jake Schwartz. He was taking out twenty-year leases, and the free-rent periods he was given at the beginning of each one was allowing him to gobble up space while he could and worry about the escalating rents when the time came.

Shlomo Silber, who ran two coworking spaces in New York, raised his hand to ask a question. How did such growth fit with the macroeconomic warning Neumann had just offered? Adam brushed him off. WeWork wasn't a real estate company like the rest of them, he said; it was a tech-enabled physical social network. He was a community builder, not a landlord.

Adam left before the event ended, leaving several of the attendees to roll their eyes at his hyperbole. A few of them came away feeling a mixture of excitement and fear. "He thought there was a utopian future he could bring about, and I remember being kind of excited to hear someone who was able to think at that level," Bacigalupo said. "But it also felt like the villain in the movie telling you the whole plot before he kills you. It would have been funny if that speech bought us time to compete. It didn't."

* * *

A **SOFTWARE COMPANY** might operate for years on Benchmark's investment, paying its employees, buying server space, and renting an office. But We-Work was not a software company. The costs of its leases, renovations, and day-to-day operations were much larger and required additional funding to keep up with the growth Adam was promising—he intended to open more locations in 2014 than he had in the company's first four years combined—as well as the increased expectations that bigger investors brought to WeWork's business. An employee on WeWork's finance team recalls Bruce Dunlevie telling WeWork that he thought the company might one day be worth as much as $10 billion. "At the time, we thought it was *crazy* to think the company would ever be worth even $1 billion," the employee said.

Benchmark had come to Neumann, but if the company was going to continue expanding, Adam needed to go out looking for money. A team at WeWork put together a proper pitch deck and presented it to a wide range of investors in 2013. JPMorgan Asset Management looked at the deal but decided to pass, as did General Atlantic, a venture capital firm, after one of its employees pointed out a new error in WeWork's model: a "-" had been replaced with a "+" in a spreadsheet, which prompted WeWork's model to assume that its buildings were operating at more than 100 percent occupancy.

Even as some investors passed on WeWork, Adam had grown confident enough in his pitch to remain picky. *Shark Tank*, the televised start-up competition that glorified the fundraising process, was interested in having WeWork appear as its first nine-figure valuation, but doing so would mean giving up equity to the show's producers. Goldman Sachs said that it was willing to invest at a $220 million valuation, more than doubling Benchmark's figure from a year before. But Adam again thought that number was too low; Airbnb was working on a deal valuing itself at more than $2 billion. Some WeWork employees weren't certain their company was worth anything close to that, and turning down a large investment with Goldman's stamp of approval seemed foolish, especially given that WeWork was running out of cash. But Adam decided to look elsewhere. "There were *no* other offers on the table," the finance team member said. "It was one of the ballsiest things I've ever seen."

If anyone was unsurprised it was Miguel. He had recognized Adam's cockiness instantly upon meeting his cofounder, and WeWork's early success only fed Neumann's belief in his own powers of persuasion. "Adam has an endless faith in his ability to convince people to do things he wants them to do," Miguel said in 2013.

Adam's faith was rewarded. Not long after rejecting the Goldman Sachs deal, WeWork raised $40 million from investors, led by DAG Ventures, a private equity firm that often invested bigger checks into companies that Benchmark had already backed. The Series B round valued WeWork at $440 million—double the offer from Goldman Sachs.

* * *

IN 2013, WEWORK MOVED into a new headquarters after years of bouncing from one floor to another inside the company's half-finished spaces. The new office at 222 Broadway had several appealing features. It occupied two floors, with Adam's office looking down upon an atrium where his two hundred employees milled about. Across the street was an even more personally satisfying view: the building where Adam once begged Stella

Templo to help him stay in the country. Adam was also tickled to find out that WeWork's new space had been used as the set for the movie *Wall Street*. WeWork put up a poster of Michael Douglas in French cuffs and suspenders to mark the location of Gordon Gekko's fictional office.

The space was a more appropriate setting than WeWork's previous offices for a visit from Jimmy Lee, a legendary banker at JPMorgan: Gekko's character was said to have been based partly on Lee, who had worked with companies ranging from General Motors to Facebook. JPMorgan had been keeping its eye on WeWork. Noah Wintroub, one of the firm's top investment bankers, had met Adam at a happy hour at a hotel in SoHo that was hosted by Michael Eisenberg, from Benchmark. Adam asked Wintroub to step outside while he smoked a cigarette, and complained about an issue with one of WeWork's accounts at Chase; Adam was impressed that Wintroub made a call, and the situation got resolved.

Wintroub lived and worked on the West Coast, and had made it a mission to help JPMorgan become more involved with young start-ups. Jamie Dimon, the bank's CEO, had emerged from the financial crisis as a leading financial voice—a Wall Street titan who managed to remain friendly with Barack Obama—but the firm had struggled to break into the tech world. Goldman Sachs and Morgan Stanley dominated the business of helping the tide of world-beating start-ups navigate the financial world and eventually make their way toward a public listing on the stock exchange. WeWork wasn't a pure tech play, but the opportunity to disrupt the real estate business seemed like a big one. JPMorgan was still Manhattan's largest private office occupier—the position that Adam had promised to usurp—so it knew the pains and costs of leasing and maintaining office space. The *Wall Street Journal* reported that after Dimon toured a WeWork location with Neumann, he tore up a design for a new JPMorgan space in Manhattan and agreed to pay WeWork $600,000 to design a new one.

In February of 2014, less than a year after WeWork was valued at $440 million, JPMorgan Asset Management and several other investors put an additional $150 million into the company at a valuation of $1.5 billion. Adam began spending time with Jimmy Lee, who became his first serious mentor in the financial world, an alternately encouraging and sobering voice in Adam's ear. (Lee chastised Wintroub after Adam was slow to thank him for giving a glowing quote to *Forbes* magazine on WeWork's behalf.) Neumann appreciated Lee, he said later, as a banker who "did business with a handshake and made bets that were first based on people and then numbers." Whenever WeWork went public, JPMorgan's early involvment figured to help it land a role in handling WeWork's IPO.

The new valuation made WeWork one of just fifty American "unicorns," a term invented the year prior to describe the growing cohort of start-ups with previously unheard-of private valuations above $1 billion. It was hard for anyone to believe how far WeWork had come in four years. Adam flew with friends and family to Turks and Caicos for a three-day thirty-fifth birthday party. Miguel had moved into a nice apartment in Manhattan with a great view, fulfilling his childhood dream of being able to see the New York City skyline from his home, but he felt bashful sharing the valuation with his friends and family.

At a party in May to celebrate an expansion of WeWork's Gordon Gekko headquarters, several of New York's biggest landlords, including Steven Roth, the septuagenarian founder of Vornado, stood under a net of white and black balloons and toasted Neumann, the young man they had once looked at with skepticism. "Adam always says, 'No schmucks and no assholes,'" Roth said. But "the definition of a schmuck is someone who rents a property at .5x and then that guy turns around and rents it at 1.5x."

Adam corrected Roth by holding up two fingers, to indicate WeWork's margin was actually even larger. That, Roth amended, was "the definition of an asshole," before ending his speech and taking a swing at a large gong that was engraved with WeWork's name. Adam and his team used to bang a gong each time WeWork signed a new lease, until there were so many that the celebratory noise became too much to bear.

* * *

AFTER THE SERIES B investment from DAG Ventures, Adam and Miguel finally offered employees a benefit they had put off: WeWork stock. If it was going to be a tech company, it needed to act like one. At WeWork headquarters, Adam and other WeWork executives called employees in one by one, and told them how much equity they would be receiving. "You're gonna make a really good millionaire," an executive told one employee while sharing the details of her stock package. On weeknights, Adam would sometimes walk around WeWork headquarters offering shares and a tequila shot to anyone working late. (Only the boldest employees followed up on the offers in the light of day.) The potential financial boon was exciting for WeWork's employees, some of whom were right out of college and barely understood how a stock option worked, or came from industries where such equity stakes were rarely handed out. Adam bragged openly about the fact that WeWork underpaid its employees, but promised that if they remained committed to the company, their options would one day more than make up the difference.

Up to that point, the benefits of working for WeWork were less quantifiable: a sense of purpose, fun parties, free beer. In August of 2014, WeWork's two hundred employees boarded buses in New York and Boston, where the company had opened its newest location, to make their way to WeWork's annual corporate retreat, called Summer Camp. The New York crowd gathered at sunrise in front of the American Museum of Natural History. "This is like a mini Burning Man," one person said, standing in front of the statue of Theodore Roosevelt on horseback. At 6:45 a.m., someone opened a bottle of Patrón and offered a toast: "To Summer Camp!"

For a third straight year, WeWork was hosting its employees and members at a children's camp five hours north of New York City that was owned by the parents of Mark Lapidus, Rebekah's cousin, who helped Adam land the Woolworth Building deal and had since joined WeWork as its head of real estate. Three hundred people attended the first camp, in 2012, which cost \$200,000—members paid a nominal fee to attend—an expense WeWork chalked up to marketing. "Thank you for being part of something that actually has a meaning," Adam said onstage a year later, at Summer Camp 2013. "Every one of us is here because we want to do something that actually makes the world a better place—but we wanna make money doing it!"

By 2014, Summer Camp had quintupled in size to include more than 1,400 WeWork employees, members, and friends. The event offered traditional camp fare—archery, s'mores, acoustic sing-alongs to Weezer's "Say It Ain't So"—in a start-up-friendly atmosphere: one attendee wore a T-shirt that read BOBA FETT WAS A FREELANCER. (Adam loved rap music, and campers were assigned to sleep in tents laid out along Wu-Tang Way, Slick Rick Road, Biggie Boulevard, Lil' Kim Lane, and 2Pac Trail.) A yoga class took savasana to the soundtrack from *The Social Network* while an entrepreneurial arts and crafts hackathon challenged attendees to come up with the worst possible business idea—something to outdo onesies with knee pads. Five Flags, an amusement park that only sold tickets through the DMV, had won the first competition. The deranged entrepreneurs of 2014 came up with a marketplace for renting babies that could be used to pick up women, a hepatitis factory with a mission to spread hepatitis, and a coworking space with dial-up internet and enforced isolation.

On Saturday afternoon, Lew Frankfort, the former CEO of Coach, who had invested in WeWork alongside JPMorgan and joined the company's board of directors, gave a talk at a fire pit in front of a few hundred campers. Adam and Rebekah sat in the front row. Frankfort encouraged the assembled entrepreneurs to embrace single-mindedness, telling them to "never be captive to your employees" in the pursuit of your vision. "A drive for excellence and a fear of failure is a double-edged sword," Frankfort said. "If you have it, embrace it."

"Lew, are you going to party with us?" someone in the crowd asked.

While some attendees viewed Summer Camp as a networking

opportunity, passing business cards between bunk beds, it was for most a weekend to forget adulthood. "This is my only vacation this summer, so I'm getting into as much trouble as humanly possible," the cofounder of a small social media company told Marisa Meltzer, a *New York Times* reporter who had purchased a ticket to the event, much to the chagrin of WeWork's PR team. The cofounder had taken psychedelic mushrooms on the first night of camp and was carrying around a water gun filled with vodka.

The campground was dotted with canoes filled with cans of Coors Light and Smirnoff Ice, and several people participated in a contest that required eating a pie, sprinting to the lake and back, and then chugging a giant boot full of beer. There were a dozen hookah pipes lined up on a table, and the scent of marijuana wafted over a "Logistics for a Start-up" talk given by a senior employee from UPS. On the second night of camp, Rebekah's old friend Michael Franti performed, leaping into the crowd to dance with the Neumanns. By the end of the weekend, a twenty-seven-year-old marketing manager from Brooklyn had success-fully hooked up with multiple strangers, consumed more tequila than she had in the previous year, and thought the weekend had even been a little productive. "I've already followed up with some people I met," she said after the event. "I'm hoping they'll evolve into real lasting friendships and business connections."

For the company's young workforce, Summer Camp was a dream weekend—the most fun they'd had since college and the ultimate collapse of work-life boundaries that WeWork promised. Drinking and partying had been ingrained in WeWork's culture from the beginning, with Neumann serving as partyer in chief ever since he sealed the Empire State deal over a bottle of whiskey. During an outdoor party at a WeWork employee's house, when they ran out of wood for a bonfire, Adam picked up a piece of picnic furniture and tossed it into the flames. The company had started hosting lavish Halloween parties, to which Adam wore elab-orate costumes. In 2013, he went as Gandalf, the wizard from *The Lord of the Rings.* A year later he and Rebekah painted their faces and bodies blue to dress up as the Na'vi, from *Avatar.* During a company ski trip, a WeWork employee remembers watching as Adam and several executives grabbed waiters' trays from the hotel bar so they could go sledding. When a hotel employee asked them to stop, Neumann yelled, "Fuck that—I could buy this hotel!" Later that night, a few WeWork designers decided that the hotel's furniture was laid out all wrong. The next morning, the entire lobby was rearranged. WeWork was asked not to come back.

✻ ✻ ✻

AMONG THE BELIEFS Adam had adopted from many founders in Silicon Valley was a lack of interest in sales—the product, whatever it was, should be so good that it sold itself. He tried to avoid using the term *sales* altogether, pushing whatever selling the company did onto its "community" team. But as WeWork opened more spaces, some of them not far from locations that already existed, the company needed to ramp up its operation to keep its occupancy rate high.

In 2014, Benchmark, which had also been the earliest major investor in Uber, helped recruit Luca Gualco, who had helped Uber expand internationally, to lead WeWork's "community team." (Adam wasn't ready to lose the euphemism.) Gualco was a forty-three-year-old former professional water polo player from Italy who made a habit of lifting weights at WeWork headquarters and bursting into song at company events. He called WeWork employees at all hours of the night to demand reports on their numbers. "There are only two things that matter in a company," he told one group of employees. "Sales, and everything else."

Gualco brought along Patrick Morselli, another senior Uber employee, to help manage WeWork's expansion. Morselli quickly recognized certain differences between the two companies and their leaders. "Travis is an analytical person. He thinks like an engineer. He's process driven, organized, meticulous," Morselli told me. "Adam is the opposite. He's charismatic. He's a dealmaker. He wins people over because they like him. But he doesn't work systematically." Adam wasn't bad with numbers; employees marveled at his ability to scan an empty building and calculate how many desks WeWork could squeeze inside. But he had built WeWork on guts and charm rather than by creating a system to support its growth. The two Uber emigrés set about trying to create a "playbook"—an idea ported from Uber and popular all over the tech world—that would contain a standardized plan for the company's expanding legion of employees. Their constant refrain became "Well, at Uber…"

The comparison annoyed WeWork employees. Uber had plenty of factors complicating its business, but taxi service was more or less universal across the globe, lending itself to a relatively uniform playbook. Workplace demands, by contrast, varied widely: when WeWork arrived in the UK, in 2014, the company had to install espresso machines because Londoners wouldn't accept drip coffee. Angelenos cared about on-site parking in a way that New Yorkers didn't. And while Uber insisted on abdicating responsibility for the cars that its drivers used—hiding behind the shield of being a "platform"—WeWork not only had to lease its buildings but fully load them with features, perform routine maintenance, and ensure they had competent humans at the wheel.

WeWork employees from this period tend to describe their experience by making analogies to fast-moving vehicles: building an airplane while flying, or pedaling a bicycle desperately so it doesn't fall over. At the beginning of 2013, WeWork had ten buildings in development; by 2014, it was working on more than a hundred. "We are in a consumption phase like nothing that has ever been seen," Adam said, describing the company's appetite for leases. He began to compare WeWork's expanding reach to conquering empires of the past, boasting in 2015 that WeWork was undergoing "the fastest physical growth in the history of the world," with perhaps one exception. "I'm not sure about Roman times," he said. "There might have been some very high-growth companies there."

Cities around the country were clamoring for WeWork, which had successfully marketed itself as jet fuel for local entrepreneurs. San Francisco's mayor rerouted police patrols when Adam agreed to build a location in a less desirable neighborhood, while Chicago mayor Rahm Emanuel pressed Adam to open a WeWork there. Anyone who got in the way of WeWork's expansion was liable to be shoved aside: Two non-profits lost their offices in downtown San Francisco when WeWork offered to pay the building's landlord double the rent in order to take over the space from the organizations, both of which worked to prevent tenants from being evicted from their homes in San Francisco.

To keep up, WeWork was hiring architects, salespeople, community managers, mechanical engineers, coders, real estate brokers, and more. At one company meeting, a newly hired software engineer yelled out, "Adam, we're hiring slightly over pi people per week." Many of the new arrivals came from jobs at dull real estate companies or from the lowest rungs of architecture firms and found it exhilarating to be given so much responsibility at a successful company that also knew how to throw a good party. One employee decided she wanted to work at WeWork because the company had the word *fuck* on its website. ("It was something about, 'We fucking break down walls!'") If the salaries were lower, WeWork's hiring managers told them not to worry: the company's stock, they reminded them, was on the rise.

Ted Kramer, an energetic veteran of several start-ups, joined WeWork's operations team in 2013, taking a pay cut in the hope that any shares he accumulated would one day be worth much more. Kramer was the kind of eager go-getter that every fast-growing start-up depended on, and in less than two years, he helped open WeWorks in New York, Los Angeles, San Francisco, Washington, DC, Austin, Boston, Seattle, Miami, Chicago, and its first overseas locations in London.

The launch of each WeWork presented new challenges, especially given Adam's insistence that every location open on time. Kramer opened the first WeWork in Berkeley, California, without a functional front door, which left him to buy breakfast for members as an apology for the cold

East Bay wind blowing into the building. A new WeWork in SoHo, half a dozen blocks from 154 Grand Street, didn't have a bathroom, so Kramer bought out all the pastries in a nearby coffee shop so that members could use the cafe's toilet. The aging HVAC system in WeWork's first Washington, DC, location required constant repair—Green Desk's founding ethos having been sacrificed at the altar of growth. Keeping expenses low was key to WeWork's model, even if the company's tequila budget could sometimes get out of control. "You've got three options: fast, right, or cheap," Kramer said. "WeWork always picked fast and cheap."

When they took a moment to breathe, Kramer and other employees sometimes had a tough time explaining exactly why they were working so hard. Many of them looked up to Miguel, who still spent considerable time in the trenches, designing and building out new spaces. But the company was beginning to form itself in Adam's image. For all his bluster, he could be an inspiring leader, pushing WeWork employees beyond their limits for the good of the cause and the promise of riches down the line. They compared his aura to the "reality distortion field" that an Apple employee once described as emanating from Steve Jobs, convincing anyone within its radius that the impossible was not only plausible, but exactly what they were going to do. After several workers installed a large stone table in a Manhattan WeWork, one employee noticed smears of blood left behind by one of the workers, which felt poetic.

Many WeWork employees were in their first jobs and uncertain about what to expect from a CEO. Toward the end of 2014, Carl Pierre, a WeWork employee in Washington, DC, arrived at the company's Dupont Circle location to find its game room trashed. They had been rushing to open the location on time, busing a dozen construction workers in from New York the night before the building's grand opening to get rid of more than five hundred pounds of trash. Now, the game room was strewn with unwashed cups, and Pierre said the place smelled like weed. When they reviewed security footage from the night before, preparing to identify and chastise whichever WeWork member had disrespected the community, they were surprised to see that it wasn't a member at all. Adam and another WeWork executive had spent the night drinking beers and playing on a Time Crisis video game console. Their employees were left to pick up the mess.

* * *

A FEW WEEKS LATER, WeWork employees arrived at the company's Gordon Gekko headquarters one morning to find that a large glass wall in Adam's office was cracked. The night before, an employee had apparently broken it with a bottle of Don Julio 1942, Adam's favorite tequila. Adam and a group of employees had been celebrating yet another funding round: $355 million, at a valuation of $5 billion. WeWork's Series D put it among the world's dozen most valuable unicorns, ahead of Spotify and just a few spots behind Theranos.

The deal allowed WeWork shareholders to offload some of their stakes. Adam and Miguel kept their shares in an entity called We Holdings, which Adam controlled, and sold roughly $40 million worth of shares in the tender offer. This was an unusually large amount for the founders of a young start-up to take out of a company while professing their belief in its world-altering ambitions. The number wasn't announced publicly, but rumors spread. Ted Kramer made a habit of checking stray papers on WeWork's printers and found details about the transaction left behind in a tray.

But Adam had another reason to be excited. A deal this large would typically diminish the founders' control over the company. Miguel wasn't especially concerned, having already transferred some control to his co-founder. But as part of the deal, Adam engineered a change to WeWork's charter with the help of Jen Berrent, WeWork's new general counsel, that gave him ten votes for each share of the company he owned. The arrangement would give him roughly 65 percent of the votes on any company matter.

These "supervoting" shares had become popular in Silicon Valley, where founders feared losing control of their companies. Mark Zuckerberg had negotiated a similar deal, as had Travis Kalanick at Uber. Many investors were so eager to get in on the small group of start-ups that could make plausible arguments for world domination that they often believed they had no choice but to accept such founder-friendly terms. But giving so much control of a company to an entrepreneur who had never run a business of this size before was a risk. As the deal was finalized, Bruce Dunlevie, Neumann's first major investor, tried pushing back on the arrangement. But Benchmark wasn't eager to lose favor with Neumann, and it didn't have much standing in the fight, having just given Travis Kalanick similar control at Uber. Dunlevie relented, but not before offering a warning to Berrent and WeWork's board. "I'll just leave you with this thought," Dunlevie said. "Absolute power corrupts absolutely."

CHAPTER EIGHT

Greater Fools

IN AN ARTICLE TITLED "Office of the Future," about the most innovative company in commercial real estate, *Fast Company* magazine explained that the global economy was moving faster than ever, aided by the internet and a rise in entrepreneurship that entrenched real estate interests weren't prepared to meet. Start-ups were pivoting every six months, doubling or halving in size along the way, and no one needed a ten-year lease anymore. The company had been founded by an entrepreneur himself, and offered furnished offices whenever and increasingly wherever anyone needed them, with new locations opening at a rapid pace. Hospitality was a top priority: employees were instructed to answer the phone with a "smile in the voice." The company was still figuring out all the ways its spaces might be used—the Backstreet Boys, who were then at the peak of their fame, had just used one to hold a global videoconference—but at its core, the business hinged on bringing a "sense of community" to shared offices.

The *Fast Company* article appeared in March of 2000, when Miguel was working on *English, baby!* and Adam was still in the Israeli Navy. The company that was supposedly building the office of the future was Regus, launched in Belgium in 1989 by Mark Dixon, a British businessman who had dropped out of school to start a lunch delivery service called Dial-A-Snack. Regus had 250 locations in twenty-five countries and was opening two more every week. Dixon had a Neumannian view of his company's future, a decade before Adam joined him in the industry. He believed that people would use Regus spaces to work, to congregate, to build community. "I tell our employees that we're just getting started," Dixon said. "If we get it right, we have an opportunity to change the world."

* * *

WEWORK'S RISE FROM nothing to becoming a multibillion-dollar company in half a decade gave many in the real estate world a sense of déjà vu. In 2000, when the *Fast Company* article ran, Regus was preparing to go public on the London Stock Exchange. The company had become a crucial cog in the booming start-up economy of the '90s, and its shares quickly shot up by almost 40 percent, reaching a total market capitalization—the stock market's version of a private company valuation—above $3 billion. But when the dot-com bubble burst, Regus collapsed with it. Tenants bailed on their flexible contracts, leaving Regus with a devastating decrease in revenue to cover the costs of the long-term leases it still had to pay for. In 2003, the US arm of Regus filed for bankruptcy.

By the time WeWork secured a private valuation of $5 billion at the end of 2014, Regus had recovered and would soon rebrand as IWG— International Workplace Group—a nicely profitable if boring company. But IWG had not returned to its peak stock market value, a number WeWork had now blown past, despite the fact that IWG had more than two thousand locations bringing in over $2 billion in revenue. WeWork, by comparison, had just two dozen spaces producing close to $150 million.

WeWork was clearly doing something different than IWG. Its spaces were vibrant and millennial-friendly, while most of IWG's were practical and bland. But it wasn't obvious that an aesthetic edge offered WeWork a competitive advantage worthy of its valuation. When critics asked Adam how his business would fare in a recession like the one that felled Regus, his response was much the same as the one Dixon had offered without success: big companies will downsize into WeWork, while laid-off freelancers will look for something beyond a home office. "What's shocking to me is that you could look at our P&L" — profit and loss — "and then you could pull up Regus's, and it's the exact same business," said a member of WeWork's finance team. "A lot of people got caught up in the hype and Adam's charisma, but when you looked at the numbers, it was always kind of clear."

The task of filling the chasm between WeWork's vision and the promise presented to investors was left to Adam and his pitch, which needed to be properly staged. He insisted that potential investors join him for a WeWork tour, and while there were plenty of occasions in which WeWork locations were naturally lively, it fell to the company's employees to ensure those moments lined up with Adam's pitches. Community managers became experts at throwing impromptu parties that could be "activated" in the precise ninety-second window Jamie Dimon or Bruce Dunlevie walked through a WeWork common area with Adam. ("You got to know which members were willing to come back for a third bagel if the VIP was running late," one community manager said.) To emphasize the company's digital qualifications, Adam placed WeWork's software engineers, rather than Miguel's team of physical designers, at desks next to his office. "These aren't architects or builders," Adam would tell visitors. "This is my tech team."

But Adam needed help as WeWork began approaching larger investors. While pitching WeWork's Series C and D rounds, which included traditional Wall Street institutions — JPMorgan, T. Rowe Price, Goldman Sachs — Adam had been joined by Michael Gross, who replaced Ariel Tiger, Adam's navy buddy, as WeWork's CFO at the end of 2013. Gross knew Rebekah from childhood, and from college at Cornell. He had spent much of the 2000s in finance; in 2011, after his private equity firm invested in Morgans Hotels, a boutique chain run by Studio 54 founder Ian Schrager, Gross was installed as CEO. WeWork had talked with Morgans about building a music-themed space—WeRock—at one of its New York hotels.

Gross was blond and boyish, and moved naturally within New York's elite circles, swimming laps with investment bankers at the New York Athletic Club on Central Park South. A few months after joining We-Work, he helped coax Lew Frankfort, the former Coach CEO whose son was Gross's friend, to invest $7 million in the company and become a board member. "Michael's the kind of guy who could take a Saudi sheik out for a night in New York and come back with $200 million," Jamie Hodari, the founder of a WeWork rival called Industrious, said. "If I was trying to get into sipping rum, Michael would say, 'There's this perfect place in Tribeca for that.' Adam would say, 'Have you thought about tequila?'" As one WeWork executive put it, "Michael was everything Adam wanted to be."

Some investors didn't know what to think when Adam ordered tequila shots at dinner or took his shoes off during a presentation, and Gross added a note of refinement to Adam's wild energy. He became Adam's right-hand man and party buddy—Gross was the other executive who trashed the Dupont Circle WeWork game room during a late night of booze and Time Crisis—and most importantly, his running mate on the fundraising trail. Adam had stopped describing Kabbalah as the inspiration for WeWork, on a recommendation from Lew Frankfort ("Wear your bracelet if you want, just don't talk about it"), but he still described the company's appeal as stemming from an ephemeral "energy" in the air. "It can't exactly be touched," he said. "It's a feeling." After Adam walked into a room and put on a bravura performance for a potential investor, Gross could reassure any skeptics that there was a steady hand directing things behind the scenes. Adam seemed to feed off of Gross's natural confidence; Rebekah lamented to another WeWork executive that "the only person who can get Adam at his best is Michael."

Adam had always leaned on his partners, going all the way back to Susan Lazar in the baby clothes business. (In 2013, Adam sold his stake in Big Tent.) His fundraising efforts with Gross were now key to the company's growth, and while Miguel made sure the company's physical product was appealing to investors, he had taken a back seat in the financing pitch. Miguel believed in the company and the quality of what they were building, but he didn't always have Adam's ability to prevaricate about its grandest ambitions. While speaking to a group of WeWork members in 2015, Miguel admitted that they still didn't know what would happen when the economy dipped. He thought the company offered something valuable, but WeWork didn't have a magic trick that would allow it to subvert the economics of the business it was in. "There's nothing that we do that isn't in line with what everyone else does," Miguel told the group, before seeming to realize this wasn't the most compelling pitch. When he tried to offer an example of how WeWork separated itself from other office space operators, he mentioned how much fun people had at its recent Halloween party, where Busta Rhymes performed. WeWork's competitive advantage, it seemed, was knowing how to put on a good show.

* * *

ONE EXPLANATION FOR the blindness investors appeared to have for the realities of WeWork's business was the fact that every private valuation of the 2010s required a certain suspension of disbelief. "The funny thing about 'hard numbers' is that they can give a false sense of security," Bill Gurley wrote in *Above the Crowd* in 2014. He was talking about the math behind valuations and how widely their underlying calculations could vary, depending on what numbers you put in. In this case, Gurley was defending an outsize valuation: Uber, another Benchmark company, had recently been valued at $17 billion. Gurley was critiquing an NYU professor who said that Uber's valuation was inflated "by a factor of 25."

The professor's analysis presumed that Uber's total addressable market, or TAM, was the $100 billion taxi-and-limousine market. Gurley believed that Uber's TAM was every single car on the road—a market theoretically worth $1.3 trillion.

This kind of blue-sky thinking was saturating Silicon Valley. When Airbnb's founders first raised money from venture capital investors, an adviser encouraged them to tweak only one item in their pitch deck: swap out a letter and boost their $30 million revenue target to $30 *billion*. "Investors want B's, baby," the adviser said. Adam was trying to position WeWork in similarly ambitious terms. "We are not competing with other coworking spaces," he said. "We are competing with offices—and that is a $15 trillion asset class in the U.S." Globally, the real estate market was closer to $200 trillion.

Real estate is a fragmented business, with none of the network effects that allowed tech companies to devour entire industries. Even the world's largest real estate firms control a fraction of 1 percent of the market. But venture capitalists weren't looking for ceilings; they wanted B's, baby. What if WeWork could break that mold? A global brand known for providing the kinds of offices that people actually wanted to work in had huge potential alongside anonymous building operators like Brookfield and Vornado. Two percent of the market could make Amazon's revenues look like a pittance.

Investors from Wall Street to Sand Hill Road were also primed to hope. The post-recession era ushered in an age of hypergrowth, where one well-timed hit could make a career. Low interest rates enabled speculative investors to fund risky bets that could produce outsize returns. Individual investors were putting more of their money into index funds, which broadly tracked the economy, leaving mutual fund managers seeking alternatives to prove they could beat a market that was already booming. At the end of 2014, the *New York Times* published an article about investors casting about for the next Uber, which was now a decacorn—a company with a $10 billion valuation. WeWork, which the

Times described as "Uber for offices," was among a group of decacorns just waiting to be funded.

Benchmark had invested another chunk into WeWork's Series D round, but a few months later, Bill Gurley returned to *Above the Crowd* to express concern about the state of the broader venture capital world in a post titled "Investors Beware." Gurley believed that venture capitalists had "essentially abandoned" risk analysis and were blindly treating the fundraising decks shared by start-ups as if they were properly audited financial documents. The new unicorns, like WeWork, were burning cash to increase market share at such an unhealthy rate that going public was unthinkable for many. Investors were only making the problem worse. "The very act of dumping hundreds of millions of dollars into an immature private company can also have perverse effects on a company's operating discipline," Gurley wrote. Investors were pushing profitability further into the future while avoiding a test of whether any given company's business model "actually works." They suffered from a fear of missing out on the next Facebook or Uber or Netflix. "There is a fool in every market," Gurley wrote, quoting Warren Buffett. "If you don't know who it is, it is probably you."

Investors wanted to believe Adam could fulfill his vision, and at least some of their faith seemed to rest on an expectation that he could convince the next person to kick in even more—the greater fool theory of finance. When Adam approached tech investors, he emphasized the money that could be made in real estate; to more traditional financiers, he talked about the promise of WeWork's technology. Around 2015, Adam came up with a new pitch: WeWork was a "community company," part of the sharing economy, with hallways that were designed to be as narrow as possible not because doing so allowed WeWork to squeeze in more paying tenants, but in order to force members to connect.

In early 2015, just a few months after WeWork's Series D, its finance team started approaching investors about another injection of capital that would allow the company to keep up with its escalating costs. Real estate prices were hitting record levels as the economy continued to improve, which meant that WeWork was now paying double or triple the amount per square foot that it had for its first locations.

Adam viewed the costs of WeWork's expansion as an obstacle with a simple solution. He told potential investors that WeWork could grow at whatever rate they wanted, so long as they were willing to fund it: demand for the company's offices was so strong that the only restriction on its growth was how much money it could spend building new ones. "Adam's attitude was, 'Tell me how much revenue you want me to produce, and I'll tell you how much capital I need,'" one member of WeWork's fundraising team said.

Among the firms that considered investing was SoftBank, the Japanese conglomerate, which had a small venture capital arm in the United States. One of its New York–based investors suggested WeWork as the kind of company on which SoftBank might want to place one of the large bets for which its founder, Masayoshi Son, had become famous. But the WeWork pitch died with Nikesh Arora, SoftBank's then-president, who didn't see how it fit the firm's focus on technology companies. The pitch never even got to Son. "The response was extraordinarily negative," the SoftBank investor told me. "It was almost like I was an idiot for even bringing it up."

Eventually, WeWork's team met with Glade Brook, a Connecticut hedge fund that was one of several East Coast investors trying to edge its way into the world of unicorns. Maintaining a "unicorn portfolio" had become a fashionable investment strategy; if just one of your companies took flight, it could cover all the duds. Unlike Benchmark, Glade Brook wasn't at the top of any founder's list of strategic investors, but the firm had money, and a strategy of potentially overpaying to make certain it could get in on recent investments in Uber, Snapchat, and Airbnb.

While new unicorns were being regularly sired in Silicon Valley, WeWork was a rare East Coast breed. At a meeting in February, the WeWork team showed Glade Brook what it considered to be an aggressive growth plan; whenever the team brought forecasts to Adam, he would always tell them to increase the projections two or three times before he showed investors. But Glade Brook was unmoved. "How much money do you need to double that?" one of its partners said of the already accelerated growth targets. If WeWork could build a model capable of that, Glade Brook said it would invest at a $10 billion valuation—doubling WeWork's value in a matter of months. After ramping up the projections to Glade Brook's satisfaction, WeWork took them to Fidelity, along with the inflated valuation. Fidelity had passed on WeWork's Series D round, judging its valuation to be wildly inflated, but several of the firm's portfolio mangers had taken a sudden liking to the company. "They just accepted it when we told them the new valuation was $10 billion," a member of WeWork's finance team said.

In June, Glade Brook, Fidelity, and several others invested $434 million into WeWork's Series E at a valuation more than three times higher than what IWG was trading for on the London Stock Exchange. The new valuation was a coup for WeWork's early investors, who had seen the value of their shares skyrocket, but it produced some internal angst. "This is a stupid number," one member of WeWork's finance team said in a meeting with Adam and other executives about the Series E deal. Investors were so enamored by the company's revenue growth, which was doubling every year, that they chose to look past the fact that its costs were escalating just as rapidly. It was becoming increasingly difficult to make projections that met investors' hopes while maintaining fiscal plausibility. The new investors would also dilute the stakes owned by common stock shareholders—employees, primarily—and new hires joining the company were at risk of having their shares be underwater if the company couldn't meet its new expectations.

Most of WeWork's employees weren't concerned. They were young and didn't care to read much of the fine print that came with their stock options package. The new valuation that Adam was crowing about—not to mention the arrival of investment giants they had heard of—only served to comfort them as word rumbled through the company that it might go public soon. Adam brushed off any concerns about overvaluation, as did investors. "When people invested in Facebook at a $10 billion valuation, people thought they were totally nuts," Michael Eisenberg, from Benchmark, told the *Wall Street Journal*. "I don't think they have a lot of regrets about that." Eisenberg believed WeWork's global community offered an opportunity to build Warren Buffett's famous "moat," in part by offering frequent business travelers a uniform experience wherever they went—although venture capitalists were perhaps a biased cohort when it came to valuing access to offices in San Francisco, New York, and London.

Ted Kramer, who had spearheaded so many WeWork launches around the United States, was opening a second location in London when he decided to put in his notice. He was grateful for the opportunities he had been given, but something about the experience had started to feel off. He was one of WeWork's first hundred employees—it now had more than three hundred—and had pushed for an equity stake he felt was commensurate with the effort he had put in, only to meet the same resistance that had nudged Lisa Skye and other early employees out of the company. When a friend with access to WeWork's cap table—a document listing how much of the company each shareholder owns—showed it to Kramer, he says he saw that many people close to Adam were being handsomely rewarded. Meanwhile, the company had forgotten to renew its corporate health-care plan, leaving rank-and-file employees without their insurance for a month. (WeWork agreed to cover any employee health care costs that month.)

Kramer left WeWork in the summer of 2015 and took a job at HackerOne, a San Francisco tech start-up in which Benchmark was also an investor. One night, Kramer attended a board meeting with Bill Gurley and took the opportunity to ask him about WeWork. Gurley had checked Adam's math, found it lacking, and then watched WeWork break seemingly every warning Gurley was presenting in public. Why had Benchmark continued to invest in the company? Gurley responded with a shrug and a short answer. "Adam," he said, "is very convincing."

* * *

AFTER CLOSING THE $10 billion Series E round, Adam told the *Wall Street Journal* that WeWork was profitable, that it wouldn't need any additional funding before an IPO, and that it had met or exceeded all its growth projections, although he couldn't get into details. None of those statements proved to be accurate. But WeWork wasn't a public company, and Adam controlled the board, so there wasn't much to keep him from saying or doing whatever he wanted. We Holdings unloaded an additional $80 million of WeWork stock. The Neumanns bought a second home in the Hamptons, next door to Rebekah's relatives Gwyneth Paltrow and Blythe Danner, as well as a $10.5 million West Village town house they were renovating to include a "stroller parking garage."

WeWork itself was moving to a new headquarters in Chelsea, its sixth in as many years. To fill the old office at 222 Broadway, the company had reached a groundbreaking deal with *The Guardian*, the British newspaper, which agreed to take over the entire space. WeWork had been trying to figure out how it could begin serving larger corporations, particularly as it became more difficult to fill the company's expanding real estate portfolio with two- and three-person start-ups. At more than a hundred employees, *The Guardian* became WeWork's largest single tenant.

The only hitch was that the companies would have to share 222 Broadway for several months while the renovations to WeWork's new space were finished. *The Guardian* moved into the twenty-third floor, where Gordon Gekko's office once stood; WeWork squeezed its employees onto twenty-two. By and large, *Guardian* employees were content with the arrangement and glad to have access to the fancy snacks WeWork kept in its office canteen. But as WeWork's renovations dragged on and the cohabitation continued, WeWork proved to be a raucous co-tenant. There were constant celebrations, with Adam giving rousing speeches in the open atrium, leaving *Guardian* reporters and editors to look on with mild concern at the WeWork employees who were fawning over their boss as if they were disciples pledging fealty to a fiery preacher.

One weeknight, Eamonn Store, *The Guardian*'s CEO, was at an early dinner with an advertiser when his phone began to vibrate. He was getting messages showing what appeared to be video of *Guardian* journalists shouting obscenities at WeWork employees on the floor below. He called Adam Amar, a WeWork employee who had brokered the *Guardian* deal, to ask what was going on.

"You need to come back, quick," Amar said.

"What do you mean?" Store asked.

"There's about to be a fight," Amar said. "Like, literally a fight."

That afternoon, Adam had given another celebratory speech, punctuated with shots of tequila and thumping music queued up on a stereo: "Empire State of Mind," "Run This Town," "I Run New York." The music kept getting louder as *Guardian* employees tried to finish their workday upstairs. Eventually, a *Guardian* reporter yelled at the WeWork employees to shut up. Adam heard the request and yelled back, "*You* shut up!"

Another *Guardian* reporter walked downstairs and found Adam dancing in the middle of the office canteen. When she asked him to please turn down the music, he locked eyes with her and silently reached for the volume knob on the stereo. Without saying a word, he turned it up, then went back to dancing—stacking his hands on top of each other, as if he were building a tower of dollar bills.

Adam would say later that it was around this time that he began to struggle with his ego. It had always been robust, even when he didn't have much to brag about. Now he had good reason to boast. He stopped going to GCUC and skipped the next meeting of the Five Families, deeming himself above the coworking fray. While touring a building in Austin with Liz Elam, the GCUC cofounder whose company he had tried to acquire, Adam pulled Elam aside to make sure she noticed how the brokers were slobbering for his business. "I bet they don't treat you like that," he pointed out with a smile. His mother had recently been diagnosed with the same pancreatic cancer that killed Steve Jobs, and Adam started talking more about immortality, and his interest in the emerging science aimed at staving off death.

At Summer Camp 2015, the cost of which had ballooned into the seven figures, WeWork hired T. J. Miller, a comedian who played the cartoonishly boastful venture capitalist Erlich Bachman on HBO's *Silicon Valley*, as well as the Chainsmokers, the popular DJ duo, whom they paid in WeWork stock. On Saturday night, Adam was in the front row, dancing with Michael Gross, when the Weeknd arrived by helicopter to play a surprise set. (Miguel performed in a talent show wearing a Sia wig and lip-synching to "Chandelier.") A WeWork employee ran between the rows of tents in a costume that might as well have been the company's mascot: a unicorn.

Late one night during camp, Adam went missing. No one knew where he was, and a few employees were starting to get nervous. Everyone had been drinking. A jet ski was missing. Mark Lapidus, whose family owned the camp, got into a boat and trawled around the pitch-black lake with a giant flashlight, looking for his cousin-in-law. The next morning, rumors spread that Adam had fallen overboard, and that the search party was only able to find him by the light of the glow sticks around his neck — a wild tale, but WeWork employees had heard crazier things. In truth, Adam had driven the jet ski a mile across the lake, to another part of the camp, and continued his night there.

Adam seemed to know that he was getting out of control. "My soul was attracted to 'We,' but it required some effort," as he put it. He turned even more toward religion, inviting Eitan Yardeni, the rabbi from the Kabbalah Centre, to address WeWork's employees at the company's first annual Summit, a wintertime retreat in 2015. (The event included a scavenger hunt that ended at a club where the rapper Ja Rule tried, unsuccessfully, to back out of a gig by claiming that WeWork hadn't provided him with the proper setup.) Adam consulted another rabbi who advised him to keep Shabbat, the day of rest that begins every Friday night, when Jews are encouraged to unplug from the world as a way of reconnecting with what matters. Adam found that it helped—at least until Thursday, when his ego would flare back up and he had to start the process all over again.

* * *

ON A SWEATY NIGHT that August, Adam walked out the front door of WeWork's new headquarters in Chelsea to address a crowd of WeWork's janitorial staff, all of whom were chanting "WeWork, shame on you!" That summer, as the company's valuation hit $10 billion, the cleaners had announced their intention to unionize; the workers made $11 an hour, with no benefits, while most New York janitors received hourly union wages of more than $20, plus benefits. A week later, the third-party company that employed the cleaners canceled its contract with WeWork, which decided to hire its own staff. That prompted a campaign—"We work here, too"—demanding that WeWork rehire the workers. Protesters hopped onto Wall Street's *Charging Bull* sculpture wearing masks depicting Miguel's and Adam's faces.

This was not the company's first dustup with organized labor. "They're not bad people, but they're doing bad things," Adam would tell employees when WeWork found itself dealing with one of the many unions that represented workers in various construction and building management fields. The company had turned over almost all its construction on the East Coast, along with the renovation of two of the Neumanns' homes, to UA Builders, a fringe player in the New York construction world that avoided union labor. UA was run by three brothers, Granit, Albert, and Jimmy Gjonbalaj; in 2015, WeWork hired Granit as its head of construction. Multiple WeWork executives told me that shirking union labor was a key part of WeWork's business model, keeping costs low and allowing its construction operation to run around the clock.

The company ran into regular pressure from unions. When WeWork sent a UA team to work on its first space in Boston, local construction unions sent a band to play outside the building for three weeks. Scabby the Rat, the giant inflatable rodent that New York unions install on sidewalks to embarrass companies that hire nonunion labor, became a regular feature in front of WeWorks around the city as well as at the Neumanns' home. One member of WeWork's construction team told several employees that he carried a gun to deal with potential threats against Adam.

As Adam tried to placate the crowd of janitorial workers outside WeWork headquarters, he told them that he, too, had come to New York "chasing the American dream" and "wanting to change the world." He said that "when I was a little kid, me and all my family lived in a house the size of my daughter's room," ignoring the fact that most of the cleaners might still be living in similarly cramped situations while the Neumanns chose between their multiple vacation homes. When Adam told the protesting cleaners that they had never been his employees, they objected by pointing out that they were required to wear WeWork shirts on the job.

Adam told the cleaners that WeWork would be hiring many of them back, at $15–$18 an hour, with benefits, plus an invitation to Summer Camp and a chance to earn equity. "This company is going very far," he said. "The stock, God willing, is very valuable." He dismissed one of the cleaners who pointed out that Neumann was, on paper, a billionaire— "That has nothing to do with this," Adam said, waving his hand through the air to swat away the question—and said that he believed the workers did not have all the facts about the union situation. "I know life is tough," Adam went on. "So I will keep doing my best to make the most difference I can—first in your lives and my employees' lives, and in the world."

Adam called for peace so that he could deliver a final soliloquy. "There's a saying, 'God truly helps those who help themselves,'" he said. "I understand your heart. I know everybody here is trying to help."

He said that WeWork would "definitely not be blackmailed, pushed, or aggressively moved into anything…not in this country, because this is a great country where freedom comes first." He turned back into the building, and the chanting continued: "WeWork, shame on you!"

* * *

WEWORK'S DISPUTE WITH its cleaning staff made it into the press and highlighted the fact that beneath its progressive rhetoric about offering a better day at work, WeWork's business depended on the same tactics any hard-nosed New York landlord might employ. The disconnect didn't necessarily come as a surprise to WeWork's employees, who were already familiar with the company's disregard for the forty-hour workweek. Adam and other WeWork executives pushed an idea that had become common at most start-ups: your company is your family. Why join a union when your employer promises they have your best interest at heart? WeWork employees quickly became one another's best friends, forging bonds over long hours, tequila shots, and the promise that one day—as soon as Adam made good on his promise to take the company public—their stock options would offer them the money and time to take a nice long vacation.

By the summer of 2015, WeWork was hiring more than thirty new employees every week—pi times ten. Among the newcomers was Alana Anderson, whose sister, Aja, was so enthusiastic about her job at WeWork in San Francisco that Alana stopped working at a family farm in Pennsylvania to take a job at WeWork—partly to make sure her sister had not joined some kind of capitalist cult from which she needed to be rescued. But when Alana got to WeWork, she loved it. "It felt like I was empowered to make change. It felt anticorporate," she said. "It was a wildly exciting first year and a half."

It was around that time that Anderson, and many other WeWork employees, began to see their experience in a different light—as if they were waking up from a tequila-infused hangover. In 2014, WeWork started holding an all-company "Thank God It's Monday" meeting to kick off each week. TGIM, as it became known, was a mandatory pep rally after work on Mondays during which Adam would typically give a rousing speech, followed by a company-wide round of shots. The events were rarely useful at the beginning of what would surely be an exhausting week. But WeWork had never shown much interest in employees maintaining a life beyond the company. Long hours became a badge of honor, and executives stayed after TGIM for weekly late night meetings with Adam. A community manager in Washington, DC, recalled working late one night and looking over at one of his colleagues who didn't seem to be doing anything. "You're here, so I'm here," his coworker said. Employees started deploying the company's motivational mantras in jest. "If you had a rough week, people sarcastically said, 'Hustle harder,'" the community manager said. When they came to work on Mondays to find WeWork's offices in whatever state members had left them over the weekend, employees would lift one another's spirits by declaring, "Thank God it's Monday!"

WeWork employees took solace in the fact that their colleagues felt like a surrogate family rather than coworkers; many employees eventually realized they had no friends outside the company at all. Adam and Rebekah often talked about the joys of building a nuclear family—in 2015, Rebekah was pregnant with twins, the Neumanns' third and fourth children—but most WeWork employees found the circumstances of their employment made that an impossibility. Multiple female employees said that when they were interviewing for jobs, Adam asked if they had plans to be pregnant soon—the implication being that this would get in the way of what needed to be done. Ariel Tiger told another WeWork executive whose wife was about to give birth that "a real man" would be in the office the next day. The executive balked at the idea but felt pressure to abide by it. "My wife had a C-section on Friday," the executive told me. "And I was in the office on Tuesday."

The lack of female employees in the company's upper ranks also became noticeable. When a woman finally joined the engineering staff, the team scrambled to rewrite the underlying code because they had described a reddish color in the design as "hooker's blood." When an employee brought up the lack of female leadership at a company town hall, Adam didn't offer much of a response except to point to Stella Templo, who was then working as his chief of staff. During another Q&A, Adam took questions alongside Michael Gross and Noah Brodsky, an executive recently poached from Starwood Hotels. The lack of diversity came up again. "Diversity?" Adam replied. "I'm a brunette, Michael's blond, and we have a Noah." Brodsky, who is gay, turned bright red.

In 2015, Lisa Skye, WeWork's second employee, came back from her honeymoon to a text message from Adam asking her to come by for a meeting. Skye had been gone from WeWork for years and spent the intervening period in and out of real estate trying to figure out what she wanted to do next. She had never been given stock options, despite her early arrival at the company, but she didn't harbor any bitterness. When Skye heard Adam was closing the Benchmark deal, she had emailed to wish him good luck.

When Skye met Adam at his office, Rebekah happened to be there and she greeted Skye with a kiss on the cheek before checking in with Adam about a forthcoming trip to Miami, asking what type of jet they planned to take for the trip. Rebekah left, and Adam got down to business. WeWork had been successful since Skye left, if she hadn't noticed, but Adam couldn't shake the feeling that something was missing. He was pitching WeWork as a "community company," but the community that had made 154 Grand Street so special had proven difficult to scale, much as Liz Elam from GCUC had warned him.

Adam wanted Skye to come back to WeWork. He would give her one of the company's buildings to tinker with, just as they had in the early days, to see if she could reignite the spirit that made WeWork feel fresh and different.

Skye told Adam she would think about it. But as she walked out of the building, bumping into Miguel along the way, she came to a realization. Adam needed her—it had just taken years for him to admit it. But why go back to work for him when she knew what it would take to build what she always wanted: a space or two, small and simple, all her own? A few months later, she and Danny Orenstein, WeWork's third employee, opened their own flexible office space right across the street from a WeWork in lower Manhattan.

CHAPTER NINE

WeLive

WHEN HURRICANE SANDY crashed into New York, back in October of 2012, there was no power below 14th Street. WeWork's three downtown locations all had to shut down, and the company canceled its Halloween party. "We tried to get one-up on Sandy, but the force of her tidal surge has proved to be too much," WeWork wrote in canceling the event, while promising more to come. "This storm will not get us down."

A few days later, Adam got a call from Bill Rudin, whose family real estate office owned buildings from Battery Park to Midtown. Rudin told Neumann that one of his towers had been severely damaged by the storm. 110 Wall Street was half a block from the East River, and millions of gallons of water had rushed into the building. Its lobby was a swamp, and the mechanical systems in the basement were destroyed. It was a 1960s skyscraper with a step-back wedding-cake design that had never done all that well for Rudin anyway. Did Adam want to take a look?

Two days later, Rudin met Adam at the building with a pair of flashlights. No one had been allowed back inside 110 Wall Street since the hurricane hit. The lights were off, and on the upper floors of the twenty-seven-story tower, Rudin and Neumann walked in the dark between empty cubicles where people had left personal mementos and Friday afternoon messes, not knowing they wouldn't be coming back. Rudin expected the repairs to cost millions and take months, so he was likely going to cancel the leases for the twenty tenants, leaving the building empty. Adam had an idea.

* * *

TWO WEEKS LATER, Adam came back to Rudin with a proposal. Just as he had in 2008, launching an office business in the depths of a real estate collapse, Adam was prepared to find a new opportunity amid destruction. He wanted to fill the building with five floors of WeWork space and twenty floors of a concept called WeLive: small apartments with big common spaces to encourage residents to hang out with one another. The idea went back to his failed attempt to pitch his Baruch professor on a more communal apartment building. It had appeared alongside WeBank and WeSail and WeConnect in the pitch deck that Adam and Miguel made in 2009, listing the "We Brand Companies," with WeLive rendered as a twenty-four-unit apartment complex on the beach in La Jolla, California.

There wasn't much evidence to suggest that New York apartment dwellers felt their homes were too big, but Rudin was intrigued. His grandfather had always built residential buildings near his office towers, and Adam thought WeLive might serve a similar purpose, allowing members to live as close as possible to their WeWork office. Plus, Adam was very convincing. "It had a lot to do with Adam and his vision," Rudin told me. "And his belief that, with two plus two, you get ten."

For Neumann, the chance to try WeLive served as both validation of his once-rejected idea and an expansion of the company's ambitions, which he could sell to investors. WeLive featured prominently in the company's 2014 pitch deck, and Adam began spinning a story to investors that WeLive would become bigger than WeWork. He pitched it as a solution to the country's urban housing crunch, while Michael Gross told investors the idea was so good that even their millionaire friends would want to move in. The deck projected that in four years WeLive would have 34,000 residents paying more than $600 million in rent.

But by 2016, when the company projected fourteen WeLives around the country, it was still scrambling to open 110 Wall Street and one other location in greater Washington, DC. Both projects were woefully behind schedule. WeWork's growing expertise in the construction of commercial office space didn't neatly translate to the more complicated requirements of a residential building. Office towers such as 110 Wall Street had deeper floor plates, which left designers puzzling over how to convert interior spaces that had no natural light. Building codes prohibited some of the common spaces Adam wanted to build, and the construction costs ballooned. Plumbing is the most expensive part of any building project, and WeLive needed much more than the single men's and women's bathrooms they put on every WeWork floor. One employee said that an initial set of drawings forgot to include a laundry room.

Adam wanted the building to make a splash. Just a few months before 110 Wall Street was scheduled to open, he told the team he wanted to double its occupancy; their solution was to add Murphy beds so that two people could fit into one studio apartment, with mattresses separated by a curtain. Employees rushed to and from West Elm and ABC Carpet & Home with company credit cards to buy last-minute furniture to spruce up the place.

In January of 2016, more than three years after Adam first toured the hurricane-ravaged building, two WeLive floors opened up at 110 Wall Street. A barista poured complimentary cortados in the lobby. The common areas had a terrace with two hot tubs and a laundry room with arcade games. The apartments came with preselected books on the shelves and decorative bowls on the coffee table. To fill each unit, as part of a beta test, WeWork employees and members paid as little as $500 a month to share a studio with a coworker. For WeWork's low-paid employees, pining for their recently lost dorm-room experience, it was an appealing offer.

But the price would have to increase to make any economic sense. At a launch party, Adam repeated his belief that WeLive would change the world of residential real estate forever and suggested that his family might become one of the millionaires Michael Gross promised would move in. Rebekah was in the audience and replied with a firm "No."

* * *

WELIVE WAS THE biggest of Adam's many efforts to expand the idea of what WeWork could become. In 2014, the company began trade-marking names for various product lines: WeLearn, for an education offering; WeBike, for a bicycle valet service; WeEat, for food delivery; and WeMove, for a gym. At one point, the company hired a scent artist to design a signature WeWork fragrance; at another, an employee asked a WeWork member about the idea of a WeWork-branded energy drink. "There's not milk for coffee consistently," the member said. "Can we fix that first?"

Many of WeWork's new initiatives felt like pet projects. The release of *Awake* had failed to jump-start Rebekah's acting career, but she had held on to her Hollywood ambitions and was now attaching them to WeWork. In 2012, Rebekah and Adam launched WeWork Studios, a production company with a goal in part of helping Rebekah land a breakthrough role. They brought in Bonnie Timmermann, a Hollywood casting direc-tor who had worked on everything from *Dirty Dancing* to *Black Hawk Down*, and gave her a free office on a floor at the Varick Street location renovated specifically to entice companies in the film and TV business. (The WeWork engineers trying to build the member network had to vacate the area and move to the building's basement, where they joked about coming down with "hepatitis W.") Timmermann set up meetings with various producers and directors, including Ted Hope, who went on to co-run the movie department at Amazon Studios.

Timmerman says she couldn't find the right role for Rebekah, but in 2013, the Neumanns got involved in the production of I, Origins, a science fiction film centered on a man who finds spirituality, and a belief in reincarnation, through his fiancée. The Neumanns invested roughly $350,000 in the film, and attended the premiere at Sundance, where Fox Searchlight bought the rights to distribute the movie, netting the Neumanns a hundred thousand dollars. They scored an invitation to Vanity Fair's exclusive Oscar party, but I, Origins tanked at the box office. WeWork Studios never made another film.

The company's scattered assortment of potential business lines was distracting for the employees tasked with maintaining the blistering growth of its core office-leasing business. But the most ambitious companies of the 2010s were no longer content to do what they were best at. Google was building a driverless car. Snapchat was getting into eyewear. Amazon was starting to make movies. In 2015, Adam had a team draw up a plan for a private club on the top floor of a Manhattan tower where Goldman Sachs once had its executive suites. (WeWork had also leased the basement, where Adam thought about opening an outpost of SPIN, a Manhattan ping-pong bar.) Inspired by the Boom Boom Room at the Standard hotel, the space would be called the Creators Club, with conference rooms named for Steve Jobs, Bill Gates, and Bob Dylan. Food would be served at the M&A Kitchen, which had a double meaning: it was a nod to Miguel's and Adam's initials, along with the mergers and acquisitions that would be discussed over glasses of Don Julio 1942, which they planned to offer on tap.

Adam was pitching investors on this expanded vision for his company—

an entire WeWorld. He wanted others to see WeWork as capable of much more than managing offices. The company referred to its Chelsea home as its "Galactic Headquarters," and Adam told a reporter in 2015 that "WeWork Mars is in our pipeline." He fantasized about working with Elon Musk. "When he gets everybody to Mars," Adam said, "we're going to build a community like there's never been."

* * *

WHILE HE WAITED to hear from Musk, Adam set his sights on occupying other territory. "Adam, more than anything, was a deal guy," one of his early investors said. "Whether he was raising money or closing a building, he loved the deal." After closing on the Woolworth Building, Adam told several employees that he wanted to buy a company. One night, he took the owner of a coding academy in Colorado out for a drink in Manhattan, ostensibly to mull over a partnership. "I've sold buildings, I've done $5 million deals, but I haven't bought a company yet," Adam said. "I don't know if I want to buy you, but this is something I've wanted to do for a long time." He made overtures to competitors in China and London and asked WeWork's engineers for their take on various software companies he might acquire. He floated the idea of buying Etsy, which was a $3 billion public company, arguing that the site's sellers were entrepreneurs in need of office space.

WeWork also looked into buying Magnises, a membership club founded in 2013 by Billy McFarland, who would achieve infamy years later, along with Ja Rule, for planning the disastrous Fyre Festival. McFarland had been a WeWork member for years. He started his first company, Spling, at WeWork Labs in 2011, and kept WeWork offices for his various companies up until the Fyre Festival fell apart, in 2017. From prison, McFarland told me that Magnises was meant to add a lifestyle component to the WeWorld, but the deal collapsed after his company got sued for trashing a town house it rented in Manhattan. He had met Adam several times and said that WeWork served as inspiration. "The concept of merging different people who wouldn't have met—that definitely helped power what I tried to do through Magnises and Fyre," McFarland said.

In the summer of 2015, Adam finally made his first big acquisition. Case was a company founded by three former architects—Dave Fano, Steve Sanderson, and Federico Negro—to bring technological innovation to the design and construction world. Case had an office at WeWork Labs and had been consulting with WeWork to streamline the latter's design and development process. The company's slogan—"Buildings = Data"—fit the tech-forward story Adam was trying to tell, and by 2015, half its sixty employees were devoted exclusively to WeWork projects.

Joining WeWork gave Case's founders and employees, most of whom weren't software engineers or product developers, the rare chance to join a fast-growing start-up with the same promise of stock-based riches that their brethren in Silicon Valley were receiving. But much of the Case staff wasn't excited about the acquisition. Fitting out one WeWork space after another wasn't the most interesting task. The pace was hectic. And Neumann's bombast didn't land as well with the company's more experienced workforce. They knew enough to be skeptical of Adam as their new leader: several Case employees had handled the architectural drawings for WeWork's new headquarters in Chelsea and there was a vent that they understood would allow him to smoke pot in his office, though WeWork's PR team disputed this.

After the deal closed, Adam, Miguel, and Jen Berrent, WeWork's lawyer, met with their newly acquired employees. Berrent had joined the company from WilmerHale, a white-shoe law firm, and was there to allay the concerns from Case employees that WeWork intended to claim ownership of their personal projects, which Case had encouraged them to pursue freely before. Berrent referenced HBO's *Silicon Valley*, which was then in its second season. The show's villain was Gavin Belson, an unfeeling business titan running a company called Hooli, who was constantly followed around by a spiritual guru and had recently laid claim to a piece of technology that one of his former employees had built. "Look," Berrent said. "We're not Hooli!"

* * *

AT THE END OF 2015, WeWork had lawyers from Skadden, Arps, Slate, Meagher & Flom start quietly making early preparations for an initial public offering. Raising money through the public markets as part of an IPO is a complex process requiring many months of detailed work, and teams at WeWork spent considerable time trying to bring the company's chaotic books into compliance with the Sarbanes-Oxley Act of 2002, the federal law instituted in the wake of the Enron scandal to require greater accountability from public companies. The company was still a year or more away from going public, but getting its finances in order seemed like a worthy step to take.

Adam had little interest in going public, fearing that doing so would mean losing control and limiting the scope of its ambition. His fundraising blitz had been a resounding success; in addition to becoming a "decacorn," modern start-up vernacular defined WeWork as a "minotaur"—a company that had *raised* more than a billion dollars in venture capital. But WeWork was again running low on cash, and the number of private investors willing to fund the company's losses at its already sky-high valuation was dwindling.

To keep the private bonanza going at the end of 2015, Adam looked to China, hiring Goldman Sachs to seek out investors interested in funding the company's expansion in Asia and elsewhere. Uber had recently raised more than $1 billion to expand into China. WeWork was a tougher sell. A member of WeWork's finance team said that a number of investors had passed. Chinese funds weren't eager to cover WeWork's escalating losses, especially when the Chinese market already had local competitors offering a similar product.

But all it took was one person willing to buy Adam's vision. "We were like, Who the hell is Hony Capital?" the finance team member said. Hony Capital was a fund started by John Zhao, a Chinese businessman who agreed to invest $600 million—the company's largest funding round yet. "The nature of the private markets is that if nine smart investors pass, it only takes one relatively dumber investor, and suddenly we're valued at $16 billion," the finance team member said.

In a meeting to discuss the deal, several members of WeWork's board of directors objected. They thought pushing into China was a fool's errand. Uber was burning tons of capital trying to keep up with local companies in a country where it had no expertise. The best thing for WeWork, and its investors, was to get its spending under control and go public sooner rather than later.

But Adam and other WeWork executives liked the deal; Miguel was excited by the challenge of expanding into China. With the Hony team in New York, hashing out the terms, Adam was at WeLive for a party when he got the idea to invite the investors to come by. WeLive offered a new stage from which Adam could deliver his pitch, and when Zhao and the Hony team arrived at the party, Adam told a dozen of his employees to join them in a freight elevator bound for the building's roof. No one was supposed to go up there, but Adam ran the entire building—who was going to stop him? A WeWork employee relayed a request by walkie-talkie to an intern to bring a tray of tequila shots to the roof. Adam grabbed a fire extinguisher on the way up.

Twenty-eight floors up, the group could survey WeWork's bright future. They were standing atop its newest product line, which Adam promised would become its biggest business. Across the East River was the site for Dock 72, a ground-up development WeWork was building in the Brooklyn Navy Yard along with Rudin and Boston Properties, which would include the largest WeWork yet. On the roof, Adam laid out his vision for WeWork, arguing that 110 Wall Street was only the beginning of the broader We revolution. When Zhao spoke, he began to tear up as he described his hopes for the new partnership.

Suddenly, Adam unlocked the fire extinguisher and started spraying it all over Zhao and the Hony team. Everyone laughed and took their tequila shots before heading back downstairs. "Should Adam not have done that? Maybe not," an employee who was on the roof said. "But you kind of have to tip your hat to him. We closed the deal the next week."

CHAPTER TEN

Manage the Nickel

JACKIE HOCKERSMITH ARRIVED for her first day at WeWork in January of 2016 and walked straight into an orientation session led by Rocky Kerns, a WeWork employee responsible for onboarding employees and sometimes lathering them into a frenzy when Adam took the stage during a company event. At orientation, Hockersmith received a copy of *Setting the Table: The Transforming Power of Hospitality in Business*, a book by the restaurateur Danny Meyer, who argued that the key to a successful business is to treat people with respect. WeWork was giving the book to all new employees.

Three days later, Hockersmith joined her new coworkers at 23 Wall Street, a few blocks from WeLive, for the company's second annual winter Summit. The building was in disrepair, having been purchased by a foreign businessman in 2008 and left to decay since then. It had no lighting, heat, or water, and the space was stripped to its concrete floor. WeWork brought in lights and port-a-potties, which were set up inside and hidden from the rest of the space behind a curtain.

On Friday morning, Adam jogged down a center aisle between rows and rows of seated WeWork employees. He jumped onstage wearing a shirt that said NEVER SETTLE and expressed amazement that, since the last Summit, WeWork had tripled in size to more than a thousand employees.

He started shouting out every city that now had a WeWork: Los Angeles, San Francisco, Berkeley—"We need more energy, Berkeley!"—Denver, Chicago, Boston, Philadelphia, DC, Miami, and Atlanta, where there was a lone employee preparing to open a space in a few months. Then: London, Amsterdam, Tel Aviv, Shanghai, Mexico City, Toronto, Montreal, and Beersheba, the "dump" where Adam had been born thirty-six years before. Neumann reserved a final shout-out for New York, where the company had twenty-six locations. "That is a city that has achieved scale," he said, responding to the roar that erupted from his local employees. "All cities are going to sound like that in the next two to three years."

Hockersmith was excited about her job on WeWork's user experience team, tasked with trying to make the company's glassy labyrinths easier to navigate. But Summit was a lot to wrap her head around. The employees learned a synchronized dance and posed for a photo with their hands above their head and their thumbs touching to form the first letter of their employer's name. At one point, a motivational speaker gave a speech in which he kept referring to the company as "WeWorks," until one employee finally stood up and corrected him, to boisterous applause from his colleagues. There was a party that night, with scantily clad aerial dancers performing in hoops hanging from the ceiling. Hockersmith wandered around the dark husk of a building, not knowing anyone; by the end of the night, the floors were so sticky she ended up ruining a new pair of shoes.

The next day, WeWork employees gathered again while the rest of New York prepared for a blizzard advancing up the East Coast. Adam told everyone not to worry. The plan was still to board buses that night, bound for a party at a large home in Westchester County owned by one of the company's executives. But by the afternoon, New York City was beginning to shut down. Rather than cancel Summit, WeWork's employees were told to go home, pack a bag, and then come back: the company had rented out every hotel room it could find in lower Manhattan.

Adam told the team at WeLive that he wanted to move the party there. Community managers who ran nearby buildings were instructed to raid their liquor cabinets and mix a different punch for each floor. Adam only showed up at WeLive for a short time, but new employees were tickled to find themselves drinking and smoking pot with other WeWork executives they barely knew. Jackie Hockersmith went home early, to the hotel where she had been assigned to share a room with a male coworker. That made her uncomfortable, but it ultimately didn't matter; he spent the night hooking up with another WeWorker somewhere else.

The next morning, while New York dug itself out from three feet of snow, WeWork's hungover employees dragged themselves back to Summit, where Adam was scheduled to deliver another speech. An hour went by without any sight of him. When he finally showed up, Adam had the audiovisual team play a video that explained his whereabouts: an SUV had driven Adam around New York while he held onto a rope and rode a snowboard through the snowy streets. "Every young kid was like, 'That's awesome,'" an executive who had recently joined the company said. "And every older person was like, 'Fuck you.'"

* * *

THE DAY AFTER ADAM sprayed his newest investors with a fire extinguisher, a contractor working on the ongoing WeLive construction walked up to the roof and found the now-empty tray of tequila shots. Word of the rooftop party spread throughout the company. When the news made its way back to Artie Minson, WeWork's new president and chief operating officer, that his boss had not only sprayed potential investors with a fire extinguisher but also violated safety regulations that might require halting construction at 110 Wall Street, he could only shake his head. Minson told Adam that if he was serious about becoming a public company, at some point, antics like this had to stop.

Minson had been at WeWork for six months, having left a job as CFO at Time Warner Cable. He had never heard of WeWork when Michael Eisenberg reached out from Benchmark to gauge his interest. At the time, WeWork had ten thousand members. "At Time Warner Cable, we did ten thousand installs a day," Minson told me, when I interviewed him at WeWork headquarters a few years later. But Minson was excited to try something new and to transition from CFO to COO—a position that would set him up to take over the company's top job if Adam decided to follow the example of many start-up founders and hand the reins to an experienced executive.

For years, Adam had depended on the circle of friends and family who populated WeWork's senior ranks. His brother-in-law was the company's COO; his cousin-in-law was its head of real estate; his navy friend was its first CFO. Rebekah herself had become more involved when it came to WeWork's branding, developing its new logo and coming up with some of its slogans, like DO WHAT YOU LOVE. Adam admitted that he especially liked hiring his countrymen when he could. In meetings, he regularly switched to Hebrew when he wanted to convey something to the Israelis in the room; one WeWork executive joked about buying Rosetta Stone for his team.

But WeWork had grown beyond the expertise of some of the employees whose primary qualification for their jobs was loyalty. The board of directors pushed Adam to bring in more outside voices. Minson was the most prominent among a new class of executives joining WeWork. "Artie was the first person who mattered outside of Adam's orbit," one senior employee said. Minson brought in Francis Lobo, a former AOL executive, as chief revenue officer. Jon Gieselman, a DirecTV executive, joined as WeWork's chief marketing officer. Many of the newer executives were enticed by the idea that WeWork was moving toward an IPO, as Minson helped bring some sobriety to the company's projections. "Artie made the projections more reasonable," a member of the finance team said. "We focused on an 'if, not when' story—it might take ten years to get there, not two, but the numbers will look good."

Whether Adam was willing to open up to outsiders was another question. Gieselman lasted less than two months at WeWork. Patrick Morselli, from Uber, left WeWork toward the end of 2015. The constant partying had become a bit tiresome, but mostly he found WeWork's leadership to be problematic. "The decision-making process wasn't transparent. Meritocracy was foggy at best," Morselli said. Uber had been exhausting, but Morselli found WeWork to be the more frustrating experience. "Travis [Kalanick] can come across as hard to work with, but he's to the point in a very intelligent and constructive way," Morselli said. "Adam was always finding ways to force teams, and people within teams, to compete with each other, as if it were all a zero-sum game."

One of the new executives Adam hired was Jennifer Skyler, a Facebook spokesperson, whom he brought in to build a communications team as the company continued to push the idea that it was more than an office-leasing operation. In the press, WeWork was talking up the new version of its member network, and the idea of a "WeWork effect"—that companies would want to join WeWork's network less for the physical space than for access to its community of entrepreneurs. Adam posed for photos in *Fast Company* with slicked-back hair and a leather jacket. Sixteen years after the magazine declared Regus the office of the future, it now saw something even grander: "Adam Neumann's $16 Billion Neo-Utopian Play to Turn WeWork into WeWorld."

But the company was still struggling to fulfill its promises, especially when it came to building the physical social network Adam had sold to investors. WeWork had parted ways with Joey Cables, its teenage IT director, but its tech infrastructure remained patchwork. Cnet.com reported that a member had recently complained to the company that its wireless network was so insecure that he had been able to see documents on other members' computers: financial records, graduation photos, a birthday card featuring Nicolas Cage's face superimposed onto a cat's body. WeWork couldn't solve every technological problem with the modern office. In early 2015, Chris Hill, Adam's brother-in-law, grew so frustrated after he couldn't get a printer to work that he picked it up over his head and smashed it on the floor in the middle of WeWork headquarters.

In 2016, an employee at Thinknum, a data analytics start-up with a WeWork office in Manhattan, was poking around the company's member network when he discovered another security loophole, one that allowed him to see information about every WeWork member. Thinknum found that WeWork's churn rate, which measured the pace at which members were moving out of WeWork's spaces, had been steadily rising. As for the company's internal LinkedIn, Thinknum found that only 21 percent of members had posted even once. Half of the most-followed people on the network were WeWork employees.

Thinknum posted the data on its blog. The next day, Justin Zhen, its cofounder, got an email from his WeWork community manager. She had direct orders to kick Thinknum out of its office, and out of the WeWork community. They had thirty minutes to leave the building. Thinknum's six employees packed up their things and started looking for a new office. It didn't take long to find another one that met their needs. The next day, Thinknum moved into an IWG office four blocks away.

* * *

WHILE MINSON AND WEWORK'S other new executives tried to bring more control to the company's operations, expansion remained its driving impulse. WeWork had built a machine capable of rapidly occupying physical space at an unprecedented rate, but now its sales team had to keep up. They worked out of unfinished spaces to try to presell empty buildings, stealing Wi-Fi from nearby restaurants while new locations were being fitted out. WeWork's occupancy rate, which it often boasted about, started to dip as it opened more and more locations. Luca Gualco left WeWork—he went on to start an adult diaper company—but the rest of the sales team was told to spare no expense. "We were just told to wine and dine," John Boozer, a WeWork salesperson on the East Coast told me. "We did $2,200 at a sushi restaurant in Chicago, and you weren't keeping track of anything." WeWork started giving out several months of free rent to new tenants with no commitment; the smartest companies in big cities would simply take the free months, then move to a new WeWork opening nearby and get another discount. No one was keeping track. When newer employees ran the numbers in their head, they didn't understand how WeWork would ever make money spending the way that they were.

In May of 2016, Adam addressed his employees at a TGIM meeting, pacing the floor of WeWork's Chelsea headquarters while his employees sat in silence. He tried to strike an optimistic note, arguing that WeWork was at less than 5 percent of its potential, both in "what we can do and probably also from a valuation point of view"—a calculation that implied a $300 billion valuation somewhere in its future. But the company was at a critical juncture. "What scares me is in ten years to look back and say we could have done more," Neumann said. "Time is the only thing you don't get back."

Adam was concerned about the company's spending. "We did not used to be this way," he said. "We used to fight for every dollar." WeWork was bleeding money as it quadrupled in size, which meant four times the salaries. It was already serving ninety thousand glasses of free beer a month—"a number we're proud of," Adam said. But the happy hours added up. During his TGIM lecture, Adam invoked a phrase Chris Hill had recently coined: "Manage the Nickel." Hill had begun handing out wooden tokens inscribed with the phrase to employees who found ways to save the company money. "I want to start receiving notes: 'Lights are on at two o'clock. This is wasting money. This is not smart. I don't accept this,'" Adam said. He warned that other high-flying start-ups were being felled by their out of control "spending culture," and insisted WeWork would not become like that. Adam was reining in certain initiatives, like WeKids, a day care in the early stages of development, and said that the austerity measures would be shouldered by everyone. He was canceling a Monday bagel-and-lox breakfast for executives that he estimated cost $300 to $400 each week. "The universe does not allow waste," Adam said.

Adam's concerns seemed out of touch to many employees. "It was funny because the bagels cost, like, $80," an assistant sometimes tasked with breakfast acquisition said. To others, he was being hypocritical. The *New York Post* reported that the Neumanns had recently passed on a $39 million penthouse on the Upper East Side, but they did buy a $15 million estate in Westchester County, near Rebekah's childhood home, with a tennis court and eight bedrooms. One employee had recently been in a meeting with Adam about the rising cost of furnishing WeLive, during which Adam suggested they start buying cheaper furniture from China, then turned to Miguel and asked if he wanted to take a helicopter to the Hamptons with him that weekend.

The TGIM speech was especially irksome to Joanna Strange, who had arrived at WeWork in 2015, as part of the company's acquisition of Case. Strange had taken on an undefined role, which was common for many new arrivals who joined WeWork only to hold on as their job shifted with the company's growth in various directions. "I'm a shit catcher," Strange told people when they asked what she did. "I catch the shit that falls from the sky."

At the beginning of 2016, Strange's boss, Dave Fano, gave Strange his company login information so that she could help him complete various administrative tasks—more shit to catch. While reading Fano's inbox one day in the spring, Strange noticed that several executives were emailing one another about what appeared to be looming layoffs; one of them was even bragging about the fact that he had managed to cut more than another manager. Strange was confused. One of her jobs had been to onboard new employees, and WeWork was hiring at such a speedy clip that it was often hard to keep up, and the company's standards sometimes slipped. Adam had recently chastised a group of employees for not googling a job applicant before hiring her as Ariel Tiger's new assistant; it quickly transpired that she was an infamous Brooklynite known as the Hipster Grifter, with a reputation for having scammed her way into a series of jobs and cheated numerous people out of their money.

Strange had experienced a growing discontent ever since joining WeWork. She was bothered by the cult of personality that surrounded Adam, and, as a new parent, she felt protective of the company's young employees, whom she thought were getting bamboozled into forgiving the low pay and crummy benefits because the job let them drink with their friends. After reading the email about layoffs, Strange confronted one of the executives, who confirmed that cuts were coming, but that WeWork was trying to keep things quiet. Strange decided that if her name was going to be called she wanted to go out making a point.

At the end of May, Strange leaked emails about the layoffs to Ellen Huet, a reporter at Bloomberg. On June 3, Huet reported that WeWork was laying off 7 percent of its staff. Adam was privately livid about the revelation, but at a TGIM event several weeks later, he gave another rousing speech. Employees carried trays of tequila shots into the room as Darryl McDaniels, the DMC in Run-DMC, walked in wearing a black Motörhead T-shirt and gave Adam a hug before running through a set of Run-DMC's greatest hits. Parties like this had long been one of the company's selling points, but many employees didn't know how to react. Dozens of their colleagues were losing their jobs. It felt like they were one of Adam's four young children being distracted with yet another new toy.

A month later, Bloomberg published details from an internal WeWork financial report that Strange also leaked. The document showed that WeWork was cutting its revenue projections for the year and slashing its profit forecast by 78 percent. The company was losing $90 million a year simply because of what it called "desk slippage" from delayed building openings as employees scrambled to keep up with WeWork's pace. The dual disclosures—layoffs on one end, curtailed revenue on the other— were a blow to WeWork's sunny narrative. To its competitors, and those who had never understood the numbers behind its valuation, the report was a validating confirmation that WeWork had not magically circumvented the realities of the office-leasing business.

Internally, the leaks made WeWork a paranoid place. A few months later, when an executive assistant put in her two-week notice, she was immediately barred from the building and locked out of her accounts. WeWork quickly discovered that Strange was behind the leaks—she had not done a particularly good job of concealing her digital snooping—and filed a lawsuit against her.

Adam and Miguel both spoke about their communal upbringings as the foundation of their community-building desire, but Adam's emergence as WeWork's alpha leader seemed to push the quirks of his childhood to the fore. A kibbutz like Nir Am had a communitarian spirit, but it was also about claiming territory, and building industries to propagate itself. "You put up boundaries around a kibbutz," one WeWork employee pointed out.

Not long after Strange was identified as the whistleblower, Adam called several WeWork employees who had worked with Strange into his office to press them on how this had happened. One employee who had been with WeWork for several years stayed behind to ask Adam why he was so insistent on going after Strange. Adam walked over to a whiteboard, took out a marker, and drew a large circle. He then wrote the word "We" in the middle. "You're either with us," Adam said, "or you're against us."

* * *

IN THE SPRING OF 2016, Bill Gurley sounded another alarm on *Above the Crowd*, expressing his concern about "the remarkable ease of the Unicorn fundraising process." In a single year, the number of unicorns had nearly tripled to 229. Founders were able to "pick a new valuation well above your last one, put together a presentation deck, solicit offers, and watch the hundreds of million [*sic*] of dollars flow into your bank account." A year later, everyone lined up to do it all over again. "The pressures of lofty paper valuations, massive burn rates (and the subsequent need for more cash)," Gurley wrote, "have created a complex and unique circumstance that many Unicorn CEOs and investors are ill-prepared to navigate."

Gurley didn't name WeWork, but the problem he diagnosed had obvious applications: few entrepreneurs were spending more money or boosting their valuation more quickly with rapid-fire fundraising rounds than Adam Neumann was. Benchmark had encouraged Adam to think big early on and participated in most of its subsequent rounds, but had bowed out of WeWork's Series E.

Gurley feared that some start-ups would begin to die not of starvation and lack of capital but from "indigestion." He cited the *Wall Street Journal*'s recent investigation of Theranos, which exposed alleged fraud at the well-funded blood-testing start-up, as evidence that "just because a company can raise money from a handful of investors at a very high price, it does not guarantee ... everything is going well." Summing up the issue as MO MONEY MO PROBLEMS, Gurley said that for young entrepreneurs, one of the biggest lapses in judgment "is the assumption that if we can just raise 'one more round' everything will be fine."

Despite the implicit warning from one of WeWork's investors, Adam and Miguel were still dreaming up ways to keep their company private. "We have a lot of fun, and from everything I heard about being a public company, it's not fun at all," Miguel said. Perhaps WeWork's members could own stakes in the company, like a collective, they wondered. Adam continued to believe that the only requirement for WeWork to achieve its ambitions was faith from the investor community. Talking to a reporter from *Fast Company*, he said that WeNeighborhoods and WeCities were "a when, not an if." He was far from the first charismatic leader to imagine himself bringing about a better world, and the *Fast Company* reporter pointed out that pretty much every utopian project in the history of humanity had failed. The kibbutz movement, for one, had shrunk from hundreds of outposts to a few dozen. Adam conceded the point but said that the reporter was missing the crucial difference that made him uniquely situated to lead this particular revolution: "The reason most people did not succeed in this idea before, is that nobody was ever able to write the check."

Adam would need another check soon. With the Hony money in hand, WeWork was heading into China, where many unicorns had charged in with confidence only to get their horns smashed. That August, Uber sold its China business to a local rival after losing billions. WeWork was burning money there too, and had more or less tapped out investors from Israel to New York to San Francisco to Beijing. The wave of venture capital funding that had ballooned since the recession had fallen off by 2016, as investors finally grew leery of skyrocketing valuations for companies with seemingly no intention of going public, or turning a profit, anytime soon. For WeWork, there seemed to be no option left but to go public. "We said, 'Nobody else in the world is going to invest,'" one senior employee involved in WeWork's fundraising told me. "Then, all of a sudden, literally the only guy in the entire world who could give the company the one drug it's craving shows up at the door."

CHAPTER ELEVEN

Mr. Ten Times

ON JUNE 25, 2010, just a few months after Adam and Miguel opened the first WeWork at 154 Grand, Masayoshi Son walked onstage and smiled at the audience packing a five-thousand-seat auditorium in Tokyo. Son was the founder of Softbank, the Japanese technology conglomerate, and he was preparing to deliver his annual address to the company's shareholders along with a thousand members of the Japanese public who were so enthralled by Masa—he only needed one name—that they had entered a lottery for tickets. Masa was fifty-two and stood just above five feet tall. Friends thought he looked like Charlie Brown, with a tuft of hair atop his bald head. His ambitions had always exceeded his unassuming appearance, and as he began talking, Masa told the crowd that he believed this speech would be the most important moment of his life. He hoped they wouldn't mind if he went long.

In the thirty years since Masa founded SoftBank, he had driven the company to great heights on the back of one risky bet after another, briefly becoming the world's richest man before losing more money than anyone in history—only to do it all over again. He liked tying his fortune to founders who shared his appetite for building a world no one had yet imagined. In 2000, Masa made what the *Financial Times* called "one of the best venture investments of all time," putting

$20 million into Alibaba, the Chinese answer to Amazon, when the company had only a few employees. Masa's Alibaba stake was eventually worth more than $100 billion. He described his interest in almost primal terms as an "animal smell" he detected upon meeting Jack Ma, Alibaba's founder. "Mr. Ma has very bright sparkles in his eyes, which are as bright as the sparkles in the eyes of Bill Gates and Steve Jobs," Masa said. "I believed in the sparkles in his eyes." He and Ma were "the same animal," Masa said. "We are both a little crazy."

Onstage in Tokyo, Masa was scheduled to deliver his vision for SoftBank's next three decades, but he told the crowd that such a timeline felt too limiting. "Why don't we talk about three hundred years from now?" he asked, wearing a light gray blazer over a white shirt with an open collar. Masa predicted that the world was about to experience "the greatest paradigm shift" in human history. A revolution was coming, and the sale of technological services that had made Masa and his company rich—computer software, then broadband internet, then mobile phone service—had taken on a new urgency. "SoftBank is now working to make people happy through the information revolution," Masa said. "This is the single thing we want to accomplish."

On Twitter, where Masa had one of the largest followings in all of Japan, he had asked his followers to identify "the saddest thing in your life." They returned a panoply of grief: loneliness, despair, the death of a loved one. SoftBank could not solve every human malady—"People long for love, and get hurt by love"—but Masa believed that his company's vision and reach should be expansive. SoftBank, he said, would strive "to comfort people in their sorrow."

When Masa's speech hit the ninety-minute mark, the lights dimmed, and he cued up a somber video that opened with a drone zooming in on a man standing amid the ruins of a castle. "Sorrow," the narrator began. "It's inherent to the human condition." He went on to dramatically describe the way Son and SoftBank saw the future.

Since the beginning of time, humans have sought to overcome sorrow. Some have turned to religion. Others have sought solace in philosophy or art. Now, we see a different solution—a new means to relieve sorrow, to multiply joy. A solution unique to our time, to our era. We call it the information revolution. A revolution that allows the thoughts of one to be shared by many, and the thoughts of many to be available to all—connecting people, thoughts, visions, and dreams, one to another, no matter how far apart they may be.

When you're all alone, in the dark of night, someone, somewhere, on the other side of the planet, can shed a ray of morning light. A technology developed in one country can solve a problem in another. A brilliant idea on one side of the globe can turn despair to hope on the other. Information technology generates an attractive force between people, ideas, and thoughts. A force that drives our destiny, and that tells us we are not alone. A force that brings people together, and sets us free—overcoming barriers of nationality, age, race, language, time, and space. We believe that this new force will help us cure disease, fill education with excitement, eliminate war, and live in peace. Ever-evolving technology, and the never-changing value of human love—together, we'll open the doors to a new century of happiness and joy.

The lights went back up, and Masa returned to the stage. He had become captivated by the growing field of artificial intelligence and believed that exploiting this coming revolution was how SoftBank would bring people happiness—one slide in his presentation showed an image of a human hand offering a heart to a robotic arm—and return value to shareholders. Masa planned to scour the globe with his checkbook, looking for entrepreneurs capable of realizing his vision. It would be five and a half more years before Masa met Adam, but he ended his presentation with an animated clip that included a message suggesting they were destined to collide. "No one should be left alone," the text said. "The 'I's' will come together to build the 'We.'"

* * *

MASA WAS BORN in 1957 in Tosu, a small town at the southwestern tip of Japan. His grandfather had emigrated from Korea, and Masa saw himself as an outsider in Japanese society, much as Adam did when he moved from Indianapolis back to Kibbutz Nir Am. Japanese society was unwelcoming to many foreigners, and the Sons adopted a Japanese surname—Yasumoto—that left young Masa with a sense that he was hiding something. His father cobbled together a living doing a bit of everything—raising pigs, hawking illegal liquor, running a fishing hole—and his son was intent on building a different life for himself. When his father opened a coffee shop, Masa suggested that he give out free drink vouchers to potential customers in the hope that he could attract enough business to make up for the losses later. "I believe you are a genius," his father told him. "You just don't know your destiny yet."

By middle school, Masa had decided that his destiny was to become one of Japan's most successful businessmen. His idol was Den Fujita, who brought McDonald's to Japan. Fujita was eccentric and highly quotable on everything from business ("There is neither clean money nor dirty money. In a capitalistic society, all methods of making money are acceptable") to burgers ("The reason Japanese people are so short and have yellow skins is because they have eaten nothing but fish and rice for two thousand years"). He wrote a number of bestselling books, including *The Jewish Way of Doing Business*—Fujita insisted the title was a compliment—and *Stupid People Lose Money*. After hours spent as a teenager fruitlessly calling Fujita's office in hopes of speaking with him, Masa traveled from Tosu to Tokyo, arrived at Fujita's office, and demanded an audience. Fujita agreed to meet for fifteen minutes, during which he encouraged Son to go to America and offered him one word of career advice: "Computers."

Masa landed in California at the age of sixteen, shrugged off his adopted surname, and enrolled in English classes at Holy Names, a Catholic university in Oakland. The campus was up on a hill, and when the sky was blue, he could see the Golden Gate Bridge across San Francisco Bay and Silicon Valley on the horizon to the south. Brimming with confidence, he thought to himself, "I'm going to conquer the world." He was immediately taken with the pace and expanse of America, though he came away unimpressed by visits to Yosemite and the Grand Canyon; his biographer, Atsuo Inoue, reported that Masa was "struck by the shopping malls and freeways more so than these natural spectacles."

He was also in a hurry. After brushing up on his English, Masa went to Serramonte High School, south of San Francisco. He entered as a sophomore, but a few days after arriving, he explained to the principal that he wanted to get to college as soon as possible—could he reclassify as a junior? A few days later, Masa persuaded the school to make him a senior, and two weeks after that he was taking a college entrance exam, where he realized he was in over his head but prevailed on an administrator to let him use a Japanese-to-English dictionary. After less than a month as an American high school student, Masa graduated.

Following a brief return to Holy Names, Masa transferred to the University of California, Berkeley, where he majored in economics. Like Neumann, his studies took a back seat, and he became a serial college entrepreneur. Masa set a goal of spending five minutes every day coming up with a new invention he could sell, and by year's end, he had more than 250 of them.

He decided that the best was a calculator-size device that would translate text from various languages. Masa combed through Berkeley's faculty directory for someone who might be able to help, but each professor kept passing him on to their colleagues until eventually Masa met Forrest

Mozer, a physics professor who saw that even though Masa's idea wasn't unique and he didn't know much about electronics, he possessed an important skill. "The beauty of his idea was not to create a translator but to sell it," Mozer said later. "It was clear from the very beginning that he was an entrepreneurial genius." While Mozer built a prototype, Masa had another Asian student sit in on the Berkeley lectures he was missing to travel around cold-pitching tech companies. (As a side business, Masa imported Space Invaders arcade machines from Japan and set them up in bars and restaurants.) After several false starts, Masa landed a meeting with Sharp, which agreed to buy the patent for hundreds of thousands of dollars. "That guy is going to own Japan one day," Mozer told his wife.

Masa graduated from Berkeley in 1980. He thought about staying in the United States, which had a more entrepreneurial spirit than Japan's conservative business world, but Masa's new vision was to build a giant corporation. He wanted his employees to be loyal, and Japanese workers were more inclined to stick with a company for life. (He had also promised his mom he would come back.) Masa mapped out forty business ideas, evaluating each based on twenty-five different metrics, including whether he could build the top Japanese business in that particular field within a decade.

A year later, Masa winnowed the list down to one: a company that distributed computer software—a software bank. This wasn't an obvious business, with personal computing still in its earliest days, but Masa was optimistic. One morning, he stood on a tangerine crate and told his two employees they had to listen to him because he was their boss and that SoftBank would one day become a billion dollar company. Both employees quit.

SoftBank struggled to take off, so Masa started several magazines, including *Oh! PC*, to help drive interest. But the publication began to tank, and Masa feared the consequences of an early public defeat. "If we stopped the magazines, everyone would say that SoftBank was in trouble—that SoftBank was going to die," he said. Masa went all in, doubling the pages in the next issue, printing twice as many copies, and spending the rest of his money on television ads. The issue sold out in three days.

By the mid-'90s, SoftBank had 800 employees and a billion dollars in revenue. Masa stood atop his Japanese peers in the software distribution business but realized that this was no longer enough. He viewed himself as an equal to the tech elite he had brushed up against in California and began working himself into American business circles. Masa would become their man in Japan. He launched a joint venture with Ross Perot to help Perot's company, Electronic Data Systems, enter the country, and worked to set up a Nasdaq stock exchange in Tokyo.

Masa's showmanship and appetite for risk were unusual for a Japanese businessman. During a night out in Tokyo with Microsoft executives, he reportedly let several bar hostesses remove his shirt and write on his chest in lipstick. He drove a Porsche and loved to golf, once shooting a seventy-four at Augusta National. When Bill Gates visited Tokyo, Masa gave him a tour of his mansion, which had a $3 million driving range that could simulate a Pacific Ocean fog rolling over Pebble Beach as a light drizzle fell from the ceiling.

By the end of the decade, Masa had developed a reputation for audacious bets. He made a big investment in a young company called Yahoo!; bought COMDEX, a Las Vegas–based computer trade show, from Sheldon Adelson for $800 million; and reportedly invested $400 million in E*Trade after a single phone call with its founder, Christos Cotsakos. "Masa is the master of the internet universe," Cotsakos said. "He has a clear vision of how technology is going to connect everyone globally in the next fifty years and doesn't let daily, weekly, or monthly fluctuations get in the way." In 1995, a *New York Times* reporter called Masa "the Bill Gates of Japan."

Throughout the '90s, SoftBank invested $3 billion into eight hundred tech start-ups—so many that the company could barely keep up. (At one point, a single SoftBank executive served as president or CEO of twelve different companies.) Some of the companies complained about Masa's flightiness, griping that he would shower attention on a start-up only to find a new toy and leave his old favorites to collect dust. Some of his bets were bad—American Cybercast, an online soap opera producer, folded—but Masa discovered the lesson that unicorn hunters would later learn: a single winner, like Yahoo!, could mask failures everywhere else.

In 2000, Masa raised the largest Japanese investment fund ever: $1.2 billion of venture capital, which he piled into hundreds of companies heading into the teeth of the dot-com boom. For three days, in the middle of 2000, Masa says that he passed Bill Gates as the world's richest man. Masa knew this because he was keeping track, but before he could tell anyone, the market crashed. SoftBank's stock sank more than 90 percent by year's end, and Masa himself lost $70 billion—more wealth than any single investor had ever lost.

* * *

MASA WAS HUMBLED but undeterred. That fall, he flew to Denver to meet with Larry Mueller, an American tech CEO looking to move his company into Japan. At the end of the night, with the deal closed, Mueller poured some Cognac and gave Masa a gift he took home and displayed proudly in his foyer: a statue of a cowboy trying to stay on the back of a bucking bronco.

Masa spent the decade after his dot-com rise and fall taking another series of risks. In 2001, he successfully forced his way into the Japanese broadband business after barging into the office of a government regulator and yelling, "This is the end. If you don't help me, I'm going to pour gasoline all over myself right here and set myself on fire." Masa launched the service, Yahoo BB, at half the price of his competitors. The *Wall Street Journal* reported that he had saleswomen in striped miniskirts handing out free modems on Tokyo street corners. Yahoo BB quickly gained subscribers, but the business lost hundreds of millions of dollars in two years; Masa hoped to one day charge for add-on services, such as on-demand video, but was "vague on when the business will actually turn a profit," the *Journal* reported. In 2006, Masa wanted in on the mobile phone business and took on an enormous amount of debt to buy Vodafone Japan for $15 billion. He later secured exclusive rights to iPhones in Japan, then gave them away with cheap unlimited data plans to eat up market share.

By the time Masa got onstage to deliver his three-hundred-year vision, in 2010, his risks had paid off. Both of his latest gambits were thriving, and his investment in Alibaba had become legendary. He wanted more. By 2300, Masa said, SoftBank might be "a telepathy company instead of a telecommunications company"—who could say how far the company would go? ("Maybe communicating with dogs could be possible," he said.) But Masa also knew he wouldn't be around to see that vision come to fruition. He told the audience that, back at Berkeley, he had developed a fifty-year life plan for himself: start a company in his twenties, build wealth in his thirties, deploy that money in his forties, tie up loose ends in his fifties, then hand things off to a new generation after he turned sixty.

Masa was approaching that final stage, and he had begun to look around for updated versions of himself—young entrepreneurs with a sparkle in their eyes and a willingness to act a little crazy. "Masayoshi Son 2.0," as he put it with a smile.

* * *

IN JANUARY OF 2016, shortly after WeLive opened, Adam and several WeWork executives flew to India for a start-up conference hosted by Indian prime minister Narendra Modi. The Indian economy was experiencing unprecedented growth, increasing its GDP by 7 percent a year—the highest rate in the world. (Like many other economic metrics from the 2010s, India's growth rate was not what it seemed, and the government's numbers were found to be a "fantastically crafted fiction" that was inflated by half.) Adam was one of the conference's keynote speakers, alongside Travis Kalanick, from Uber, and Masa, who was planning to invest $10 billion into Indian start-ups.

Marc Schimmel, one of WeWork's Kabbalah Centre investors, had been pushing Adam to make a large commitment to India as well, and Adam used the trip to make a frenzied tour of the country. When the WeWork team landed in Mumbai late at night, Adam met several local businessmen Schimmel had connected him to and asked them to drive him around the city, looking at buildings, so that he could do so when there was no traffic. The group then flew to Bengaluru. After a late night of drinking, Adam slept through a breakfast meeting with a group of potential business partners, including Jitu Virwani, a real estate tycoon and one of India's wealthiest men. The other WeWork employees on the trip had to send hotel security to Adam's room to check on him. Adam eventually met with Virwani, at the billionaire's home, where he baked a loaf of Challah bread in Virwani's kitchen to present to Modi at the conference in New Delhi. (The prime minister's security team rejected the baked gift, citing the traditional fear it could be poisoned.)

Adam delivered his address wearing a traditional Indian garment that was inspired by a guest he had met at a recent birthday party for his friend Jared Kushner. Both Modi and Masa, along with Neumann's father, were in the audience as Adam laid out his vision. "I just came here five days ago for the first time, so I'm still an early student of India, but here is what I've observed," Adam said onstage. "For a very spiritual country—and I can definitely tell you this is the most spiritual country in the world—I'm surprised a little bit from the amount of talk I heard about valuation and raising money and bubbles." The crowd laughed nervously. Adam insisted this wasn't what he was after. He believed that India's budding democracy and growing economy embodied an idea he had been talking about with increasing frequency: the "We Generation," an ageless demographic defined by a faith in the sharing economy and a belief that doing well could come from doing good. "I swear to you success will follow; the money will follow," Adam said. "And you will change the world."

On his last night in India, Adam met Masa at a bar on the top floor of a building in New Delhi. The meeting had been arranged by Nikesh Arora, Masa's top deputy at SoftBank, who had previously spurned WeWork as a potential investment. At first blush, Masa harbored many of the standard doubts about Neumann's business—insofar as he had thought about We-Work at all. Masa had never even been inside one of its spaces. But Adam had told others that if he could connect with Masa, founder-to-founder, he believed that he could convince SoftBank to invest.

Masa also prided himself on his ability to see past the numbers and into the soul of a business—and its entrepreneur. When he met founders who "did not have true belief in their heart," he often passed; when he met ones like Jack Ma, he gave them more than they could imagine asking for. (Masa had initially wanted to invest even more into Alibaba, but Ma turned him down, arguing that it was too much for him to know what to do with.) Adam and Masa were separated by two decades in age and more than a foot in height but recognized something innate that they shared as they sat talking for half an hour on a small couch in a corner of the bar. Adam told Masa about WeWork's growth, with the company on pace to open its hundredth location later that year—a number Adam had been dreaming of since he had just two. Masa was unimpressed. He told Adam that if he set his sights high enough and was willing to move quickly, the opportunity in front of him was even bigger than Adam himself could imagine.

* * *

ADAM WAS GIDDY with excitement from the conversation; he nearly missed his flight back from New Delhi to New York that night. He and Miguel had talked about WeWork as a "hundred-year challenge," and here was someone who thought that timeline was too short. That fall, Adam and Rebekah painted their entire bodies white for WeWork's 2016 Halloween party, which had an appropriately forward-looking theme: "3016."

A few weeks after the party, on the first Tuesday in December, Masa made plans to visit WeWork headquarters while he was in New York on other business. "Ladies and gentlemen, this is Masa of SoftBank...one of the great men of industry," Donald Trump told a bank of cameras in the lobby of Trump Tower. A month after Trump's surprise electoral victory, Masa was the first in a line of business-world supplicants to visit the president-elect's building to curry favor. Masa was interested in reviving a proposed merger between T-Mobile and Sprint, which SoftBank owned; the deal had run afoul of Obama administration regulators concerned about a lack of competition in the mobile phone market. There was a bit of Trump in Masa, who summed up his interest in the merger by saying, "I'm a man, so I want to be number one."

Wearing a red V-neck sweater and tie in front of Trump Tower's golden elevators, Masa told reporters that he had come to celebrate Trump's new job. "Because he would do a lot of deregulation, I said, 'This is great'— US will become great again," Masa said. He held up the piece of paper that he had just shown Trump, explaining that SoftBank would invest $50 billion in the United States and create fifty thousand new jobs over four years, a timeline neatly tied to the span of Trump's first term.

The plan was light on details other than Masa's suggestion that the money would come from his newest project. In October, he had announced the launch of the Vision Fund, a $100 billion venture capital vehicle that was eighty times bigger than the record-setting $1.2 billion Masa had raised in 2000 and four times larger than any other fund in history. The Vision Fund's limited partners included Foxconn, the government of Abu Dhabi, and Apple, which had so much cash on hand that there weren't enough productive places to put it. Masa and SoftBank would choose the fund's investments, and each of the limited partners would receive returns relative to the amount it had put in.

The bulk of the Vision Fund was coming from the Saudi Arabian government. Mohammed bin Salman, the next Saudi crown prince, had been on a worldwide tour expressing his hope of expanding the country's economy beyond oil. There was only so much real estate the Saudis could buy in Manhattan and central London, and they had come to Masa hoping he could identify the next Yahoo! or Alibaba. When an interviewer asked Masa whether it was true that he had persuaded bin Salman to invest $45 billion into the Vision Fund after a single hourlong meeting in Tokyo, Masa objected to the idea it would take him that long: "Forty-five minutes, $45 billion—one billion dollars per minute."

The Vision Fund, which initially had the code name Project Crystal Ball, was meant to supercharge the work of Masa's three-hundred-year plan. He believed society was approaching the singularity, when artificial intelligence would become so advanced that humans and machines would be indistinguishable. This shift could be accelerated, and monetized, with enough capital, and the Vision Fund had more money than most venture capitalists would be trusted to invest in their lifetimes. Masa intended to spend the money over the next five years, promising bin Salman "a Masa gift" on his investment—a tenfold return. He would model the fund on Warren Buffett's Berkshire Hathaway, building a portfolio of companies defining the new economy much as Buffett had taken large stakes in banks, railroads, and airlines. Masa liked to think of the Vision Fund's companies as a flock of migratory birds flying in formation.

In the months since Masa and Adam met in India, their respective companies had discussed the possibility of an investment, and the Vision Fund had supercharged what might be possible. On the same day that Masa visited Trump Tower, he scheduled a tour of WeWork headquarters. Masa was known for running start-ups through a car wash, giving founders fifteen minutes to wow him before moving on to the next pitch. But SoftBank had agreed to block out two hours for a full tour and presentation from WeWork.

That morning, however, a SoftBank representative called to let Adam know that Masa was running late. Adam grew nervous, pacing back and forth in his office as the morning dragged on and Masa still hadn't shown up. A circle of employees prepping for the meeting were tasked with ensuring the pitchers of fruit water looked fresh, the music in the office was at the right volume, and the religious paraphernalia had been removed from Adam's desk. By the time Masa arrived, the two hours were almost up. "I only have twelve minutes," Masa said. "Go."

Adam knew that the Vision Fund was focused on technology, not real estate, so after walking through a floor of the building that was filled with WeWork members, to show how lively it could be, he took Masa straight to the company's "R&D lab" on the third floor. There, Dave Fano, the co-founder of Case—the Buildings = Data company Adam had acquired—showed off various systems WeWork was developing: a standing desk that automatically adapts to a member's height; a keyless entry system; a phone booth with smart lighting. None of this was likely to bring about the singularity, but after the twelve minutes were up, Masa told Adam to join him in his car.

Adam grabbed his investor deck and hopped into the back seat; he was used to meeting on the move, and often asked WeWork executives to debrief him in his chauffeured Maybach, tailed by another vehicle that would drive the executive back once Adam arrived at his destination. But Masa was in charge, and he told Adam to put the presentation away. Despite his doubts, Masa was impressed by the speed at which WeWork had been able to execute a labor-intensive expansion. That month alone, the company had opened new locations in thirteen cities in seven different countries. WeWork also presented a unique opportunity for the Vision Fund. It would be impossible to invest $100 billion in five years by funding a flock of nimble sparrows; Masa needed to find albatrosses that could use his cash to overcome barriers to entry in industries where the theoretical returns were also large enough to justify the costs— an industry like real estate, with expensive leases and significant capital expenditures to go along with an enormous total addressable market.

As Adam and Masa drove away from WeWork's headquarters, Masa pulled out an iPad and began sketching the terms of a deal: SoftBank and the Vision Fund would invest more than $4 billion into WeWork. The investment would be the Vision Fund's biggest to date, and many times larger than any funding round Adam had managed thus far. Masa signed his name, drew another line next to it, and handed Neumann the stylus. Adam had gotten WeWork this far in large part by making shrewd deals—acting coy when it suited him and playing hardball when necessary. But that morning, Adam had met with a spiritual adviser, as he often did before making big decisions, and received some advice: in life, it was sometimes necessary to do "the opposite of our nature."

Adam also knew a good deal when he saw one. After Masa dropped him off, Neumann got into his white Maybach, which had been trailing Masa's car, turned up some rap music, and drove back to WeWork head- quarters. A photo of the digital napkin, with Masa's signature in red and Adam's in blue, was soon circulating among WeWork executives. The entire exchange, from Masa's twelve-minute tour to signatures sealing one of the largest venture capital investments of all time, had taken less than half an hour.

* * *

THINKING BACK TO the meeting with Masa, Adam would often get goose bumps. At the precipice of needing to go public to continue funding his business, he had found more money than ever. He also had a new mentor—someone whose vision exceeded his. Jimmy Lee, the JPMorgan banker Adam had connected with back in 2013, had died two years later, leaving Adam without a north star in the world of big money. Masa could now fill that role.

A few months after their visit in New York, Adam and a group of WeWork executives, lawyers, and advisers prepared to fly to Tokyo to hammer out the deal. Adam insisted they arrive with a gift. Specifically, he wanted to send the large eight-foot-by-four-foot piece of artwork hanging in his office. The collage, commissioned from an Israeli artist, spelled out "WeWork" on a canvas of household items: screwdrivers, floppy disks, a keyboard, paintbrushes, cassette and VHS tapes. It weighed 150 pounds and couldn't fit on the private jet ferrying Adam and his team across the Pacific. So on Wednesday morning, WeWork hired a logistics company at a cost of $50,000 to pack up the piece, rush it to JFK, and put it onto a flight that would get the piece to SoftBank headquarters before the close of business on Friday.

Masa was enamored by Adam, but others at SoftBank and the Vision Fund were less convinced. Many of Masa's deputies told him they didn't understand why a technology company like SoftBank, managing a fund dedicated to artificial intelligence, would pour so much money into a company that, despite Neumann's grandest articulations, seemed to be a real estate leasing business. The Saudis had invested in the Vision Fund as a way of diversifying their economy, and when Masa initially proposed investing as much as $5 billion in WeWork, Saudi Arabia—along with Abu Dhabi, the fund's second-largest investor—threatened to use the veto power they held on any Vision Fund investment that exceeded $3 billion.

After the meeting in New York, a team from SoftBank put WeWork through several months of "the most intense diligence we'd been through," a member of WeWork's finance team said. "We were talking to these guys every day, and their body language, the questions they were asking—you could just tell they were skeptical." Several months into the negotiation, SoftBank's team asked to see WeWork's projections from previous investment rounds to assess whether the company had fulfilled its promises. "There were some projections we missed by [roughly] 80 percent," the WeWork employee said. "You figure that's the 'gotcha moment' where they say, 'You guys are full of shit.'"

But SoftBank was not a democracy. Masa liked to say that while his team might perform months of diligence on a company, "my first insight in the first few minutes is sometimes more meaningful." He often compared his deductive powers to another diminutive guru: "Yoda says use the force. Don't think, just feel it." He viewed the future of WeWork's industry as a land grab in which the person with the most territory would ultimately win. Masa's money would allow WeWork to box out any competitors. His only objection, as Adam and his team laid out their plan, was that they were still being too shortsighted. "Why only a million members when you can have five?" Masa said at a time when WeWork barely had a hundred thousand. If WeWork could do that, growing to fifty times its size, Masa said its valuation would look cheap. The company might be worth $1 trillion.

As the negotiations wore on, Adam pushed his executives to find ways to live up to Masa's expectations. Employees responsible for managing projections in markets around the world were asked to return to their models for the next five years and crank them up. "It just kept getting more and more ludicrous," a WeWork executive on the West Coast said. "Every time we turned the numbers in, we would get on calls and be told, 'You have to keep getting bigger.'" WeWork as a whole had generated $400 million in revenue in 2016; Adam wanted the region alone to bring in more than $1 billion.

The West Coast team met in Seattle to come up with new projections that could satisfy Adam. For WeWork's rent arbitrage to work at any given location, each space needed to meet certain physical requirements—size, shape, location, available infrastructure—that would allow the company to keep its costs at a minimum while squeezing in enough people to turn a profit. But as the West Coast team surveyed the real estate market in cities up and down the coast, they came to a troubling realization. "There was *literally* not enough real estate in these cities to reach these numbers," one person involved in the discussion claimed. New construction was popping up all over Seattle, for example, but the team found that WeWork could have occupied every new building going up in the city and still not hit the goals set before them.

Investor pitch decks are not audited financial statements, and it was difficult for even the skeptical members of SoftBank's team, who weren't real estate experts, to question WeWork's projections or push back too forcefully on Masa's desire to do the deal. During a meeting in Tokyo, as the negotiation closed, Masa wanted to send Adam off with a message. Whatever strategy they had, Masa said, "make it ten times bigger." This was a refrain Masa repeated so often to companies he invested in that Alibaba executives had taken to calling him "Mr. Ten Times." Masa told Adam not to be proud of the fact that WeWork was growing without much of a sales team or any real marketing. Where were the free coffee vouchers? The women in miniskirts?

Masa shot Adam a look. "In a fight, who wins?" Masa asked. "The smart guy or the crazy guy?"

Adam replied that an unhinged combatant, willing to scrap and claw to survive, could beat even the most skilled fighter. "You are correct," Masa said. "But you and Miguel are not crazy enough." In Adam, Masa had found not only a vessel for his cash but also a visionary eager to be molded in his image—Masayoshi Son 2.0. When WeWork's executives returned to Tokyo for another meeting later on, they noticed Adam's collage was still hanging up at SoftBank headquarters.

* * *

MASA'S INVESTMENT IN Adam and his company was officially announced on August 24, 2017. It totaled $4.4 billion, some of which came from

SoftBank itself, and $1.4 billion of which was earmarked for WeWork's continued expansion into Asia—a deal structure that kept it below Saudi Arabia's veto threshold. WeWork's valuation leapt from $17 to $20 billion, making it the fourth most valuable start-up in America, after Uber, Airbnb, and SpaceX. The deal also included $1.3 billion earmarked for buying stock from existing WeWork shareholders. Benchmark cashed out $129 million, realizing an eight-fold return on its 2012 investment. Sam-Ben Avraham and Marc Schimmel, Adam's friends and early investors, cashed out tens of millions, while Joel Schreiber, the man who had given WeWork its first injection of capital, passed his stake on to SoftBank for a poignant amount: $44.6 million, just shy of the $45 million valuation Adam and Miguel pulled out of thin air back in 2009.

The biggest winner was Adam. We Holdings sold $361 million worth of its WeWork stock—the maximum amount, and nearly three times more than every other WeWork employee was able to cash out combined. This was an even more shocking amount than the earlier stock sales. Why cash out so much now if you believe the potential spoils to be even greater down the line?

One answer was that the Neumanns needed to fund their increasingly lavish lifestyle. At the end of 2017, Adam and Rebekah spent $35 million to buy four apartments in a single Gramercy building, combining three of the units into a mega penthouse. Adam bought homes for his sister and grandmother, paying them back for the rent and tuition they had covered during his early years in New York. WeWork employees could only roll their eyes when Adam and Rebekah spoke about their embrace of the sharing economy and lack of interest in material wealth. "We believe in this new 'asset-light lifestyle,'" Rebekah told one interviewer, at a time when the Neumanns owned five homes. "We want to live off of the land. I'm like a real hippie." WeWork's 2017 Halloween party had another apt theme: *The Great Gatsby*.

With Masa's money in hand, a calm seemed to settle over Adam. He was set for life, no matter what happened. Executives at WeWork said the chaos that so often permeated the company settled down. A day before the start of Hanukkah, in December of 2017, Adam invited Cheni Yerushalmi to visit him at WeWork's Chelsea headquarters. The two men hadn't seen each other much in the years since Yerushalmi called Adam a "fucking piece of shit" for seemingly mimicking his business and running with it after his mother had connected them. Like many office-space operators, Yerushalmi didn't have Adam's gift for fundraising, and Sunshine Suites had gone out of business. As Yerushalmi's mother pointed out, it wasn't the idea that mattered, but what you did with it.

Yerushalmi settled into Adam's large office, with its Peloton bike and punching bag. Adam said he had been thinking of Yerushalmi, and while he acknowledged they weren't going to be friends, he wanted to clear the air. He was embracing religion and encouraged Yerushalmi to meet with Eitan Yardeni from the Kabbalah Centre. He was also spending more time surfing. Adam said it brought him some peace.

Not long after, Adam left for vacation in Hanalei Bay, on the Hawaiian island of Kauai. Hanalei Bay is a surfing mecca that maintains an eclectic vibe. The celebrities and CEOs who visit try to tread lightly. One morning, two start-up employees who worked at tech companies back on the mainland were paddling out to sea when they spotted Adam in the water nearby. He was flat on his board, holding on to a pair of ropes attached to the back of two surfboards, from which two local guides were pulling him out to the waves. It was the surfing equivalent of a cross-country skier holding on to someone else's pole—or the start-up equivalent, his fellow surfers noted, of propelling yourself with a $100 billion venture capital cannon. Back in the Hamptons, Adam kept a motorized surfboard.

A few days later, Adam was back in Hanalei Bay with a group of friends. He had two boats this time, one of which carried a drone operator, along with a pair of jet skis whizzing in and out. While an extreme version of surfing involves jet skis pulling riders into giant waves that are otherwise difficult to reach, the breaks in Hanalei Bay are among the smoothest rides in the ocean. The horsepower was unnecessary, eliminating the struggle and patience and timing that surfing required, not to mention unsporting for the others in the bay. They could only watch as Adam leaped from the back of a jet ski onto his board, stood up, and surfed a perfect wave. When he got to the end, Adam spread his arms wide like Christ the Redeemer and looked up at the drone flying above, filming his every move.

CHAPTER TWELVE

Me Over We

IN JANUARY OF 2017, WeWork's employees arrived in Los Angeles for the company's third annual Summit—its first outside New York—to find that the era of Managing the Nickel was over. The SoftBank deal was still being finalized, but WeWork felt flush enough to fly all two thousand of its employees to California for the weekend. A contingent from the Kabbalah Centre hosted Shabbat services on Friday night, and Eitan Yardeni addressed the company again. WeWork seemed to be back at its most audacious. The company rented out Universal Studios Hollywood for a night and brought the Chainsmokers back to perform. During their set, Adam leaped onstage, sweating heavily, and pumped his fist in the air while one of the Chainsmokers yelled, "Everybody fucking jump!"

The weekend was a blast for most WeWork employees during an otherwise disorienting time. Donald Trump was set to be inaugurated as president of the United States in a few days, and given that many WeWork employees had been attracted to the company's public rhetoric of Obama-era inclusivity and togetherness, Trump's election had been a gut punch. Many of them found solace in believing that their company was building a better world. At Summit, WeWork was collecting bone marrow swabs to help build a registry, after an attempt to find a match for an employee who needed a transplant. Miguel sat down to join a group of employees on a picnic blanket as if he were just another bearded community manager wearing sneakers and a T-shirt; later, he gave a speech encouraging WeWork employees to always make decisions from a place of love. When a company scavenger hunt challenged employees to prompt passing cars to honk, Rocky Kerns, the orientation leader, held up a sign that said HONK 4 OBAMA.

In addition to Trump's inauguration, WeWork's Summit overlapped with the Women's March, the worldwide protest that had a stated goal of harnessing "the political power of diverse women and their communities to create transformative social change." This was a version of the way Adam described WeWork's mission, and on Saturday morning, a hundred or so WeWork employees skipped several Summit events to join 750,000 Angelenos gathering downtown. That afternoon, Los Angeles mayor Eric Garcetti stopped by Summit to give a speech, having just come from the Women's March himself. He thanked the WeWork employees who had done the same.

A few days later, Jen Berrent, the company's lawyer, got up to speak at a town hall back in New York. Berrent said that WeWork had noticed an increase in absences on Saturday morning. "You think I didn't want to be at the Women's March?" Berrent said during the town hall. She was the only female executive on WeWork's leadership team besides Rebekah, who had been installed as chief brand officer, so employees were surprised when Berrent accused those who joined the Women's March of being selfish, implying that any community building needed to take place within WeWork's walls. "That," Berrent said, "was a 'Me Over We' decision."

* * *

A FEW WEEKS LATER, Adam received an invitation to the White House from Jared Kushner. Neumann and Kushner had both gotten into the New York real estate world in the 2000s, when Kushner was pushing his family's real estate business from New Jersey into Manhattan. Kushner didn't trust Neumann when they first met in the early 2010s, but the aspiring moguls were devoutly religious, and connected as self-identified disruptors in an industry averse to newcomers. WeWork leased space in several Kushner buildings, and Neumann resolved one negotiation by insisting they go to a bar and take shots. Adam and Jared settled another dispute with an arm-wrestling match in Adam's office at 222 Broadway while several WeWork employees looked on. "I used to arm wrestle all the time in the navy," Neumann told Kushner. When Adam won, Jared complained that Adam's elbow had come off the table; they clasped their opposite hands for a rematch, but Adam won again. "They've built a good mousetrap," Kushner said of WeWork at the time. "I capitulated."

As Kushner's profile grew alongside his father-in-law's, Adam wasn't afraid to boast about the connection. "I find Jared to be one of the most sophisticated real estate developers on earth," Adam told *Bloomberg Businessweek* shortly after Trump sealed the Republican nomination. "I take cues from his behavior just to learn how to act—to act a little bit better myself." During the campaign, Adam ran over to a group of WeWork employees with a smile on his face and told them he had just spoken to Kushner, who said that if Trump won, he would consider Adam's suggestion that WeWork take on the task of reimagining America's post offices and libraries. It was hard to figure out what was exaggerated in Adam's statement—a perpetual problem at WeWork—but the Kushners and Neumanns clearly remained close, dining together at Carbone in Manhattan after Trump's victory. When an acquaintance traded phone numbers with Rebekah in 2017, Rebekah said, "You have almost the exact same number as Ivanka."

Adam was conflicted about whether to accept the White House invitation. He valued personal loyalty above almost everything else; plus, Masa, his new benefactor, had already visited Trump. What was the harm? But WeWork's public affairs team lobbied heavily against the idea: Trump's presidency, and all that it stood for, was the antithesis of the world

Neumann claimed WeWork was creating. Hobnobbing with the Trumps would appear hypocritical at best. It could also hurt the company's business: *The Guardian* backed out of a deal to move into a WeWork location in a Kushner property in Brooklyn, worried the landlord might bug the building.

For years, WeWork had studiously avoided taking stands that didn't fall under the banner of the "We revolution." This insistence on neutrality made certain things more difficult. An employee in Washington, DC, grew frustrated when she was told not to invite politicians to WeWork events in the city, which was a little like trying to throw a party in LA without any actors. But the nonpartisanship also served a business purpose. Several progressive members became upset when Adam changed the name of one DC WeWork from Metropolitan Square to White House shortly after Trump's election—but the company leased space to two writers from Breitbart, too.

In early 2017, around the same time Adam was mulling his invitation to the White House, the Trump administration released its executive order banning travel from a group of Muslim nations. The order produced outcry across the country, and protesters swarmed airports. Both people and corporations took sides; a Twitter campaign, #DeleteUber, erupted after the ride-hailing company was seen as trying to profit from the protests.

The travel ban seemed to be a natural place to take a stand for WeWork and for Neumann—an immigrant building a global company predicated on bringing people closer together. WeWork's public affairs team presented Adam with several possible responses. A group of New York tech companies was writing a letter opposing the order, and cosigning would allow WeWork to take a leadership role in that community. The team also drafted a letter for Adam to send himself, making the case that what made America great was the ability of an immigrant to meet a guy from Oregon and start a multibillion-dollar company together. Adam said that he understood the issue and was sympathetic. But if WeWork took a stand, he feared the imperative to speak up would become constant. He believed the company should talk with its actions, not its words. "Can we write letters every day?" Adam asked. Against the advice of his public affairs team, Adam quietly made the trip to DC, visiting Kushner at the White House, and he decided to stay silent on the travel ban. At the end of the day, why cause trouble for a friend?

* * *

ADAM NOW HAD a pair of models for success in the late 2010s: Masa and Trump. His friend's father-in-law had become the most powerful person in the world through a mix of chutzpah, bluster, and a willing-ness to pander to his audience. An employee who joined WeWork from Hillary Clinton's campaign—the unicorns of the 2010s were popular post-campaign jobs for political operatives seeking a lucrative and phil-osophically palatable gig—experienced flashbacks while watching Adam stride onstage at Summit after another WeWork executive tried to work the crowd into a frenzy. What kind of CEO needed a hype man? Adam seemed to want the fawning crowds Trump had on the campaign trail, but the need for a forced display of adulation reminded the Clinton staffer more of Jeb Bush's desperate efforts to build enthusiasm rather than the natural fervor Trump's supporters felt for their candidate.

But Adam ran his company with a Trumpian hubris. In the spring of 2017, his chief of staff called Matt Fry, a WeWork real estate executive who was touring several locations in San Francisco with another WeWork employee. Adam wanted them to look at a space with him in San Jose—right now. When Fry said they had plans to look at another building elsewhere in the Bay Area, Adam grabbed the phone. "You should be with me," he said. "When you have the opportunity to spend time with the greatest real estate mind in the world, you do it." (The next day, Fry rode with Adam in his car; Adam pulled out a joint, asked if it was okay if he smoked it, then did so without sharing.) Adam began invoking the phrase "fake news" when something negative about WeWork appeared in the press, telling an audience at the New York Stock Exchange it was "a great term."

Masa, meanwhile, had become one of the world's wealthiest people through a willingness to light himself on fire when necessary. Adam had not resorted to self-immolation, but his confidence grew as each of his gambits worked out. He began spending some of his SoftBank spoils to build a miniature Vision Fund to match his own interests, investing in a biotech firm dedicated to increasing human longevity; a "Shazam for TV" app that would identify shows playing on bar televisions; and a medical marijuana company headed by former Israeli prime minister Ehud Barak.

On a drive from Marin County into San Francisco in 2017, Adam met with John Cole, the founder of skyTran, a start-up that was developing a transportation system involving pods gliding along elevated tracks. Adam was considering an investment, but first he had some advice for Cole, who had raised $13 million in venture funding. If Cole wasn't trying to raise a billion, how could he expect to be taken seriously?

There was something to admire in Adam's ambition, but his proclamations about WeWork's world-changing power often seemed disconnected from reality. "Our valuation and size today are much more based on our energy and spirituality than it is on a multiple of revenue," Adam said after the SoftBank deal closed. "We are here in order to change the world— nothing less than that interests me." He began telling people he would become the richest person they would ever meet. "I want to have the biggest valuation I can, because when countries are shooting at each other, I want them to come to me," Adam said during a conversation about the ongoing Syrian refugee crisis and how WeWork might help solve it.

Adam believed that WeWork was uniquely capable of doing good in the world, and subscribed to the prevailing ethos among American start-ups that they were best suited for coming up with new models to solve old problems. Adam's and Miguel's unorthodox backgrounds, along with their incredible financial success, seemed to incline them toward what one executive described as "a general disbelief in and distaste for how society works on problems." WeWork's employees often felt that Adam lacked a willingness to engage in the complexity of the issues he hoped the company might solve. When an employee came up with an idea to hire refugees for open positions, WeWork's public affairs team proposed making an official commitment to hiring a few hundred refugees over the next five years. Adam told them that wasn't enough: they should hire 1,500, never mind that the company had only recently passed the 1,500-employee mark in total. During one meeting, Neumann told two employees from his public affairs team that he believed WeWork was going to have more of an impact on a whole host of issues than any government would.

"Who knows?" Adam said. "Maybe I can be president of the United States one day."

One of the employees pointed out that, of the three people in the room, only two of them could legally become president, given that Adam wasn't born in the United States.

"President of the world, then!" Neumann tossed out cheerfully. The situation was another occasion when it was hard to know whether to take Neumann literally—he later joked to a congressional aide that he hoped the Constitution could be amended to allow foreign-born citizens to occupy the Oval Office—but the ceiling on his ambitions was getting higher. On a trip to Israel, during which Adam held a town hall with the mayor of Jerusalem, one of his staff members joked that he was prepping his run for prime minister, the job he once told Stella Templo that he might want. In Jerusalem, Adam said the position was no longer "big enough."

In June of 2017, Adam delivered the closest he had come to a stump speech for his We-focused platform. A decade after dropping out of Baruch, he was asked to give the commencement address to its class of 2017. "We are *we*," Adam said at the Barclays Center, in Brooklyn. "If we work together, we cannot be stopped. Or else…divided we fall." Adam seemed to have picked up some talking points from his new mentor: "As exciting as technology might be . . . it is us who will blaze the path forward, paved not with algorithms, not with software, but with values, with friendship, with common goals, and most importantly, with humanity."

He offered the graduates a blueprint for success: pick the right partner, one "who will see your potential of who you are tomorrow, and love that"; find a therapist; do something meaningful. "If it doesn't have a purpose, why are you wasting your time?" he said. "Hang out at home and chill." But doing something with meaning, he admitted, wasn't enough. He offered a warning to the entrepreneurs in the room. "I'll tell you another secret," he said. "Your business has to make sense. If the business is not making sense, if you're not profitable at the end—yes, there are a few companies, we hear about them, they lose a lot of money every month. Don't build that."

CHAPTER THIRTEEN

Blitzscaling

A FEW WEEKS AFTER WeWork's gargantuan SoftBank deal was announced, Jamie Hodari met Adam early one morning at Francis S. Gabreski Airport, which serves private jets flying in and out of the east end of Long Island. Hodari was the CEO of Industrious, a WeWork competitor with a large presence in the second-tier American cities that Neumann was only just getting into. While Hodari was among Neumann's nearest rivals, he didn't have a beach house in the Hamptons, let alone two of them, so he took a two-hour Uber ride from New York the night before and booked a motel room so that he could board the jet flying Adam out at six o'clock the next morning.

By 7:30, the group was on its second round of Bloody Marys. Michael Gross was encouraging Hodari to try surfing. Hodari sipped his drink slowly. They were flying to Atlanta, where Industrious had three locations and WeWork was opening its second. Adam wanted to show Hodari what it meant to have WeWork moving into his turf.

As they flew down the coast, Adam asked Hodari to join him in a pair of lounge chairs at the front of the plane for a private chat. According to Hodari, Adam laid out his argument for why Industrious should partner with WeWork. The two companies would be stronger together than if they battled for customers in Atlanta or St. Louis or Phoenix, Adam said.

He promised to arrange any deal with Hodari so that it would be more beneficial to his fellow founder than to Hodari's investors.

If Hodari didn't want to join forces, Adam presented an alternative. "I'm going easy on you, because we're both Jewish," he said. "But I've got 150 people ready to bury you."

As they approached Atlanta, Adam explained what would happen if Hodari turned him down. WeWork employees would descend on every Industrious location, in Atlanta and beyond, and offer Hodari's tenants a year of free rent. If they resisted, Adam would offer them two years, and if there was anyone left after that, he would give them three—all subsidized by the multibillion-dollar war chest Masa had just given him.

Hodari was rattled. Next to Adam's billions, he had raised less than $100 million. Industrious couldn't compete with discounts like that. At the same time, giving out free office space was a lot more expensive than handing out free modems on the streets of Tokyo, and it was hard to imagine an investor—even one as flush as Masa—who would be willing to weather losses on that scale. Hodari had given serious thought to the possibility that Adam had figured out some trick that broke the realities of the office-leasing business—that he saw something Hodari couldn't. But he also wasn't interested in hitching himself to something he couldn't understand. Hodari refused Adam's offer. If nothing else, he figured Adam was bluffing.

* * *

LINDSEY ISBELL'S FIRST few weeks managing the inaugural WeWork locations under construction in Nashville in 2017 were a quick introduction to the company's culture. Before she took the job, a WeWork executive had opened Isbell's final interview by saying, "I'm a little hungover right now. Do you have any questions for me?" Isbell, who was twenty-five, spent a few weeks in Nashville before jetting off to WeWork's 2017 Summer Camp, which the company had moved from the Lapidus family's campground to a field outside London. She danced until 3:00 a.m. only to come back to her tent and have a male coworker she didn't know stumble in behind her; he was heavily intoxicated and expressed no intention of leaving. During a few days of training, which she completed at a WeWork in Austin, Isbell grew confused about what exactly her job entailed. "This is Lindsey," an employee said, introducing Isbell, who had been hired as a community manager. "She's in sales." As construction finished up in Nashville, Isbell started giving tours while stepping over dead birds in the construction zone and pitching prospective tenants on a dream and the heavy discount WeWork was now offering.

A few weeks later, Isbell was told to get on a flight to Atlanta. Adam wasn't bluffing, and the blitz against Industrious was on. Following his attempt to partner with Hodari, Adam sent Isbell and other WeWork employees from cities around the United States to lead a guerrilla marketing campaign in Atlanta. One tactic involved driving a flatbed truck carrying a glass-walled office and parking it in front of Industrious locations while employees handed out the free rent deals that Adam had threatened to unleash.

Atlanta was just one front in a worldwide marketing assault. In New York, a WeWork employee started showing up at locations operated by Knotel, another competitor, claiming to be the CEO of a start-up urgently seeking office space. He then took a tour and surreptitiously jotted down the names of each tenant, in order to send them all a discount for switching to WeWork. (Knotel put up a "Wanted" poster charging the employee with "espionage" and offering a $2,500 reward.) WeWork employees in San Diego sent out the offer—"A year of office space, on us"—so indiscriminately to tenants at a local coworking space run by Wolf Bielas that they sent one to Bielas himself, who kept a personal office there. A few days later, WeWork set up an outdoor living room with several couches and a snake plant in front of the building. When Bielas confronted them, a WeWork employee replied that they were simply "spreading the love."

At the end of September, Shlomo Silber, who ran a coworking space called Bond Collective—he had questioned Adam about his growth plans back at the meeting of the Five Families—put his phone away to celebrate Rosh Hashanah, the Jewish new year, when the names of the righteous and wicked are said to be separated for judgment. (Adam reportedly celebrated the holiday at a Kabbalah Centre party, dancing onstage at Manhattan's Hammerstein Ballroom alongside other Kabbalah VIPs.) Two days later, when the holiday was over, Silber turned his phone on to find more than two hundred emails from his tenants reporting the discounts WeWork was offering. Silber was already acquainted with the fact that Adam could present in public as a prophet for a beneficent workplace revolution, then play the part of hard-nosed real estate tycoon in private: after Silber leased a building in Brooklyn that WeWork also wanted, Adam called the landlord to say that he intended to put Bond Collective out of business.

By 2017, Neumann had threatened to crush or buy virtually every one of his competitors. In the UK, WeWork's biggest rival was the Office Group (TOG), which launched in London in 2004, when Neumann was still in college. Its founders had pursued a more conservative path, owning some buildings and leasing others while forgoing giant injections of venture capital. No one was going to become president of the world, but the company was nicely profitable. When one of its founders met Adam in New York, back in 2012, Adam casually suggested that he might buy the Office Group—never mind that WeWork had just four locations in two American cities.

The Office Group deflected further overtures from Neumann over the years, as WeWork entered London and quickly passed TOG as the city's largest flexible office provider. In 2017, Blackstone, one of the world's largest investment firms, acquired a majority stake in TOG at a $640 million valuation. Adam was so incensed that he complained to Jon Gray, Blackstone's head of real estate, who controlled more buildings worldwide than practically any other real estate executive, including several that WeWork occupied. He then set about putting Masa's money to use. WeWork hired a steel drum band to play outside a new TOG location, offering the same lavish discounts. Adam bragged to an investor that his efforts had slashed his rivals' occupancy rate. "I destroyed the Office Group," Adam said. "And I can obliterate any coworking company that I want."

Poaching tenants was only one front in WeWork's campaign to crush its competition. WeWork's legal team filed lawsuits against three different coworking companies—UrWork, WE Labs, and Hi Work—claiming their names infringed on WeWork's intellectual property. (The suits were eventually settled.) The latter two were tiny operators, but UrWork was a Chinese entity valued at more than $1 billion, with plans to expand into the United States; Adam had tried to buy the company in 2015, but UrWork rejected his offer. (UrWork wanted cash, not stock, and it didn't help the negotiation when Adam welcomed the company's CEO to his office by kicking his bare feet up on his desk.) In one lawsuit, WeWork's lawyers said that while the company didn't claim "exclusive rights to the ordinary word 'Work,' " it did object to "the combination of a two-letter pronoun followed immediately by the word 'Work.' "

Adam's competitors weren't averse to hardball, and he was far from the only eccentric rogue in real estate. WeWork drove a double-decker bus around New York, handing out ice cream at Knotel locations, only after Knotel sent a retrofitted school bus of its own to WeWork locations in the city. When Jamie Hodari arrived for a meeting with Amol Sarva and Edward Shenderovich, the cofounders of Knotel, there were copies of Plutarch stacked up in the conference room, as a taunt. (Hodari had once appeared on *Jeopardy!* only to miss the final question about Plutarch.) Real estate was a dirty game, and if there was an objection to Adam, it wasn't that his tactics were especially dastardly, but that he was pretending to be something he wasn't. WeWork's warpath mentality undercut its rhetoric about changing the world and doing what you love, which had attracted members and employees to the business in the first place. Avril Mulcahy, the owner of a coworking space in London, decided to shut down rather than battle a new WeWork that opened next to her at five times the size. "Their emergence in our building did make a question that had been lurking in the corners for a while very obvious," Mulcahy wrote. "Is what we are doing still meaningful?"

* * *

MASA'S MONEY ALSO turned the game that WeWork's competitors thought they were playing into something unrecognizable—a pattern that was repeating itself around the world in industries of all kinds. Massive amounts of venture capital, much of it flowing directly from Masa and the Vision Fund, were flooding into everything from scooters to food delivery to all-you-can-watch movies. The money was being funneled to consumers, who were happy to receive heavily subsidized services, while Bird and DoorDash and MoviePass all burned cash to acquire customers, hoping that one day they could charge full price. For businesses without Warren Buffett's "moat" protecting them, a new model existed: "capital as a moat." Can't beat them? Drown them in cash. Almost none of the companies spending so profligately was anywhere near profitable, and the discounts made it difficult for anyone to figure out the natural demand for their product. The deals also made it hard for competitors to keep up. Hodari and other WeWork rivals said they lost only a small chunk of their tenants to WeWork's marketing blitz, but if the campaign continued, none of them would have the cash reserves to survive what amounted to predatory pricing.

Prior to SoftBank's arrival, back in the era of Managing the Nickel, WeWork executives had been talking about finding a more balanced growth trajectory. T. Rowe Price, which invested in WeWork in 2014, had pushed for a more sustainable strategy and was so skeptical of the SoftBank-funded bonanza that they sold as much as they could when SoftBank agreed to buy stock from existing shareholders. In 2016, WeWork had explored a revenue-sharing model with landlords much like the one employed by hotel chains. While the company might bring in less revenue with such a strategy, it would also have to shoulder much less risk.

But Masa had not invested $4.4 billion to pursue moderate growth. If Adam was going to achieve the full effects of the "physical social network" he promised to build, he needed space everywhere. The company's existing plans were ripped up and doubled, or more; WeWork's marketing team tripled its spending. Masa told Adam he should have ten thousand salespeople—never mind that he didn't yet have ten thousand employees. WeWork was hiring thirty people each week, then fifty, until eventually more than a hundred people were joining every Monday. As Artie Minson described it, WeWork was "building and selling at scale." In December of 2017, just a year after opening its one hundredth location, in Berlin, WeWork opened its two hundredth, in Singapore.

WeWork was by then on five continents and figuring out how to expand into markets where it had little expertise. "Is that a city or a country?" Adam asked one WeWork executive during a conversation about opening in Kuala Lumpur. The rents it could charge members in Latin America were so low that getting buildings to break even was going to be difficult, while landlords in many Asian countries were less willing to fund WeWork's renovations, which had been a crucial part of keeping the costs of its domestic growth under control. "The expansion here was just as haphazard and aggressive as it was in the rest of the world, and the economics of the deals were worse," Matt Fry, who helped the company expand in Asia, said. "But we were on autopilot." In one meeting, about ballooning costs in London, some of WeWork's team thought they should put the brakes on growth in the city to get its operations under control. Adam rejected the idea. WeWork could charge exorbitant rents in London and thus bring in more revenue, which was how people were judging the company's valuation. If anything, Adam wanted to step on the gas. At one point, according to a person familiar with the conversation, Adam suggested that WeWork lease the entirety of 22 Bishopsgate, a new sixty-two-story tower set to become London's second-tallest building—a lease that could have cost upward of $150 million a year.

The demands for space became so aggressive that the company's real estate team loosened its diligence on the deals it was making, paying to occupy space where it wasn't clear WeWork's model would be feasible. There was also plenty of competition in the market. After initially passing on a lease in Los Angeles, WeWork reportedly decided to put in an offer only after it found out that IWG was making one. WeWork began offering commercial real estate brokers a shocking commission: 100 percent of the first year's rent paid by new tenants. On some two year deals, where WeWork was already giving a year away free, that meant the company was bringing in no revenue at all for twenty-four months.

Sales and growth remained the company's focus, but after years spent trying to institute a playbook, everything still felt patched together. "There was no training. There was no sales model. There wasn't a sales department," said John Boozer, who helped build out a sales team on the East Coast in 2017. During one Monday night meeting of WeWork's global real estate team, with senior employees dialing in from the middle of the night in Europe and Asia, Adam walked in a few hours late from a dinner and began holding court. The team was 20 percent behind its ambitious targets for leasing new space. "He *raised* the targets by 20 percent, based on nothing," one executive in the room said. "Based on, *I think you should do more.*"

* * *

AS WEWORK'S OTHER investors adjusted to life alongside Masa, Benchmark was in a particularly complicated situation. The firm was dealing with a tumultuous moment at its other prize investment, Uber, which Benchmark had invested in shortly before Michael Eisenberg and Bruce Dunlevie met Adam. Uber was wading through a morass of public relations nightmares and internal cultural issues, many of which were tied to Travis Kalanick, the company's brash founder and CEO. In June of 2017, Benchmark led a coup against Kalanick, forcing him out of his own company.

No one at Benchmark was prepared to make a move on Adam, especially given the ongoing battle with Kalanick. Developing a reputation for ousting start-up founders was a sure way to have the promising entrepreneurs of the future look elsewhere for funding. Bruce Dunlevie remained Adam's champion, expressing his belief in Adam's expansive vision and comparing him to a new-age Jeff Bezos.

But several of the firm's partners, including Bill Gurley, who handled Benchmark's Uber investment, were beginning to fear that Neumann might eventually present the same kind of problem that Kalanick had. In 2017, five Benchmark partners, including Gurley, flew to New York to confront Adam in his office. (Dunlevie didn't attend, in an effort to maintain good relations.) The Benchmark investors chastised Adam for selling so much of his WeWork stock; even with all the trouble Benchmark was having with Kalanick, he had not sold a single share of Uber stock. The Benchmark team also critiqued Adam's strategy and the fact that WeWork had missed its projections yet again. In 2014, Adam told investors that WeWork would be spitting off more than $500 million in profit by 2017. Instead, the company was on pace to *lose* nearly $1 billion as the costs of its rapid expansion grew. WeLive, which was projected to have dozens of locations producing hundreds of millions in revenue, still had only its two original buildings.

What worried some of the Benchmark partners was the fact that WeWork was facing some of these issues even before the distorting effects of the Vision Fund's outsize injection of capital took effect. (Uber negotiated its own multibillion-dollar investment from the Vision Fund, and

Dara Khosrowshahi, who replaced Kalanick at Uber, made the counter-argument in favor of taking Masa's money: "Rather than having their capital cannon facing me, I'd rather have their capital cannon behind me.") The Benchmark partners didn't necessarily think that encouraging Adam to act even crazier was a prudent strategy, but the decision was also largely out of their hands. Dunlevie had ceded control to Adam when the board agreed to give extra votes to each of his shares, and unless they wanted to risk being ostracized or kicked off the board entirely, many of the partners felt like they could only make suggestions and hope that Adam listened.

But practically every atmospheric force of the 2010s was encouraging Adam to do precisely what Masa was enabling. WeWork's growth-at-all-costs plan epitomized an increasingly popular Silicon Valley strategy known as blitzscaling, a term coined by Reid Hoffman, the cofounder of LinkedIn, who had begun teaching a course on the subject at Stanford—"CS183C: Technology-Enabled Blitzscaling." In a follow-up book, Hoffman acknowledged that blitzscaling could seem counterintuitive. "It involves purposefully and intentionally doing things that don't make sense according to traditional business thinking," he wrote. The idea was to not worry too much about risks and costs that might bother a traditional businessperson. The goal was "lightning" growth. Network effects were key. Building a nicely profitable business was a quaint idea in Silicon Valley—"Investors want B's, baby"—and the effect of the Vision Fund was to break some of the foundational rules of capitalism, allowing WeWork and other companies to price products not to make a profit but simply to acquire market share. In a perfect world, you became too big to fail.

Hoffman admitted that blitzscaling had its dangers. In a final section, titled "Responsible Blitzscaling," he said there was a difficult balance required "in marrying responsibility and velocity" and that while start-up founders "may benefit from behaving like ethical pirates, they should never behave like sociopathic criminals." He was worried less about ethics than the kind of negative PR that befell Kalanick and Uber.

Adam expressed little interest in slowing down. One morning in early 2018, with his own blitzscaling campaign fully operational, Adam flew to Seattle to meet with Howard Schultz, the former CEO of Starbucks. WeWork was thinking of expanding into retail. When they met, Schultz gave Adam a piece of advice. After Starbucks started to take off—blitzscaling before the word even existed—Schultz said that he wished he had taken six months to stop growing so that Starbucks could have ironed out various problems that would plague the business for years. This was precisely what many WeWork executives had been pressing Neumann to do: systematize its sales and leasing operation, get a handle on the construction process, stop moving into peripheral businesses. On a private jet flying him out of Seattle, Adam shared Schultz's advice with several WeWork employees who were on board, then told them what he thought of it: "Fuck that."

CHAPTER FOURTEEN

The Holy Grail

AS SOON AS ADAM landed in San Francisco after his visit with Howard Schultz, he drove to a dinner party at the home of Marc Benioff, the founder of Salesforce, with whom Neumann had become friendly. Benioff launched Salesforce during the last dot-com boom and came out the other side as a majordomo of the start-up world. He was preparing to move his company into an eponymously named tower that would be San Francisco's tallest. Salesforce, which offered back-end technological solutions for corporations, was at the leading edge of the software-as-a-service movement. The new business model centered on selling subscriptions to a variety of computer applications that could be accessed through the cloud. Masa had built his fortune selling floppy disks and CD-ROMs, but thirty years later, SaaS businesses were producing some of Silicon Valley's largest valuations: Salesforce, Slack, Palantir, and a host of largely anonymous companies that offered new cloud-based services forming the backbone of the new economy.

But the flock of Silicon Valley unicorns had grown so large that Benioff himself had become nervous. The kind of rapid expansion that venture capital made possible wasn't sustainable without discipline. In the middle of the decade, Benioff had issued a warning: "There's going to be a lot of dead unicorns."

Neumann had begun pitching WeWork as a new breed of SaaS business: "*space* as a service." The idea was that companies of all sizes would no longer handle their own real estate portfolios but would instead turn over the management of their physical space to WeWork, transforming the company into something like a real estate cloud—a "platform." This was a goal shared by every ambitious start-up of the decade, no matter how specious the claim. Facebook, Uber, and Airbnb identified as platforms, as did Beyond Meat, the pea-protein burger maker ("plant-based-product platforms"); Peloton, the indoor exercise bike company ("the largest interactive fitness platform in the world"); and Casper, the mattress company (a "platform built for better sleep"). It was no longer good enough for companies to simply be what they were.

Connecting WeWork to the SaaS trend was only the latest way Adam and other WeWork executives had tried to tie their company to the rising titans of Silicon Valley. WeWork needed office buildings like Uber needed cars and Airbnb needed apartments. Its member network would be a better version of LinkedIn, and the "data" they were collecting from each location would make the next one better—"Google Analytics for space." A WeWork was like "an Amazon warehouse with a lot more soul." Dave Fano, the Case founder who had become WeWork's chief growth officer, said the company's goal was to "shed ourselves of any remnants of being like a real estate company."

Adam bristled at critiques from the real estate world that WeWork's success had less to do with technology than with his storytelling abilities, especially when the criticism came from landlords who were leasing him space. "If you don't have something nice to say," Adam told an audience at the New York Stock Exchange in 2017, "and if that person is a customer—and let's say that person is going to be the largest tenant on earth—it doesn't make sense" to be so critical, he said. Landlords and real estate investors understood the value of what WeWork offered; its fresh design, flexible terms, and happy hours were a hit with customers, and landlords were having to adapt their own office spaces to keep up. But IWG operated *five* times as many spaces as WeWork did globally, and was still valued at just $3 billion. What exactly WeWork was doing to merit a tech company valuation of $20 billion remained a mystery.

* * *

TWO YEARS AFTER declaring that "WeWork Mars is in our pipeline," Adam finally got his meeting with Elon Musk. Adam was nervous, as he often was before big meetings, when he seemed to course with anxiety until his audience was in front of him and whatever pitch he was making hit a groove. Tesla was one of the hottest tech stocks on the market, and Musk was the Valley's leading eccentric visionary—a rare entrepreneur whose ambition and self-regard outpaced Neumann's.

Adam met Musk, along with Michael Gross, at SpaceX headquarters in Los Angeles; Musk was late, as Adam usually was, and he spared only a few minutes for Neumann. Adam told Musk that if he could get humans to Mars, WeWork could help build them a home, and a community, that would allow them to thrive on another planet. Musk planned to have humans on Mars by 2024, and in the meantime, Adam offered to set up a simulated WeWork Mars on Earth so they could begin working on the problem. Sustaining life would be the hard part, Adam said. But Musk brushed him off. Getting there was the hard part. Musk said he didn't need WeWork.

The meeting was a disappointment to Neumann. While WeWork had plenty of tech start-ups as members, it was having a harder time convincing Silicon Valley that the company itself was one of them. Adam still rarely used a computer, and WeWork had only recently hired a chief technology officer. Another chief product officer, with experience at Yahoo! and Adobe, had come and gone without making the WeConnect dream a meaningful reality.

The Neumanns spent some of 2017 living in the Bay Area, as did

Michael Gross and his family, partly in the hope that Neumann and Gross could woo Silicon Valley much as they had New York's real estate and investment world. In the fall, WeWork announced it was looking to hire a hundred software engineers and that it was taking over three floors halfway up Salesforce Tower, the most expensive real estate in all San Francisco, to entice them. The plans for the office called for cutting holes in the floor so a grand internal staircase could be installed, plus a full spa, modeled after a Turkish hammam, with lounge chairs upholstered in a Maharam mohair, vintage rugs dotting the floor, and $9,400 Børge Mogensen chairs. Employees working on the project said there would be a speakeasy in the sky and another ventilation system allowing Adam to smoke in his office.

A gleaming skyscraper was a far cry from the basement where WeWork's old engineering team had staved off hepatitis W, but the company needed to pull out all the stops to attract new talent. While the tech world was beginning to see physical space as the next frontier ripe for conquering, WeWork wasn't used to paying top-tier Silicon Valley salaries or dealing with employees better informed in the intricacies of negotiating stock options than the recent graduates and real estate world expats it was used to hiring. Jen Berrent, the company's lawyer, got frustrated when one new tech hire came in with a spreadsheet laying out various kinds of equity payment schemes. "You have to trust us," Berrent said.

To build out the tech team, Adam poached Shiva Rajaraman, an engineer who had bounced among jobs at YouTube, Spotify, and Apple; Adam told Rajaraman he should leave Apple because what WeWork was building would be "bigger than the iPhone." WeWork's tech team had grown from half a dozen people in 2013 to more than two hundred, but the first task facing Rajaraman remained fixing Space Station and Space Man. The insistence that WeWork build and maintain its systems in-house rather than outsourcing to an established software provider had lingering consequences. For a period of several months, Space Man was unable to process the payments that were coming in when the company launched in Mexico; when WeWork opened in India, where most tenants wanted to pay in cash, the engineering team had to drop everything to figure out how to build cash payments into its system. There was only so much time to improve the in-house LinkedIn when community managers were complaining that the button allowing them to report a broken toilet to the facilities team wasn't working.

The search for a technological validation of the company's valuation took many forms. WeWork had been trying to wring usable data from its spaces in any way possible, and in 2017, a team led by Tomer Sharon, a former senior employee at Google, unveiled Polaris, an internal WeWork system that gathered more than a thousand interviews with members and organized them into "nuggets" of information that would allow community managers to improve their spaces in specific ways. (*Polaris, what do WeWork members in the Midwest think about the light bulbs we use in our kitchens?*) The results were often underwhelming: San Franciscans complained about the quality of coffee; people generally liked square offices more than rectangular ones; noise was an issue in every glass cubicle, but it was an especially terrible fate to rent space in a WeWork that also rented an office to a call center. The Polaris team had a macabre favorite among the nuggets describing the experience of being inside WeWork's labyrinth of glass walls: "It feels like you're in a future jail."

But Silicon Valley's ethos was to distrust the opinion of humans alone, and the "Google Analytics for space" team began scraping WeWork spaces for physical data, installing sensors under conference room tables to determine how many people were using them during the day. The result: not many, so make them smaller. They experimented with cameras and microphones that could track facial expressions and tones of voice. (At one point, SoftBank suggested that WeWork partner with SenseTime, a Vision Fund company in China with facial recognition technology that had come under fire for its use in surveilling the country's dissident populations.) WeWork thought it might be able to use the readings and turn them over to members: *Seventy percent of the people in your meeting right now are either disengaged or demonstrating negative sentiment to the subject that's being discussed.*

The company was applying some of the world's most advanced technologies to relatively mundane problems, and the revelations seemed to offer minor advantages at best. One team used machine learning to predict conference room usage "with 80 percent accuracy" so they could recommend the right space for each kind of meeting. Another team was proud of an algorithm that could produce a rough layout of a new space faster than one of the company's human architects; all told, the algorithm could save an architect a few minutes. Sensors by the coffee station revealed that lines in the morning could get long. A team at WeLive found that people who lived close together and used the same common spaces tended to be better friends than residents at opposite ends of the building. When I toured a new space in Manhattan, its manager told me that "one of our best learnings" since the space opened was that people liked several desks in the back of the room that were near the windows. This, he said, was something they hadn't guessed, although he admitted that it "makes a lot of sense."

The most concrete way in which WeWork could move itself toward profitability was to streamline the process by which it opened new locations, and a new team—real estate and development technology, or REDTech for short—was tasked with finding ways to get control of the process. A team from Case, the Buildings = Data start-up, developed Stargate to fit alongside Space Man and Space Station in WeWork's software galaxy, allowing the company to keep track of buildings around the world from pre-leasing through construction. But much of WeWork's needs resisted optimization. Construction was a grubby business, and it was hard to plug handshake deals between subcontractors into an algorithm. The company had streamlined its furniture supply chain and bought more in bulk, but that meant they were simply getting discounts, not reinventing the industry. "If you were to line up the way we did it compared to the way a hospitality company does it, or how the Gap picks out its fixtures, it wasn't any different," Alison Littman, who managed the furniture acquisition process, said.

Beyond making the company's core business more efficient, the hope was that one or another of these new technologies could help WeWork figure out how to diversify its revenue. Conference room sensors might detect when members used rooms without paying for them. Masa and Adam talked up the idea of a "virtual membership," whereby people would join the WeWork community without renting a desk. At TechCrunch Disrupt in 2017, Adam crowed about the launch of WeWork's Services Store, which promised again to turn the company into a middleman hawking everything from Salesforce software to Lyft discounts.

None of these avenues proved fruitful. By the end of 2017, services made up just 5 percent of WeWork's revenue. As for the virtual membership, it wasn't clear what benefit members would receive, or how WeWork would make money from them. The network still had fewer users than *English, baby!* had at its peak. WeWork hired IDEO, one of the world's premier design firms, to reimagine the app, but the consultants couldn't come up with much that would seem to make a difference: one of their ideas was a "beer button" allowing users to alert other members that they were looking for a drinking buddy if anyone wanted to meet at the office keg.

WeWork's engineering department quintupled to more than one thousand employees—a huge jump, but Uber had five times as many—and the team was proud of its work. But many came to realize that none of it was helping WeWork build a moat, or connecting its physical social network, or justifying its valuation. Many of the projects were just marginally more successful variations on ideas Miguel and his brother Kyle had dreamed up years earlier. The only truly meaningful innovation would have been to invent a human-shrinking machine, allowing the company to squeeze more rent-paying customers into tighter and tighter spaces. "We didn't want to admit that none of this was successful or producing revenue," one senior manager on the tech team said. "We were spending money trying to find the Holy Grail."

* * *

IF WEWORK couldn't engineer its way into the Silicon Valley elite, Adam could try using Masa's war chest to buy his way in. Over a six-month period, Adam bought five companies, including a coding academy and a marketing company started by a classmate from Baruch. "Adam was focused on beating Airbnb in terms of the number of M&A deals he could do," one senior WeWork employee involved in the acquisitions said. Neumann talked about buying Slack and Zoom, which was then a little-known videoconferencing company. One of the biggest acquisitions was Meetup, an online platform for people looking to plan in-person events. Meetup had struggled to find a viable business model fifteen years after its launch, but WeWork agreed to pay $156 million for the company, hoping it could figure out how to use WeWork spaces after work hours and perhaps help the company reach Masa's goal of a million members.

In 2017, Adam tried to buy Comfy, a tech company with an app to manage the various systems needed to run a building—a natural fit for WeWork. The Comfy founders were interested, but the negotiation dragged on for months, culminating in a tequila-filled night at WeWork headquarters. Comfy's three founders wanted cash, in addition to the WeWork stock that Adam was offering. But Adam refused to budge, insisting that they were being fools for not taking shares whose value was sure to grow. Around 3:00 a.m., one of the Comfy founders developed enough liquid courage to walk over to an iPad that was playing music and queue up Kendrick Lamar's "Humble." The song's pulsing refrain— "Sit down / Be humble"—didn't seem to break through.

For many medium-size start-ups, whose ambitions had reached a ceiling, hitching a ride on WeWork's rocket ship was compelling. Over the Fourth of July holiday, Shaun Ritchie, the cofounder of Teem, a tech company based in Utah that Adam wanted to acquire, rode in the passenger seat of Adam's Maybach as they drove away from WeWork headquarters, while Neumann met with Jen Berrent in the back. When the car reached the East River, Berrent hopped out and got into a black SUV that was trailing them, leaving Ritchie to take her place and discuss WeWork's potential acquisition of Teem while they drove to one of Adam's houses in the Hamptons. Teem built conference-room scheduling software, and Ritchie, who was Mormon, connected to both Adam's fervor and the mission he ascribed to his work.

"What's the purpose of WeWork?" Ritchie asked Adam as they drove across Long Island. "Is this your life's work?"

"No, no, no," Adam said. "WeWork is just a tool. My life's work is to prepare for the Messiah."

Adam's zeal made Ritchie feel he wasn't aiming high enough. Neumann often asked the founders of companies he was thinking of acquiring what they would do if they could do anything—then told them to come do that at WeWork. There were details to work out—Ritchie's investors only wanted cash, not WeWork stock—but Adam was insistent. "We're doing this deal," he told Ritchie. It was only later, after WeWork paid around $100 million for Teem and Ritchie joined the company, that he learned from other executives that when Adam said something would happen, it usually did.

Many WeWork executives were confused by Adam's acquisition spree. They would approach other companies to forge potential partnerships only to have Adam enter the conversation and push the negotiation toward an acquisition. "The strategy was to not let Adam meet founders, because he always just wanted to buy them as opposed to partnering," an executive who joined WeWork after Neumann acquired his start-up said. "He thought, 'If I control it, it will do better.'" The company was spending money so wildly that when one competitor in the office-space business got questions from investors about how he planned to beat WeWork, he said that he didn't: he saw Masa's money, and Neumann's rapacious appetite for acquisitions, as a potential exit strategy for himself and his investors.

WeWork was flush, but buying companies was expensive, and some of Adam's deals seemed to have little to do with WeWork's core business. The strangest of all was the $13.8 million Adam spent to acquire a significant stake in Wavegarden, a Spanish company that manufactured inland wave pools for surfers. Adam claimed that he saw Wavegarden as a potential anchor attraction for corporate campuses that WeWork might start building, but it felt like a vanity play to go along with the large photograph of himself surfing that Adam installed in an executive conference room at WeWork headquarters. "The wave pool made people go, 'What the fuck?'" one employee said. "Not out of anger, just confusion."

CHAPTER FIFTEEN

WeGrow

IN THE FALL OF 2017, a member of WeWork's communications team called a friend who worked as a professor of education at Hunter College. He needed help. The communications team had woken up to a surprising Google Alert. A local blog in Tribeca had just broken news about a new elementary school in the neighborhood: "the first iteration of WeWork's educational endeavor; a network of conscious entrepreneurial schools that will be launching around the world."

This was news to pretty much everyone at WeWork. That summer, the Neumanns had surveyed the public and private educational options available to parents with limitless resources, on both coasts, and decided that none of them were good enough for their eldest daughter, who was about to enter first grade. In the spirit of a true entrepreneur, Rebekah decided to start her own. The Tribe School, as it was known, had seven students in a single classroom at Chabad of Tribeca. The school planned to expand into a nearby building, where WeWork had paid a premium to kick out the existing tenant, a Montessori school that had been there for more than a decade. It was supposed to launch quietly—stealth-mode kindercare, in Silicon Valley speak—until the blog picked it up and sent WeWork's executive team scrambling to figure out what it meant to suddenly be operating an elementary school.

The idea had come up before. In 2016, an executive assistant at We-Work who was a new mother proposed offering an affordable corporate day care for employees and members: WeKids. Rebekah latched on to the idea. She talked about it with Adam, who also liked it. "If you really want to change the world, change kids when they're two," Adam started to say. But the project fell victim to Managing the Nickel, and Adam protested when Rebekah told a reporter she was still having conversations about it. "When was your last meeting about that?" Adam said.

"Last week," Rebekah said.

"Okay, well, I just put that project off, so hopefully you won't have any other meetings about it," Adam said.

But Masa's money put all the Neumanns' dreams back on the table. In 2017, WeWork acquired the Flatiron School, a programming boot-camp for adults. The acquisition served as fulfillment of a threat Adam had lobbed at General Assembly a few years earlier, when GA bailed on the coworking business to focus on education. In 2014, WeWork had struck a deal to open GA classrooms in WeWorks around the country, but Adam told the GA founders that while he wasn't ready to get into education yet, he wouldn't hesitate to do so once he could, and at scale.

Running an elementary school was more complicated than teaching programming classes for a certificate. Rebekah had no formal training in education; her biography on the school's site would eventually say that she had spent time "apprenticing and studying under many Master Students, such as His Holiness the Dalai Lama and Mother Nature her-self." But her ideas on the topic were in line with progressive thinking on modern education, and the Hunter College professor WeWork had reached out to in a pinch saw some virtue in the idea. WeWork offered possible solutions to the biggest problems facing new schools: opening and operating a space and finding parents willing to enroll their kids. The company had an expertise in the former and a membership base of potential parents from which to recruit the latter.

Over dinner with the Neumanns, the professor, who agreed to consult on the project, listened as Adam predicted that just as WeLive would one day outgrow WeWork, the school would ultimately eclipse them both. WeGrow, as they were calling it, would become a network of private schools in every major city, allowing global citizens like the Neumanns to move around the world with their kids in tow. The Neumanns imagined creating a replacement for college and spoke about offering education "from birth to death." Rebekah started using the slogan "School of Life for Life," or SOLFL for short—"soulful" without the *u*'s. As WeGrow began enrolling students for the 2018–19 school year, Rebekah sent out admissions certificates welcoming incoming kindergartners to the class of 2031, when they would all be graduating from WeGrow's high school. Rebekah signed the certificate with her name, and a heart.

* * *

EVERY START-UP OF THE 2010s needed a foundational myth. WeWork's had shifted over time. Early on, Adam spoke about the critical role Kabbalah had played in how he thought about the company, until Lew Frankfort convinced him that wasn't the most marketable idea. The story morphed to emphasize Adam and Miguel's respective childhoods, and how those experiences had taught them the importance of community. The only debate was how to get Miguel more comfortable with referring to his upbringing as a "commune," which was more easily explained than "matriarchal collective."

"He doesn't like calling it a commune," Adam told a reporter in 2015. "Did he say 'commune' to you?"

He did, the reporter said.

"Then maybe he broke down," Adam said. "Maybe he is ready to call it a commune."

By 2016, the story had changed again. Rebekah was suddenly being identified as the company's third founder, appearing alongside Adam in magazine profiles with photographs that presented both Neumanns as entrepreneurial rock stars. Miguel, meanwhile, stood off to the side. The company's founding moment was no longer Adam and Miguel's meeting, but Adam's first date with Rebekah, when she told him he was "full of shit."

WeWork employees were taken aback by Rebekah's sudden emergence as a WeWork founder. She gave interviews recalling nights spent scrubbing WeWork's glass dividers and cleaning the floors until 4:00 a.m. before opening a new space. But she wasn't listed among the company's leadership team in the 2014 pitch deck sent to investors, and a *Forbes* magazine profile that year referred to her only as Adam's "filmmaker wife."

Rebekah had given up on her acting career, and spent several years in and out of the chief brand officer role at WeWork. She encouraged Adam to attach WeWork to the word *creator*, over his objections that people would think doing so was blasphemous, and came up with the title CWeO for employees with oversight of individual regions. She sometimes left the role to take care of the Neumanns' expanding family—their fifth child was born in 2017—while maintaining a quiet influence that could prove vexing to employees. "What does Rebekah think?" Adam would ask, even when his wife was nowhere to be found. At the end of 2017, WeWork recruited Julie Rice, one of the cofounders of SoulCycle, to become the company's new chief brand officer. But after a few months she was quietly pushed out of the job, and Rebekah was back in the position. "Julie was presented as a 'walks on water' type of person," one WeWork executive said. "And then one day Adam emails to say that Rebekah is chief brand officer again." When WeWork's board of directors expressed concern about Adam installing his wife on his executive team, he reportedly told the board they could have both Neumanns or neither of them.

As Rebekah began making more public appearances on behalf of the company, WeWork's already flowery rhetoric began to mix business and spirituality even more deeply. "Something I've been thinking about a lot is becoming the founder of your life," Rebekah told a reporter. She had an office next to Adam's with no desk and a stack of books that included Ayn Rand's *The Fountainhead* and *Many Lives, Many Masters*, which was written by a psychotherapist who claimed to be able to connect people to previous incarnations of themselves. Employees were asked to remove their shoes before stepping into her office, which had white shag carpeting. One team nicknamed Rebekah's office the Sheep Meadow.

While no one within WeWork took seriously the notion that Rebekah was a cofounder of the company, no matter how many times she and the company said it, there was no doubt that We-Grow was hers. In early 2018, Rebekah sat for an interview with her cousin Gwyneth on her website, Goop. Rebekah had shed the maiden name she previously insisted on using, and neither relative acknowledged the familial connection as Rebekah spoke about the school's launch and how it fit into the company. "WeWork is a physical structure through which we can put positive energy and consciousness into the world," she said. "We're all students of life for life."

The Goop interview irked some of the educators working on WeGrow, who thought they should finalize the practical details of launching the school before promoting it. They were already behind schedule after Rebekah left for the Neumanns' vacation in Hanalei Bay at the moment when the curriculum and logistics of the upcoming school year needed to be nailed down. To manage the project, Rebekah initially hired Lindsay Taylor, a high school friend and the maid of honor from her wedding, to serve as WeGrow's chief operating officer. She then brought in Adam Braun, who ran an education nonprofit called Pencils of Promise that was funded in large part by Justin Bieber, whose manager was Braun's brother Scooter.

The school's launch felt like an early-stage start-up entering beta mode. Priorities shifted constantly—Rebekah came back from Hawaii and suggested that WeGrow offer surf lessons—and often seemed beside the point. WeGrow employees were told their shoes shouldn't have laces and needed to be black, white, or beige. Teaching candidates were rejected for a variety of minor reasons: the pitch of a teacher's voice, their "energy." Rebekah was plotting second and third locations in San Francisco and Israel before the first WeGrow was even open—early education, blitzscaled. Speed and adaptation had been crucial to WeWork's early success, but education wasn't necessarily the best place for constant experimentation. "They would always say, 'This is how start-ups work,'" one WeGrow consultant said. "To which I would say, 'This is not a start-up. You're a billion-dollar company.'"

* * *

WEGROW OPENED in the fall of 2018 on the third floor of WeWork's headquarters in Chelsea as a "conscious, entrepreneurial school committed to unleashing every child's superpowers." The inaugural WeGrow class had forty-six students, including four Neumanns and several of their friends, from pre-K through fourth grade. Tuition was as high as $42,000, though financial aid was available: "Mini-creators from all walks of life are welcome."

Each school day at WeGrow began with a music circle during which teachers played ukuleles, bongos, and tambourines—there was sometimes a conga line—followed by a twenty-five-minute meditation period called WePractice and a midday "moment of gratitude."

WeGrow offered classes in Hebrew and robotics, two art periods every day, and a weekly trip to the Neumanns' Westchester estate, where students picked fresh produce they then sold from a farm stand at WeWork headquarters. It was all a bit goofy, but many parents loved it, including Anja Tyson, who enrolled her daughter after seeing Rebekah on Goop. "If they have an MFA program, she'll be there," Tyson said.

The public reaction was less kind. "Is this NYC's most obnoxious elementary school?" asked the *New York Post*. The school's entrepreneurial focus struck many as shamefully capitalist for early education. WeGrow's head of learning bragged about one student "who just loves to project-manage" and had been working with the WeWork events team to practice her craft. "In my book, there's no reason why children in elementary schools can't be launching their own businesses," Rebekah said. "Children are ready to start creating their life's work when they're five." It was only a matter of time before the first WeGrow-educated entrepreneurs would need their own WeWork office.

WeGrow made more sense to the company's employees than a wave pool, but only slightly. What has real estate got to do with educating children? Steve Jobs had once asked his most senior employees to come up with a list of Apple's top ten priorities, then said the company could manage only three. The Neumanns didn't seem to share that sense of focus—apartments, wave pools, schools—and it was becoming difficult to see how the company could possibly develop an expertise in the range of businesses it was entering while still maintaining the growth of its core office-leasing operation.

But the WeWorld was expanding whether anyone was ready or not. "Great entrepreneurs like Adam don't listen to guys like me," Bruce Dunlevie said in 2018, of his efforts to convince Neumann to focus on WeWork's primary business. After Rebekah replaced Julie Rice as chief brand officer, Rice began working on WeWork's push into retail. Many WeWork locations had an Honesty Market offering snacks for sale without a cashier—a video camera kept tabs on just how honest members actually were—but the company was in the process of converting them into WeMRKTs with more robust offerings. Rice was also put in charge of conceiving a new space called Made by We inside an old Jennifer Convertibles showroom in Manhattan's Flatiron District, where visitors could buy merchandise made by WeWork members and rent seats for $6 per half hour—a coffee shop with reserved seating, caffeine not included.

The company also opened Rise by We, a boutique gym. (WeRun and WeWorkOut were rejected.) Rise by We was in the basement of the WeWork in lower Manhattan where Adam had once considered putting a ping-pong bar. It offered yoga classes infused with an "entrepreneurial spirit" and was run by Adi Neumann's husband, a former professional soccer player in Israel. Michael Gross said that the company's goal was broad: to become the arbiter for the We Generation of "ultimately where to live, ultimately where to work out, ultimately where to meet their friends for a drink after work." Adam did him one better: much as Amazon expanded from books to the broader e-commerce world, he wanted WeWork to expand into "the larger category of life."

In 2018, WeWork hired Bjarke Ingels, the youthful Danish starchitect, in the largely ceremonial role of chief architect, a position meant to help thought-lead Neumann's ambitions of expanding beyond the walls of WeWork's locations. "In 2018, we want to have an impact on the buildings we occupy," Adam said, in a statement announcing Ingels's hiring. "In 2019, it will be the neighborhoods WeWork is part of, and by 2020, the cities we live in." (Ingels's firm also designed WeGrow's extravagant classroom space.) Adam spelled out a vision of the near future in which a twenty-four-year-old graphic designer would describe himself as part of the WeWork community, having access to hotels and apartments and offices around the world, spending a few months each year working from New York and Tel Aviv and Shanghai, building a family and a fortune along the way.

* * *

JIM, JORDAN, AND JAKE DECICCO, three brothers from New York, were among a select few willing to give the full WeLifestyle a try. The DeCiccos were college athletes—Jim and Jake played football at Colgate and Georgetown, respectively, while Jordan was on the basketball team at Philadelphia University—and frustrated by the fact that they couldn't responsibly gulp down a sugar-filled Frappuccino. Jordan did some tinkering and came up with a drink he called Super Coffee: caffeine with a hit of protein. He gave some to Jake, who spread it around Georgetown, and they persuaded Jim to quit his job in finance to help launch their Super Coffee company.

In 2016, Jake met Artie Minson, a fellow Georgetown graduate, at a networking event. Minson invited him to visit WeWork's Chelsea headquarters. "Halfway through the meeting, this guy with long hair and a T-shirt walks in," Jim said. Within minutes, Adam told Jake that he loved his energy and that not only would WeWork be investing in the DeCiccos' company, but he was also offering the brothers free rent at WeLive, in New York, with a WeWork office downstairs. When Rise by We opened, the DeCiccos canceled their gym memberships; if any of them settled down and had kids, WeGrow seemed like a good option. "In the case study of the DeCicco brothers, we live everything Adam dreamed of," Jim said. "There's days where we don't leave the building."

The DeCiccos had met with Adam only occasionally since his initial investment in their company, Kitu Life, but they had soaked up whatever they could. "He's gotten us to think so much bigger than we were," Jim said. He and his brothers no longer thought of Kitu Life as a humble protein shake company. Their Neumann-size goal was to "change America's food paradigm." Jim knew that sounded lofty, but Adam had taught him a lesson in the value of setting outsize expectations. "Changing that paradigm is difficult," Jim said. "Until you believe."

CHAPTER SIXTEEN

Game of Thrones

IN THE SPRING OF 2017, IBM was in a pinch. The company needed to quickly find an office in New York to house six hundred employees from its marketing department. After considering various options, it decided to lease space in a skinny eleven-story building at 88 University Place in Greenwich Village. The building was operated by WeWork, which planned to rent out individual offices on every floor to a mishmash of companies, as it typically did. But IBM said that it wanted the whole thing. WeWork had leased an entire building with a single sale.

The deal was a coup for WeWork, as it tried to convince large corporations to start using its "space-as-a-service" offering. But issues quickly emerged. The building's Wi-Fi was spotty, and one of the two elevators was almost always out of order. The other one stopped working altogether, forcing IBM employees to spend several months taking the stairs. In most buildings, the landlord was responsible for things like elevator maintenance, but the terms of the lease with this particular landlord were unusual, and WeWork was responsible for the repairs. "There were so many problems with that building," one senior WeWork employee said. "And it was like, *snicker, snicker, snicker.*"

The snickering resulted from the fact that the building was owned by Adam. He had purchased it for $70 million with Elie Tahari, a fashion designer he knew from the Kabbalah Centre, before leasing the space to WeWork. Adam had not made the board aware of his stake in the building, but his ownership of it was nonetheless ethically dubious. He was collecting rent from his own company.

As IBM grew increasingly fed up with the state of its new office, Adam went to the building himself to assure the tenants that he would take care of the situation. Back at WeWork headquarters, several executives met to address the crisis. The group agreed that someone's head needed to roll. Since the landlord couldn't be punished, the person in charge of IT was axed instead.

Unbeknownst to most WeWork employees, Adam and a small circle of WeWork executives had collected rent checks from the company for years. Adam, Mark Lapidus, and Ariel Tiger were part-owners of WeWork's Varick Street location, its fourth in New York; after two years of owning the building, with WeWork as a tenant, the owners flipped it for more than $25 million. They would argue they avoided any conflicts by not getting involved in any negotiations, but by the time Adam purchased the IBM building, he was well aware that being his own landlord was potentially problematic. Who wins in a negotiation with yourself? In 2013, WeWork's board pushed back on Adam's attempt to buy part of a Chicago building that WeWork planned to lease, pointing out the conflict of interest. That objection became largely moot once Neumann gained control of the board, and by the spring of 2018, WeWork had paid Adam more than $12 million in rent, with more than $100 million to come.

Adam had long insisted that WeWork was not in the business of owning buildings. "We definitely do not buy the properties," he said in 2015. "That would make us a real estate company." But by the end of 2017, WeWork had launched a new arm of the company, called WeWork Property Advisors, which would do just that. WeWork paid an estimated $850 million to buy Lord & Taylor's flagship location in Midtown, spending $150 million above the next closest offer. Lord & Taylor had opened the space in 1914 as an early version of what Adam now imagined for his own buildings, with a gym, a school, and a dentist for the department store's employees. WeWork planned to put its new headquarters in the building; a rendering of the potential renovation replaced the cursive Lord & Taylor marquee on the exterior with a sign reading DO WHAT YOU LOVE.

The plan for WeWork Property Advisors called for raising money from investors to help WeWork buy buildings. The team setting up the fund hoped to raise $1 billion. Adam had a better idea: Why not $100 billion? It would be a Vision Fund for buildings, and instantly among the largest such piles of money in the world. The number was unreasonable, but the lesson from Adam's early fundraising days had stuck. "Adam would put $100 billion in the deck so he would end up getting $1 billion," a person involved in the fund said. "You shoot for the moon and land higher than anyone else."

Investing in real estate at this scale was new for Adam, and he peppered the team with questions. "The thing he most wanted to understand was how it would tie back to the value of WeWork," the employee said. "We'd say, 'If we raise a billion, you can buy three million square feet of real estate.' Then he would do the math: 'Okay, we average two hundred bucks per square foot, so that's $600 million in revenue, then you put a 20x revenue multiple on that'"—the lavish multiplier WeWork was being given by investors—"'and that's an extra $12 billion in valuation.'" WeWork employees had always been impressed with Adam's ability to swiftly tabulate large numbers, and several of them had watched as he took this type of calculation to its next logical conclusion. "We were working on a deal," one WeWork real estate executive said. "And he goes, 'That's so many square feet, which means this many desks, and since we make so much per desk in revenue, and we're valued at 20x, *and* I own this percentage of the company—this deal is worth $20 million to me, personally.'"

* * *

THE JOB OF EDUCATING Adam on the finer points of real estate investing fell in part to Rich Gomel, who did not expect to find himself in this position. Gomel had joined WeWork at the beginning of 2017 as the company's president after more than a decade at Starwood Hotels and another five years running a real estate investment firm at JPMorgan. For someone like Gomel, and the other mid-career executives joining WeWork's senior ranks from more traditional companies, this was a rare opportunity to experience blitzscaling outside the tech world, and to reap the riches that could come with it.

It quickly became clear to many of Gomel's new colleagues that he was being groomed to potentially be WeWork's next CEO: Adam would step down, having led the company through its blitzscaling phase, becoming chairman of WeWork's board, where he could continue pushing his vision while a seasoned operator like Gomel led WeWork into a new phase as a public company. But much as Masa had recently backed away from his promise to begin looking for his successor, Adam seemed to be having second thoughts about handing over the reins. After a few months, Gomel was moved out of his job managing WeWork's core office-leasing business and tasked with WeWork's tangential push into real estate investing.

Shifting fortunes were a familiar pattern for WeWork executives. Gomel had taken his initial title from Artie Minson, who had been Adam's heir apparent during two years as the metaphorical adult in the room—the Sheryl Sandberg to Adam's Mark Zuckerberg. Minson was a foot shorter than Adam and had followed a more traditional path to the upper echelons of American business: private high school in New York, an accounting degree from Georgetown, then an MBA at Columbia. He had worked for founders before, and in each case, the brazen impulses that led them to start their companies in the first place had tempered as they grew into large corporations.

But Neumann had only grown less cautious over time. Adam and Artie battled constantly over WeWork's direction. Artie was skeptical of

Adam's push to position WeWork as a tech company, believing instead that it made more sense for WeWork to position itself as the Nike of office space—a premium brand that consumers would pay extra for. But Adam wouldn't hear it, and grew frustrated when Artie expressed doubts about the hundreds of millions Adam was spending on acquisitions. After one company town hall, Adam didn't realize he was still miked up and that WeWork's employees could hear him as he walked offstage and told Michael Gross, "We need to get Artie out."

Artie and other WeWork executives found themselves hesitant to press Neumann too hard. Those who did often found themselves kept out of meetings they should have been in, or sent to new jobs in far corners of the business. "Artie was in the shithouse for a long time," a fellow executive said. "The only reason he wasn't kicked out is because he was too big of a name."

The drama led to infighting between executives, who found themselves constantly shuffled in and out of Adam's inner circle. "He pitted us all against each other," one of his lieutenants said. More than one described it as living through *Game of Thrones*. One executive who left to join a rival explained his decision to a colleague as, simply, "I was tired of Adam yelling at me." Neumann seemed to wield his overstuffed schedule as a tool of control, forcing executives to meet at all hours of the night, at one or another of his houses, or on a private jet flight across the country if that was the only time Adam could squeeze in a half-hour meeting. Several executives suggested that Adam's occasional lack of concern for the personal lives of those around him was his true superpower. "We had meetings at 2:00 a.m. where he joined us forty-five minutes late," Francis Lobo, the former chief revenue officer, said. "But that meeting was worth millions."

When Miguel tried to explain his cofounder's leadership style, which he had been observing for nearly a decade, he said that Adam had often motivated by fear. At one company off-site with WeWork's executive team, Adam stood up from a large table around which his executives were sitting and began to pace. He had a tendency to go on and on in such settings, serving rounds of drinks to make sure his audience was sufficiently lubricated while everyone in the room sat around wondering when they would get to eat. In this case, Adam seemed to be in a good mood, boasting about the company's growth.

But his tenor quickly turned. He had recently learned that someone had purchased a number of $20,000 coffeemakers. WeWork was flush, but Adam didn't want to have to start Managing the Nickel again. "Who approved this?" Adam said, demanding that the culprit stand up before anyone got to leave. One executive in the room was reminded of the scene from *The Untouchables* in which Robert De Niro, playing Al Capone, circles a table of Mafiosi while carrying a baseball bat, delivering an inspiring speech right up until the moment he suddenly beats to death a lieutenant who dared to betray him.

* * *

IN THE SUMMER OF 2017, Adam reshuffled his executive team again, ousting Artie as COO, pushing him into the CFO position and promoting Jen Berrent to replace him. While other members of WeWork's executive team dipped in and out of favor with Adam, Berrent was among the few who seemed to consistently consolidate more and more power over the years. She had cultivated a reputation as a stoic foil to Adam's hyperactive energy. Whenever Adam made one outlandish promise or another at an all-hands meeting, Berrent would sometimes shoot him a look, call him over, and then whisper something in his ear that would prompt Adam to return to the microphone and say, with a smile, "Jen doesn't want me to say that." Berrent struck many employees, sympathetically, as a bit like Hillary Clinton, donning her pantsuit every day to do battle in an overwhelmingly masculine world while rarely expressing what anyone would recognize as a genuine emotion. "People think I don't have empathy," Berrent lamented to a colleague.

Berrent herself identified as an outsider. She had come out late in life, and explained her decision to leave the world of big law by emailing her fellow attorneys at WilmerHale an E. E. Cummings quotation: "To be nobody-but-yourself / in a world which is doing its best, night and day, to make you every-body else / means to fight the hardest battle which any human being can fight." Berrent said she felt comfortable at WeWork, and when she got married, she and her wife held the ceremony at a WeWork on Bryant Park.

Berrent publicly extolled the more magnanimous aspects of WeWork's culture, and her position as the company's top female executive was a source of inspiration for many WeWork employees. But she became known to those who worked closely with her as "Adam's henchwoman," as one fellow executive described her. For more than two years, Berrent's legal team had continued to press charges against Joanna Strange, the employee who had leaked internal company documents; the ostensible goal was to recover Strange's $2,000 severance, but the primary reason seemed to be making her an example of how the company would treat dissent. Strange was advised not to attend a court hearing in the case and WeWork secured a default judgment against her for just over $3,000.

In addition to her role as WeWork's top lawyer, Berrent had taken on the job of running human resources, which many early start-ups leave to their attorneys. She often echoed a goal Adam had set out for the company of laying off 20 percent of WeWork's staff every year—a blitzscaled version of Jack Welch's belief that the bottom 10 percent of a company's workers should be regularly culled. "We met those expectations, and I'm not proud of that," one member of WeWork's HR team said. He started referring to the quiet, rolling rounds of layoffs that regularly took place at WeWork as "Jen-ocides."

Adam seemed to value Berrent for not only her sharp legal mind but for her loyalty—a quality he had long sought in his executives. At an executive retreat in 2018 at the Surf Lodge, a hip outpost in Montauk at the end of Long Island, Adam said that he was going to surf the next morning before dawn, and encouraged everyone to join him. Some did, and some didn't. When the group met later the following day, Adam called out to the people who had joined him on the water. "Where are my warriors?" he said. Michael Gross handed each of them a copy of *The Art of War*.

Adam had surrounded himself with friends and family since the company's early days: childhood buddies, navy pals, friends from Kabbalah, not to mention his wife, sister, multiple in-laws, and two nephews. WeWork employees were at one point asked to reserve a company email address for Adi Neumann's toddlers. Some of Adam's relatives were as qualified as anyone else for the jobs they occupied, but the overall feeling was that proximity to Adam was the key to advancement at the company. In Montauk, Adam stood to give a toast before dinner and told an executive sitting next to him to get up and make room for Gross. "Michael," Adam said, "what's that word you always say—when you hire your family and friends?"

"Nepotism?" Gross said.

"That's it," Adam said. "To nepotism!"

CHAPTER SEVENTEEN

Operationalize Love

A YEAR AFTER the Women's March in Los Angeles, WeWork's 2018 Summit returned to Manhattan, where the company planned to introduce its latest shift in focus. Artie Minson, a New York native, fulfilled a childhood dream by giving a speech while wearing a Knicks jersey at Madison Square Garden in a theater below the fabled basketball court. Rebekah teared up while speaking about WeGrow. A yoga teacher from Rise by We, the gym–slash–wellness club, played a harmonium and held a five-minute meditation. Rocky Kerns led the company in a series of chants:

> *When I say "We," you say "Work"!*
> *When I say "better," you say "together"!*

Kerns then invited any brave employees to come onstage and deliver an open-mike performance of their own creation. One person took him up on the offer and delivered a freestyle rap that included the following verse: "Adam Neumann / He ain't human."

The 2018 Summit was also the setting for the grand finale of WeWork's first Creator Awards, a pitch show in which start-ups auditioned for grants from WeWork. The company hired Adi, Adam's sister, to serve as an emcee, and held shows all over the world—Detroit, Tel Aviv, Washington, DC—during which Adam would often speak. "You're a creator, and you're a creator," he would tell the audience, as if he were Oprah Winfrey handing out free cars. In New York, Adam wore a black leather jacket over a HIGH ON WE T-shirt and explained how the show's idea of giving away money to young start-ups had become a reality. "Of course that makes a lot of sense, but who's going to pay for that?" Adam told the crowd. "We said, 'Well, Masa might!'" SoftBank was funding the Creator Awards with more than $180 million on top of its $4.4 billion investment. After confetti fell on Adam and the winners—he decided to give out two separate $1 million grants rather than one—Macklemore, the rapper, walked out to perform after observing the bonanza from backstage. "I was just watching it, chugging a Red Bull," Macklemore said. "And I immediately thought, 'Damn, I should have got into technology.'"

With the confetti swept away, WeWork presented its employees with the company's newest initiative: Powered by We, an offering meant to appeal to so-called enterprise clients—companies like IBM that had thousands of employees who would need more than a few glass cubes. In 2016, Adam had flown to Los Angeles with Dave Fano, at the invitation of Barry Diller, the chairman of Expedia, to pitch him on redesigning a new headquarters for the travel website. Adam ripped up the existing design and assured Diller that WeWork could do better. Fano and a team spent two weeks putting together a presentation, promising it could slash the $1 billion Expedia planned to spend on the project.

WeWork lost the bid to an architecture firm that already specialized in hip corporate headquarters, but Dara Khosrowshahi, who was then Expedia's CEO, hired WeWork to redesign a large satellite office in Chicago. The idea for Powered by We was born: find, furnish, and operate entire offices on behalf of corporations. This was the platform— the WeOS, as they were calling it—that would allow companies to outsource all their real estate needs to WeWork. The benefit was less about access to WeWork's fruit water supply chain and in-office keg delivery than access to more flexible lease terms and the opportunity to offload some risk. New corporate accounting rules in the United States would soon require companies to report office leases as debt, which meant that America's CFOs were suddenly looking with disdain at their real estate portfolios. If Adam wanted to take on the liability of holding long-term leases on their behalf, companies were happy to let him.

Adam got some pushback on the move to serve large organizations. Community managers in buildings where one company had taken over a floor or two found that a caste system emerged. "It's just like high school or college, where people sit with their friends in the dining hall," said a community manager in a Boston WeWork where Amazon and Liberty Mutual had space. Several members of WeWork's board of directors argued that inviting large corporations would disconnect the company from what it did best. "You are all wrong," Adam told them in one meeting. Just as Masa couldn't spend all the Vision Fund's money investing in small companies, Adam couldn't fill all the space he was gobbling up with freelance graphic designers. If corporations were willing to house large chunks of their employees at WeWork, rather than simply leasing a few satellite offices here and there, the revenue opportunity was enormous.

Powered by We also promised to do more than transform a company's physical space. As Adam began pitching the idea, he argued that the internal problems that had swelled into a public relations nightmare for Travis Kalanick and Uber were issues that WeWork could help solve. "It's not news that affected Uber over the past twelve months," Adam said at the time. "It's a culture that was created over time that started to bubble up." WeWork was struggling to sell its technological expertise. Maybe it could sell corporate culture.

At the Summit in New York, Veresh Sita, the head of Powered by We, walked onstage to explain the offering. He cited a study showing that 87 percent of employees at big companies didn't feel engaged and half were looking for new jobs. He put up several slides with images from a recent project. The first picture showed faded yellow chairs around white cafeteria tables. The second presented the same space as an open loft with parquet floors and succulents dotting the room. "I don't know what you even call the first one," Sita said. "Death row?" The key, he said, was understanding what made an office work: the narrow corridors that forced interactions between colleagues and the lack of offices that made executives work alongside their underlings. Companies thought they needed to be like Facebook or Twitter, Sita said, with a big fancy office. They were wrong. "You don't need that," Sita said. "You need a chief culture officer!"

* * *

AT WEWORK, that job now fell to Miguel. As part of the reshuffling that pushed Artie Minson aside and elevated Jen Berrent, Miguel left his role managing WeWork's design team to take Berrent's place as CCO. The title was a modern start-up invention, adjacent to HR but reserved for an executive concerned less with pay and benefits than with ensuring a company's social coherence. At Summit 2018, Miguel's first in the new position, he objected to the notion that WeWork was selling out by catering to large corporations. "These are real human beings you're talking about," he said. "Don't they need us as much as the cool people?"

Miguel's role had changed in the decade since he and Adam opened Green Desk. He was crucial to their early success, defining WeWork's aesthetic and handling the dirty work of its physical growth—wiring the internet, sandblasting the walls. When Adam promised the world to investors and landlords, Miguel was usually sitting nearby, his mind racing to figure out how they were going to pull off whatever his partner had just guaranteed they would do. If Adam fancied himself a successor to Steve Jobs, Miguel was his Steve Wozniak, building the machine to make his partner's dream a reality.

But there wasn't much of a role for a do-it-all handyman in a company with several thousand employees. Miguel had let his architecture license expire, and his role in the design process had diminished as the job became a blitzscaled version of American Apparel's expansion from a decade before. Managing a team of architects and designers that had grown to more than a hundred people was not his area of expertise. At heart, Miguel was still the shy designer most comfortable with his headphones on and a set of drawings in front of him.

He had also never become entirely comfortable with the increasingly public role he was expected to play, even if his calming presence served to balance Adam's exuberant sermons. ("If Adam was Red Bull, Miguel was chamomile tea," as one employee put it.) Telling others what to do felt self-indulgent, and being the center of attention made him squeamish. Why should anyone listen to him? He preferred standing just offstage while his cofounder let the confetti rain down upon him. Miguel watched over the years with a sort of dumbfounded awe at Adam's ability to "turn it on," adapting his manner and message to whatever audience appeared in front of him. When it came time for Miguel to do the same, he struggled. "I'm just the same person, no matter what, in every context," he said. Miguel wasn't keen on inspirational quotes, but he did have one that he liked: "Work hard and in silence, then let success make the fucking noise."

Miguel had gotten over early skepticism of Adam's hyperambition in part because he realized that the biggest impact he was likely going to have on the world would come at Adam Neumann's side. The fact that he had become rich also helped. Miguel wasn't the start-up rock star Adam had become, but he was still happily collecting royalty checks and cashing in on the perks of playing bass guitar. He had his own home in the Hamptons and bought land to build another in an elite mountain community in Utah populated by young start-up founders. The early deal he made with his partner had curtailed some of Miguel's earnings, but he didn't mind. Two decades after writing his mom a postcard saying he wanted to move to New York and do something great, he had done just that, opening more than a hundred WeWorks and touching every part of what had become a global business. After opening a WeWork in an old opium factory in Shanghai, which he thought might be the best yet, he started to wonder how many more times he wanted to figure out where the fruit water dispensers should go.

The chief culture officer job presented a fresh challenge. The feeling of togetherness that naturally filled WeWork's first spaces had become even harder to maintain in the two years since Adam tried to recruit Lisa Skye to bring that feeling back. As CCO, Miguel set about creating what he and others began referring to as CultureOS—a WeOS component by which WeWork would help Powered by We customers improve their internal culture. Dara Khosrowshahi, who left Expedia to replace Travis Kalanick at Uber, could now hire WeWork not only to house his employees, but to help the company rebuild its culture, too.

WeWork often tested new designs and layouts at its headquarters before trying them out with customers, and Miguel's first task was to take a look at WeWork's own culture, which had morphed and twisted as the company added thousands of employees. When Miguel realized that he barely knew any of them, he set a goal of introducing himself to three new people each day. In his speech at Summit 2018, Miguel said that he wanted WeWork to rally behind a new slogan: "Operationalize Love."

It wasn't immediately obvious that Miguel was the best person to understand and improve the lot of WeWork's employees. He had no training in human resources, and by the time he took over as chief culture officer, it had been a decade since he worked for anyone at all. Miguel estimated that he had slept four or five hours a night for the past two decades; a girlfriend once told him, "I wish you would look at me the way you look at that building."

But Adam liked to put people into unfamiliar positions and see how they performed. Miguel was replaced as chief creative officer by Adam Kimmel, a fashion designer who was friendly with the Neumanns, along with his wife, the actress Leelee Sobieski. Kimmel had real estate in his blood—his father founded a company that became the largest builder of strip malls in America—but he was an unorthodox choice for the role. Like Masa, he had never set foot in a WeWork, nor had he worked in architecture or design. He had also never managed a team anywhere close to the size of WeWork's design department, which was trying to keep up with a pace that had already proven overwhelming to Kimmel: he shut down his eponymous men's fashion label several years earlier because he feared it was growing too fast for him to control.

Kimmel set about instituting a complete refresh of WeWork's aesthetic, replacing the boutique-hotel look with white walls and bright kilim rugs that felt more like a retrofitted motel in Palm Springs. He encouraged WeWork's designers to think in seasons, as a fashion designer would. There was occasional aesthetic confusion—when questions about branding came up, teams would sometimes ask, "Are we doing this in Kimmel colors or Rebekah colors?"—but, in general, Adam referred to Kimmel as a genius who should be given a wide berth to carry out his vision.

In 2018, Miguel went to a senior member of WeWork's HR department with a problem at the intersection of his old and new jobs. Two female employees on the design team, both of whom had been at WeWork for years, had been kept out of meetings with Kimmel. His orders were instead being filtered through other employees, who were men. Apparently Kimmel and Sobieski had a rule: neither party in the relationship was allowed to meet privately with a member of the opposite sex—a version of the restriction Vice President Mike Pence and his wife had set for each other. When the HR representative met with the women, he found that they feared losing their jobs if they couldn't properly implement what Kimmel wanted. A few days later, the HR rep was called in to a meeting with Neumann.

"Did you recommend that we fire Adam Kimmel?" Neumann said.

The rep said that he had.

"Firing isn't your job," Neumann said, arguing that Kimmel deserved a chance to change his behavior. "Your job, first, is to decide, Is this person brilliant at what they do? The number two question you need to ask is, Are they a good person?" Kimmel, Neumann said, was both.

* * *

ONE MORNING in July of 2018, Adam addressed WeWork's employees by videoconference from Israel, where the company was converting its first location in Tel Aviv to an office that would be occupied entirely by Microsoft employees. The hourlong address included a surprise announcement, tossed in almost as an afterthought: WeWork, Adam said, was banning meat.

This wasn't the strangest declaration Adam had ever made, but it took almost everyone, including his executive team, by surprise. Even Miguel didn't seem to know what his cofounder meant when a group of executives sat down to decode the proclamation. Could a WeWork employee bring a turkey sandwich to the office for lunch? What about members? How would the company enforce such a rule? And why? Adam was a meat eater, so they assumed that the instigator behind the ban was Rebekah, who was vegan. "When you eat something, you're also absorbing the energy of that thing," Rebekah said on a podcast in 2018. "So if the animal is sad, then you're kind of taking in that."

After some debate, the executive team came up with a plan: as part of a broader push to lower the company's carbon footprint, it would no longer pay for employee meals that contained meat. Lindsay Baker, who had just joined WeWork as its first head of sustainability, pushed back against the rationale, fearing that it would come across as insincere. Meat was far from the company's biggest environmental concern; all the resources that went into the gallons of almond, oat, and cow's milk they put out for coffee had a much greater impact on the environment, not to mention the wood and aluminum

WeWork used in construction and the aging HVAC systems in its spaces.

While the meat-free policy seemed to be in keeping with the company's progressive ethos, the response from WeWork's employees was swift and overwhelmingly negative. Employees who had various health issues pointed out that their diets required eating meat, while those in countries such as Uruguay and India noted that this was a culturally sensitive issue. A Republican politician in Texas mocked the policy on the campaign trail. A Slack channel emerged solely to debate the issue, and employees began dining out at Michelin-starred vegetarian restaurants, expensing lobster, and maxing out their per diems with airport sushi rolls. At a Creator Awards event in Nashville, Lindsey Isbell, the community manager, had to apologize to G-Eazy, the rapper who had been hired to perform, because she couldn't fulfill his request for a pepperoni pizza.

For many WeWork employees, the random audacity of the announcement summed up the experience of working at the company. Michael Bravo, a member of WeWork's tech team in Tel Aviv, shared a six-page "manifesto" with his colleagues laying out concerns he had about the trampling of individual liberties. Bravo had grown up in the Soviet Union and objected in general to the "energetic flag waving" at WeWork; he was exhausted by how often his colleagues declared how "excited" they were about one thing or another. "In your average day at WeWork, you might hear that word a hundred times," Bravo said. "If someone is permanently excited, he or she should seek help." Like many employees, he thought eating less meat was probably a good idea—he just didn't want his boss to be the one telling him to do it. Bravo's manifesto circulated widely around the company, and in a farewell email written when he left WeWork, a few months later, he included an image of the yellow Gadsden flag, a symbol of resistance from the American Revolution to the Tea Party.

It was clear that no matter how much power Adam gave to Miguel or Artie or anyone else, WeWork remained Neumann's company. Everything at WeWork revolved around him, and the charm he deployed to woo investors had a similar effect on employees. Adam was a master orator who used his physical size to dominate a room. He had an unnerving ability to maintain intense eye contact. "When he looks at you, it's what I imagine it feels like to have Julius Caesar stare at you," said Alana Anderson, the community manager who had joined WeWork in 2015 to sort out whether her sister had fallen prey to a cult. "There's an intensity, a self-understanding, a belief."

WeWork was at the leading edge of a growing movement among American companies to commingle spirituality and mindfulness with the pursuit of profit; at TGIM events, employees would sometimes snap their fingers in response to sentiments they admired, as if they were at a poetry reading. When the company's human resources team complained that WeWork's below-market salaries made it hard to attract talent, Adam insisted that people wanted to join the company for its purpose and mission, not the salary or benefits.

But its sloganeering—DO WHAT YOU LOVE—became harder to rally behind the longer employees stayed with the company. They were regularly working sixty-hour weeks or more, and chastised for leaving at 6:30 p.m. to relieve their nanny or to make it to an exercise class. Stella Templo's credit card company alerted her to possible fraud when she used her card to see a movie for the first time in forever. People who considered leaving the company worried about the fact that all of their friends were other WeWork employees, or that they couldn't afford to buy their stock options if they left. The means of escape were also limited: until 2018, WeWork forced employees, including janitors and baristas, to sign a noncompete agreement preventing them from working for competitors until the New York attorney general stepped in to say that WeWork's agreements were illegal.

Employees began to recognize a WeWork life cycle. New hires would arrive buoyed with excitement for six months—maybe nine. A slow decline would begin until they hit the eighteen-month mark, by which time they would be exhausted and disillusioned and something like the company's meat ban would push them over the edge. Those employees would leave and be replaced—rinse and repeat. At the end of 2018, as WeWork rapidly approached ten thousand employees, half of them had been with the company for less than six months. Many employees began to see WeWork less as a company than a cult. Adam's preaching attracted a constant influx of fresh devotees who kept the machine running. "From a business perspective," one HR executive told me, "the cult is working."

CHAPTER EIGHTEEN
A WeWork Wedding

AUGUSTO CONTRERAS JOINED WeWork at the beginning of 2018. He was thirty-five and living in Texas, where he ran a community arts program with his girlfriend. A friend in Mexico City was opening one of WeWork's newest locations there and pushed him to join. "I've got a life; I've got a mission. Why should I leave?" Contreras asked his friend, who replied that he should think about what his life and mission would look like with a bigger budget. Contreras had gone through a spiritual phase, and connected with the speeches he saw Adam deliver on YouTube about his plans to "humanize Earth." He decided to give WeWork a shot.

Contreras was hired as a community manager at a WeWork on the Paseo de la Reforma in Mexico City. He loved his job: the work, the members, the team, which regularly went out for dinner without thinking twice about spending a few thousand dollars. "To work at a company that says, 'Here's your Amex: do whatever you want, so long as you keep the numbers up'—it was like a dream," Contreras said. His coworkers became his closest friends. "That cult kind of vibe is absolutely true," Contreras said. "They don't force you to do things, but the energy is so strong you just go with it."

Contreras was also trying to maintain a connection with the outside world. He wanted to get engaged to his girlfriend, who had stayed in Texas to run the arts program, but the pace of his job at WeWork left him little time to plan a proposal, let alone make one happen. Contreras asked his boss if he could skip Summer Camp to spend the weekend in Texas proposing. The event was mandatory, his boss said, before offering a compromise: "Why don't you propose at Summer Camp?"

Contreras agreed and brought his girlfriend with him to Tunbridge Wells, an hour south of London, where WeWork was hosting its seventh Summer Camp in 2018. He thought about proposing on Friday night, in the middle of a performance by the rock band Bastille, but the logistics were too tricky to sort out in time. The following afternoon, during a dodgeball tournament, Contreras grabbed a microphone as hundreds of his coworkers and several of the company's videographers looked on. "She said yes!" Contreras yelled after bending down on one knee while wearing a WeWork-branded T-shirt. His colleagues cheered. In remembering the moment, Contreras said that he felt as if he were "surrounded by my extended family." He had been at WeWork for seven months.

* * *

NO ONE KNEW that WeWork's 2018 Summer Camp would be its last, but there was plenty to celebrate: SoftBank had just agreed to invest an additional $1 billion in the company. WeWork flew its six thousand employees to London, hired Lorde to perform, and had to quickly find replacement food trucks to meet the company's new dietary restrictions. Employee accommodations remained humble—air mattresses in tents— but a pair of campsites was set aside for the company's founders, with only those holding a VIP wristband allowed to access them. WeWork's event team had a one-page list of requests for Miguel's campsite: a fire pit, some Popchips, and enough beer, wine, and coconut water to last the long weekend.

Adam and Rebekah had a longer list. The Neumanns had flown to Summer Camp on WeWork's brand-new Gulfstream jet, which the company had purchased for more than $60 million at Adam's behest under an LLC called Wildgoose I. Adam and Rebekah's list of items to be stocked in their Summer Camp compound went on for three and a half pages.

Accommodation & Compound

- Standard Tent House Suite via Raj Style
- Heating
- A/C (3 aircon units)
- 1 king bed (+ mattress pad)
- 4 twin beds (2 in each of 2 rooms)
- 1 crib
- 1 high chair
- Towels, blankets, citronella candles
- 4 Vienna Two Seater + chairs (for 12)
- 8 Picnic tables for 40 people
- 1 Stockholm large coffee table
- 2 fridges
- 2 fire bowls
- 1 Woodsman's awning
- RV

Transport

- 3 buggies (two for our office team, 1 set aside for family)—dinosaur themed
- 1 buggy for WW security team
- 1 Shuttle bus to bring wristband guests to and from the main arena

- Signature Range Rover for Rebekah/Adam use
- Mercedes V Class

Staffing

- 24/7 security guard
- 2 24/7 drivers
- 2 dedicated bartenders

Supplies

- 4 cocktail shakers
- At least 400 plastic shot glasses—bring extra from the office
- Plastic cups
- Thick paper plates
- Wooden utensils
- Paper towels
- Straws (sealed in paper)
- 6 wine keys
- 6 bottle openers
- 4 Aesop Geranium Hand Soap
- 4 Aesop Gardenia Shower Gel
- 4 Aesop Gardenia Shampoo
- 4 Aesop Gardenia Conditioner
- Printer

Market

- Sliced red peppers x 6
- Cucumbers x 6
- Platter of fresh sliced fruit (two per day)

- Nuts (unsalted)
  - Cashews x 3
  - Pistachios x 3
  - Almonds x 3
  - Walnuts x 3
- SkinnyPop popcorn (12 packs)
- Lemons x 10
- Limes x 30
- LaCroix Lime 6 packs x 4
- Hot Water—or the ability to get boiling water—ideally having an electric tea kettle setup
- Dairy-free Oatmeal packets
- Dates x 3
- Sugar Free Red Bull 12 pack x 3
- Regular Red Bull 12 pack x 3
- Ice
- Ginger root
- Chocolate bars
- Edamame packets
- Kind Bars
- Guacamole singles
- Peanut butter squeeze packets
- Tea
  - Chamomile
  - Hibiscus
  - Peppermint
  - Mother's Milk
- Filtered Water
- Fresh squeezed orange juice
- Oat milk or soy milk
- Wasa Multigrain
- Wasa Crisp 'n Light

- Wasa Light Rye cracker x 4
- Sliced green apples
- Organic fresh-pressed peanut butter
- Mixed berry jelly
- Avocado
- Crudite platters (whatever veggies are fresh)
- Heirloom tomatoes
- Fresh basil
- Fresh mozzarella
- Extra virgin olive oil
- Vegetarian sushi rolls
- Baguette
- Salt and pepper (in the grinders)
- Health Warrior Pumpkin seed bar packages x 3
- Enlightened Broad Beans (snack pack size) x 6
- RX Bars variety pack x 3

The rider ended with a list of alcohol requests that could have covered most of an entry-level WeWork salary, beginning with two bottles of Highland Park thirty-year-old single-malt Scotch—retailing at $1,000 each—and concluding with a request from Rebekah for the ingredients necessary to make Bellinis, mimosas, and white wine sangria.

Booze

- Highland Park 30 yrs x 2
- 17 year Hibiki x 1
- 3 Hibiki Harmony
- 18 year Macallan x 4
- Stoli Elit / Tito's x 24
- 12 cases of Don Julio 1942

- 16 bottles Kosher red wine (Chateau Pontet-Canet 2003)
- 8 bottles Kosher red wine (Petit Castel 2014)
- 24 bottles Kosher white wine (Château Clos Haut-Peyraguey Sauternes 2014)
- 72 bottles of Peroni
- 72 bottles of Heineken
- 72 bottles of Corona Light

One afternoon at camp, WeWork's employees were herded toward the Creator Stage, coaxed along by a small marching band playing the White Stripes' "Seven Nation Army" on an endless loop. Adam, Miguel, and Rebekah were scheduled to host a panel; the vegetarian food trucks were told to hold off on serving meals, leaving their employees to fend off desperate bribes from drunk and hungry WeWorkers. For those attending their first Summer Camp, the crowd had a strange energy, erupting into a cheer of "Olé, olé, olé" when the three founders appeared onstage. An employee from India started chanting, "Let's go, WeWork, let's go!" Another, from California, screamed, "You're changing the world, Adam!"

Neumann had certainly come to believe in his ability to do just that. "The influence and impact that we are going to have on this earth is going to be so big," he said, wearing a T-shirt that read LET'S MEAT IN THE MIDDLE. A few weeks earlier, after the shocking news that both Kate Spade and Anthony Bourdain had died by suicide, Adam had stood up at a company town hall and told his employees that if they were ever feeling depressed or suicidal they should reach out to him directly. At Summer Camp, he relayed what he described as good news: one of his employees had done just that, and was in the crowd today, doing fine.

As he had on other occasions, Adam shared some of the difficulties of his childhood, and he and Rebekah expressed a desire to solve the problems plaguing children in even less fortunate situations. "One of my biggest dreams for We," Rebekah told the crowd, "is that we'll be able to build communities around the world where children who are not in the right situation could come and live forever, basically."

Adam jumped in. "There are 150 million orphans in this world today," he said. "If we do the work right, we could wake up one day and say, 'We want to solve the problem of children without parents in this world'— and do it, within two years."

"And children who are in abusive situations," Rebekah said.

Adam agreed. "Then we can go to any minority, and anyone who is weaker, who is getting taken advantage of by someone who is more powerful," he said. "And from that we can go to world hunger. There's so many topics that we can take one by one, and we will be able to tackle anything that we set our minds to."

Rebekah went on to express her gratitude to Adi Neumann, who was in the crowd, for funding Adam's early life back in New York. "You helped him create the biggest family in the world," Rebekah said. "A big part of being a woman is to help men manifest their calling in life."

* * *

THE COMMENT caught many women off guard: Was Rebekah, WeWork's most prominent female executive, telling women at the company that their primary job was to assist the men around them? Rebekah often referred to herself as a muse; translated into start-up vernacular, she described herself as "a platform for other people." But her Summer Camp comment seemed to limit the way women at the company should expect to view their roles. After the comments were reported by Thomas Hobbs, a writer for the British real estate publication *Property Week*, who had snuck into Summer Camp as if he were infiltrating a Rajneeshi gathering, Rebekah doubled down on a podcast when she was asked about what made her most proud. "Probably helping my husband and other people around me manifest their callings," she said. "I think it's a specific superpower that women have, because we can conceive life and bear life."

Whatever efforts WeWork was making to improve its culture had done little to eliminate the issues women faced in the workplace. The company's senior ranks remained overwhelmingly male. On multiple occasions, Adam jokingly encouraged female employees to date his cousin-in-law, Mark Lapidus, the company's head of real estate, who had a relationship with one of his subordinates. When Medina Bardhi interviewed for a job as Adam's chief of staff in 2013, he asked if she planned to be pregnant anytime soon, according to a complaint she later filed against the company alleging pregnancy and gender discrimination. (The complaint is still open.) In 2016, Bardhi told Adam she was pregnant and could no longer join him on private jets, having recently accompanied him on a flight during which he and several other executives smoked pot in the air, according to her complaint. While Bardhi was on leave, Adam hired a male chief of staff to replace her at double her salary; when she returned, in the spring, Bardhi was relegated to a table next to Neumann's multiple assistants. A few months later, Adam pulled her aside. He was worried that his new chief of staff was too concerned about his "own personal brand" and he needed someone who was committed to him. Bardhi returned to the job for a year before going on maternity leave again, in 2018, at which point Adam hired another man to replace her.

Two months after Summer Camp 2018, Ruby Anaya, who had recently been let go after more than three years at WeWork, filed a lawsuit against the company alleging that she had been sexually harassed at multiple company events. Anaya had most recently worked on Miguel's team, as director of culture, and launched the Women of WeWork support group. Just a few months earlier, Anaya had been interviewed by a research team at the Harvard Business School as part of a glowing case study about Miguel's efforts to improve WeWork's company culture. Now, she was alleging that Adam had offered her a shot at her job interview; that a human resources representative responded to her complaint about a male colleague who groped her at Summer Camp by saying he was a "high performer"; and that Miguel, as chief culture officer, had known about her concerns and done nothing.

WeWork's executives had a heated discussion about how to respond, and several executives instructed WeWork's communications team to leak photos of Anaya from Summer Camp and WeWork parties, in an effort to present Anaya as a willing participant in company debauchery. (The PR team refused to do so.) Because Anaya had worked on the culture team, under Miguel, Adam told his cofounder that the company's communication to employees on the issue should come from him. A day after Anaya's lawsuit was filed, and reported in the press, Miguel sent an email to every WeWork employee claiming that Anaya had been "let go because of poor performance."

Many WeWork employees were taken aback. The #MeToo movement was in full force—Brett Kavanaugh's Supreme Court hearings had been held the month before—and it felt tone-deaf for the company's chief culture officer to express anything but deep concern and a promise to conduct a thorough investigation. Whatever the merits of Anaya's case—the lawsuit remains pending—it was not a surprise to any woman at WeWork that attending Summer Camp or Summit or any of the company's parties often put female employees in uncomfortable positions. One woman woke up during Summer Camp to find one of her male colleagues peeing on the tent above her head.

The company's response to Anaya's lawsuit further sidelined Miguel. Those who had been with the company for years wondered if his voice was still being heard at the executive table, while those who had arrived recently thought he should resign altogether. Beyond this situation, his attempt at creating a CultureOS had produced nothing groundbreaking.

Building company culture was a labor-intensive task that resisted standardization. It was hard to operationalize love, and it surprised no one at WeWork to discover, later on, that the phrase was a slogan deployed by Marianne Williamson.

* * *

FOR MANY LONGTIME EMPLOYEES, the close of Summer Camp 2018 felt like the end of an era. The event had grown so large that it lost much of its charm, and many employees wished the company would just give them a week off to rest and spend the money it poured into Summer Camp on giving them all a $2,000 bonus instead. After camp was all over, several members of WeWork's events team ventured into the Neumanns' compound to see what remained. They found a mess, including an unsmoked joint that was left behind in the RV. With nothing left to do, they passed the joint around.

Three months after his Summer Camp proposal, Augusto Contreras was fired by WeWork. Throughout the fall, he had continued traveling back and forth between Mexico City and Texas to visit his new fiancée. On occasion he charged a dinner with her to his company card. Given how often Contreras had heard from Adam and other WeWork executives that the company was one big family, he figured it was safe to assume his fiancée was part of the family now, too.

In November, an employee Contreras had never met—the WeWork family had grown in less than a year from three thousand employees when he joined the company to nearly ten thousand—called him into a conference room. WeWork had found out about the dinners with his fiancée, and told Contreras he needed to refund the money. He was a bit miffed but did so the following week; in full transparency, he admitted that he had been charging meals to the company for months. He was let go immediately.

When I spoke to Contreras a few months later, he expressed remorse for his actions, having realized that he had been a bit foolish to believe that WeWork was a family in any real sense of the word. But he also felt a sense of betrayal and disappointment. He was now back in Texas with his fiancée, running their community arts program. In the end, the bigger budget hadn't been all it was cracked up to be.

CHAPTER NINETEEN

Fortitude

IN AUGUST 2018, just a few weeks before WeWork's final Summer Camp, Masayoshi Son told SoftBank's shareholders that the dozens of companies he was investing in through the Vision Fund would "join us as our family." Among his growing brood, Masa seemed to have a favored child. "WeWork is the next Alibaba," he said. The company was doing "something completely new," using technology and "proprietary data systems" to build and connect communities in a way no one else had. He was thinking of moving SoftBank's headquarters into WeWork offices in Japan and told those scrutinizing WeWork's business to stop worrying so much about the math. "Feeling is more important than just looking at the numbers," he said. "You have to feel the force."

But numbers remained an issue. WeWork was on pace to lose almost $2 billion in 2018, and was again running low on cash, despite receiving more than $5 billion from investors since Adam declared in 2015 that WeWork wouldn't need any more private investment. In April, WeWork had secured an additional $702 million in debt financing, an oddly specific number that was arrived at when Adam, who was celebrating his thirty-ninth birthday, multiplied his age by eighteen, a lucky number in Judaism.

The bond offering required WeWork to release quarterly financial statements. The magical thinking that pervaded its forecasts throughout the decade needed to be tempered with more sober assessments that would make the bond appealing to institutional investors, such as the Teachers Insurance and Annuity Association of America, which was now among the largest holders of WeWork's debt. Honesty could be humbling. "We have a history of losses and we may be unable to achieve profitability at a company level," WeWork wrote in the bond prospectus.

But there were plenty of ways to apply "the force" to WeWork's numbers. The prospectus included a unique metric: "Community Adjusted EBITDA." The acronym stands for "earnings before interest, taxes, depreciation, and amortization," and is a standard way of measuring financial performance. The phrase "Community Adjusted" was a WeWork creation, meant to apply the company's rhetorical flourish to a metric that would present its financial picture in a rosier light. By removing certain costs like design, marketing, and administrative expenses, which the company argued would dissipate over time, Community Adjusted EBITDA transformed WeWork's $933 million loss in 2017 into a $233 million profit.

Those costs were unlikely to disappear, and the cringeworthy term struck many as another attempt at convincing investors that WeWork was something it wasn't. Many of the high-growth, money-losing unicorns of the 2010s had produced their own bespoke metrics showing how much money they believed their companies would make once they stopped spending so much on growth. (Uber's version was called "core platform contribution margin.") A New York Times economics reporter offered a less upbeat way of looking at the measurements: "earnings without all the bad stuff." The Financial Times dubbed Community Adjusted EBITDA "perhaps the most infamous financial metric of a generation."

By any measure, Adam seemed unworried by WeWork's mounting losses. The company's revenue was still doubling every year, and he constantly repeated Masa's exhortation to move faster, telling executives that Masa believed WeWork could be worth $1 trillion if the company ruthlessly pursued its goals. Adam bristled at input from advisers within the company and began referring to himself as the "Mark *and* Sheryl" of WeWork, dismissing suggestions that he bring in a trusted lieutenant to run the business now that he had pushed away other internal candidates. Neumann reportedly missed several board meetings in 2018, during which the company's directors expressed concern about WeWork's growth rate. Both Bruce Dunlevie and Ron Fisher, one of two SoftBank-affiliated representatives on the board, pressed WeWork to establish a timeline for when the company would go public.

But the disclosures required by the bond prospectus had already made Adam uncomfortable, and the thought of going public remained an undesirable prospect. He wasn't alone. Start-ups were staying private much longer than their peers even a decade before: the median age of companies going public had tripled from four years to twelve since the late '90s. The restrictions of the Sarbanes-Oxley Act encouraged many entrepreneurs to avoid public scrutiny as long as they could, while the geyser of private capital now available to them removed the pressure to do so. Jeff Bezos had raised just one Series A round of venture capital before taking Amazon public; Mark Zuckerberg got to a Series E. Adam had kept WeWork private long enough for Masa to invest in a Series G.

Masa himself had long dreamed of taking SoftBank private, freeing himself from the restrictions that came with being a public company. By lavishing the Vision Fund's largesse upon start-ups, Masa believed that he was giving young companies "the gift of being private." Because the Vision Fund's investments often included large secondary share purchases, such as the $1.3 billion worth of WeWork stock that SoftBank and the Vision Fund bought from existing shareholders in 2017, early investors began describing the Vision Fund's investments as a new kind of exit strategy: the "Masa-PO."

Over the summer of 2018, Masa began talking with Adam about bestowing such a gift. WeWork was already among the Vision Fund's largest investments, but part of the fund's conception was to pursue "blockbuster" deals that would pour not just billions but *tens* of billions of dollars into individual companies. In some ways, the strategy was a necessity. There were only so many good ideas to spend $100 billion on, and the Vision Fund already seemed to be pushing that limit: Masa was investing in food delivery, virtual reality, vertical farming, genomics, driverless cars, car rentals, dog walking, pizza-making robots, and the online sale of sports apparel.

The plan Masa and Adam began sketching out would dwarf their record-setting deal from 2017. It called for SoftBank and the Vision Fund to buy out many of WeWork's existing shareholders, from Benchmark to the Chainsmokers to the former community managers in Austin and London who had taken out loans to buy their vested options. That would leave Adam, Masa, and a handful of other true believers as the company's remaining partners, excising any heretics skeptical of their shared vision. The plan called for an infusion of as much as $20 billion. It would put WeWork's value well above $40 billion, doubling the amount SoftBank had decreed the company was worth just a year earlier. Adam could maintain control of his company and his vision, while his theoretical net worth would rise above $13 billion, making him one of the wealthiest people in the world.

* * *

THE CODE NAME for the plan was Fortitude. Teams from SoftBank and WeWork bounced from New York to Tokyo to Boston, where WeWork's legal team at Skadden, Arps was based, hammering out the details. SoftBank had made a habit of fueling price wars by investing heavily in multiple companies in a single industry—DoorDash and Uber Eats, for example—so WeWork insisted that Masa not finance one of its competitors. SoftBank, in turn, made Adam pledge not to leave and launch a competitor himself. If WeWork's revenue increased to $50 billion in the next five years—a nearly unfathomable pace, but Masa and Adam were dreamers—Neumann's stake in the company would grow.

For WeWork, and Adam, Fortitude would cap another big year. The company was on target to overtake JPMorgan as New York's largest office tenant, just as Adam had promised it would, and he hoped to make a splash in doing so: WeWork was planning to lease a dozen floors in One World Trade Center, where the Twin Towers once stood, including space occupied by Condé Nast, the once-glamorous magazine publisher—another bastion of the old guard pushed out by Adam and Masa's expansion. Andrew Ross Sorkin, the *New York Times* reporter who wrote the book *Too Big to Fail*, about the 2008 financial crisis, thought that the phrase Adam had long hoped would define his company might now realistically apply to WeWork. "The idea of 'too big to fail' has long applied to banks and whether the government would come to the rescue to prop them up," Sorkin wrote. "In this case, landlords all over the world might find themselves in the uncomfortable position of having to help save a failing tenant simply because the tenant is so large."

As Halloween approached, WeWork began planning yet another party with a timely theme. How to summarize the surrealness of a New York real estate leasing company, with an elementary school on the side, becoming one of the world's most valuable private companies thanks to a pile of Saudi oil money funneled through a man in Japan who was eager to invest even more? The theme for 2018: "What Is Real?"

Throughout the fall, Adam spoke about Fortitude as if it were an eventuality. "With Adam, a deal was done with the handshake," one WeWork executive said. There were any number of things WeWork could do with the money. At one point, Adam threw out the idea of buying Cushman & Wakefield, the $4 billion commercial real estate giant. He made a bid to acquire Sweetgreen, the salad maker. The name WeWork no longer seemed broad enough to encompass the breadth of Adam's ambition, and the company started conceiving a rebrand much like the one Google had managed in renaming itself Alphabet. It had three major product lines—WeWork, WeLive, WeGrow—and many more just waiting to be dreamed up. With Masa's billions to back it up, WeWork would become the We Company.

* * *

"SUNSHINE IS THE GIFT OF THE GODS," Masa told a crowd of investors in October. It was a hot day, and he was back in New Delhi, where he had just committed to investing as much as $100 billion into India's solar power industry, promising to reduce the cost of electric power to zero. Masa was moving quickly to dispense his Vision Fund war chest, with an eye toward Vision Funds 2, 3, and 4.

The same day Masa delivered his speech in India, news broke that Saudi-Arabian journalist Jamal Khashoggi had vanished inside the Saudi consulate in Turkey. Khashoggi had written critically of Mohammed bin Salman and the Saudi regime, and as details emerged, it became clear that the Saudi government was behind the killing. Few people in global business were more directly tied to Saudi Arabia than Masa. He kept quiet in the immediate aftermath, meeting privately with bin Salman and coming away reassured that Saudi Arabia's $45 billion commitment to a second Vision Fund was still on the table. (A month later, Masa condemned Khashoggi's killing.)

The next circle of business leaders most implicated in Khashoggi's death were the dozens of companies Saudi Arabia was funding through the Vision Fund. Uber was the only American start-up that had taken more money from the fund than WeWork, and Dara Khosrowshahi, its CEO, backed out of the Saudi government's Future Investment Initiative conference, nicknamed "Davos in the Desert," in Riyadh. Adam decided to back out of the conference as well, but as with Trump's travel ban, he chose not to speak up about doing so.

Internally, Adam boasted about WeWork's relationship with Saudi Arabia. The company spent much of 2018 plotting a large Middle East expansion in Saudi Arabia and Abu Dhabi—the second-largest backer of the Vision Fund—including plans to bring the Flatiron School to the kingdom to help women learn how to code. Adam said that he was talking with the Saudi government about incorporating WeWork into Neom, a futuristic city being built from the ground up in northwestern Saudi Arabia near Israel. Neom was expected to have robot housekeepers, artificial rain clouds, and a beach with glow-in-the-dark sand. Adam thought WeWork's role in the project could be worth billions.

Adam often talked about his hope that he, and his company, would help bring peace to the Middle East. Jared Kushner now had the region as part of his White House portfolio, and Adam believed that he, Kushner, and bin Salman were millennial leaders bringing about a better world. He seemed largely unmoved by the geopolitical complications that came with doing business as an American company in Saudi Arabia. Shortly after Khashoggi's death, WeWork's public affairs team brought Stephen Hadley, President George W. Bush's national security adviser, to meet with Adam at WeWork headquarters to explain the situation and what some of the Saudi government's motives might be in bringing WeWork to the country. During the meeting, Adam told Hadley that bin Salman simply needed the right mentor. When Hadley asked who that might be, Adam paused, and then replied, "Me."

But the Saudis and Emiratis had never been as enamored of WeWork as Neumann was of them. They had come to Masa, and the Vision Fund, to diversify their economy into knowledge-based industries that would define the future, not to invest in real estate. As Fortitude was being hashed out, it didn't help matters when Adam showed up late to a meeting at the St. Regis hotel in Manhattan with Khaldoon Khalifa Al Mubarak, the head of Abu Dhabi's sovereign wealth fund. *Vanity Fair* reported that Adam wore sunglasses and looked as if he was hungover.

* * *

ADAM REMAINED CONFIDENT in Fortitude, and in Masa. Adam's deputies had come to believe that Masa served as a father figure for Adam, whose own dad had not been around for much of his childhood. Adam described the connection with Masa as a "special realationship," and Masa proudly told Adam that "the last person I felt this with was Jack Ma," the Alibaba founder. But Adam's status as Masa's favored son could be taken away. That fall, the Vision Fund invested an additional $1 billion in Oyo, the fast-growing Indian hotel start-up, which was led by a founder fifteen years younger than Adam. "Your little brother is really outperforming you," Masa told Adam, in a meeting during which Masa showed off Oyo's ambitious growth plans.

Within SoftBank, the resistance to Fortitude was just as strong as it had been to the original deal Masa and Adam agreed to in the back of a car. Several SoftBank executives, including Rajeev Misra, who ran the Vision Fund and was publicly saying that WeWork could become a $100 billion company, started arguing against the deal. WeWork was losing too much money, the detractors said, and WeLive and WeGrow—to say nothing of the wave pools—were pushing the company into industries where it had no expertise or advantage. SoftBank investors seemed to share their concern: its shares dropped 5 percent when the Fortitude details were first reported in the press.

Tensions between the two companies were growing. When Vikas J. Parekh, who helped manage the Vision Fund's investment in WeWork, began expressing his concerns about the company's business model, Adam barred him from some future meetings. WeWork's side began referring to a "deep state" within SoftBank, burrowed within the company's legal and finance teams, that was intent on souring Masa's view of the deal. SoftBank pushed for a clause allowing the firm to oust Neumann if he went to jail for a violent crime. In one meeting, Adam name dropped his friendship with Jared Kushner, which read as a reminder of Adam's connection to the White House at a time when SoftBank was still seeking government approval for the merger between Sprint and T-Mobile. (In

August of 2018, Neumann met Trump at the president's golf course in New Jersey, when Trump stopped by the table where Adam and Rebekah were having dinner with Jared and Ivanka.)

In November, the two sides came to a preliminary agreement for SoftBank to invest an additional $3 billion in WeWork while the two sides worked on Fortitude. But as the negotiations wore on, Berrent and Minson, who led WeWork's team, recognized that SoftBank could be as tactical as it was profligate. WeWork would soon be running out of money yet again, and the company's executives came to worry that SoftBank might be running out the clock as a tactic to force WeWork into less favorable terms.

They began to consider a backup plan: going public. In 2018, WeWork started receiving pitches from investment banks outlining what an IPO in the near future might look like. The company started preparing its S-1, a document presented to the Securities and Exchange Commission that would mark a first step toward a public offering. One hope was to show SoftBank that, despite Adam's hesitations about going public, the company could forge on without its benefactor if necessary.

But Fortitude was moving ahead. The rough outline had leaked into the press, and WeWork employees were excited to realize the payday they had been promised. Adam was close to achieving his dream of keeping WeWork private. In early December, he delivered the keynote address at a Wall Street fundraiser for a Jewish charity. After being introduced by Lloyd Blankfein, then the chairman of Goldman Sachs, he got onstage in a black suit and a yarmulke and gave a speech in front of three giant screens displaying his face. Adam announced that WeGrow would be adding a "Jewish track" for Torah-curious students and noted that they had recently celebrated Hanukkah—the holiday of miracles, his favorite. "In life, it's not about being afraid of shortcomings," he said. "It's about having the courage to fully live, and be the full light that we can be. It's very scary to be all that we can be, and if each one of us allowed ourselves to be our fullest, there would be no stopping us, there would be peace in the world, and *Moshiach*" — the messiah — "would be here."

* * *

JUST BEFORE CHRISTMAS, the Neumanns boarded Wildgoose I for another winter holiday in Hanalei Bay. Adam was planning to surf again, this time with Laird Hamilton, one of the sport's legends. WeWork was finalizing a deal, modest by Fortitude standards, to lead a $32 million investment round in Laird Superfood, Hamilton's company, which sold turmeric and mushroom-infused coffee creamers. Adam's wave pool investment hadn't panned out, and WeWork slashed the value of its stake to zero after Wavegarden had trouble selling its $16 million "coves." But the Laird Superfood bet had less to do with surfing than with doubling down on the nutritional coffee-creamer industry, much as Masa poured money into multiple food delivery apps. If the DeCicco brothers couldn't change America's food paradigm, maybe Laird Hamilton would.

Adam arrived in Hawaii feeling optimistic. WeWork was opening seventy-nine new locations in December — more than it had in its first six years, including its brand-new Salesforce Tower office, with views across much of San Francisco. The One World Trade Center deal had fallen through, but WeWork still managed to pass JPMorgan as New York City's largest tenant. The company was completing a renovation of its Chelsea headquarters that included the elimination of many individual desks after the "Google Analytics for space" team found that most people spent their days in meetings. One of the few personal spaces being expanded was Adam's office. It would have special privacy frosting in the shape of a wave on its glass wall, and an infrared sauna and cold tub in an attached room — some employees found out about it when water started leaking into the floor below — as well as another large-scale photo of Adam on a surfboard.

Most importantly, the documents sealing Fortitude had gone to the printers. The deal was done. While surfing with Hamilton in Hawaii, Adam worked up the nerve to stroke into the cresting barrel of a wave that he later boasted was swelling up to eighteen feet. Adam had come to surfing later in life, which meant that his skills were still developing. He rode the rising wave as best he could, but struggled to maintain control as it picked up force. When he came up for air, he had a broken finger.

While Adam surfed, the support for Fortitude was quietly falling apart. Saudi Arabia and Abu Dhabi were refusing to allow the Vision Fund to invest more money into WeWork, which left Masa stuck figuring out how to fund the deal himself. On December 18, SoftBank's Japanese mobile-phone arm went public in what was the second-biggest IPO ever, after Alibaba's. Masa expected the IPO to make him flush again, and he hoped to direct some of its proceeds toward Fortitude. "One hundred billion dollars is not nearly enough," he said, explaining why he needed more than the Vision Fund could offer. "My dreams are too big."

But the stock tanked, losing $3 billion in its first day of trading—one of the worst debuts in Japanese stock market history. Markets around the world were wracked by volatility as America's trade war with China dragged on, and stocks fell at a rate not seen since 2008. By late December, SoftBank stock itself was down more than a third since the summer, when Fortitude was just a vision in Masa's and Adam's heads.

On Christmas Eve, Masa called Adam from Maui, three islands to the east, where he was spending his holiday. Fortitude was dead, Masa said. The market crash had scared off potential investment partners and a deal of this size was simply too risky. Several financial institutions had placed margin calls on Masa's personal holdings after the dip in SoftBank's stock. His hands were tied.

Adam was stunned. His advisers had tried, at various points, to temper his expectations and warn him that Masa could be trusted only as far as WeWork was useful to him. But Masa had always seemed to be the only person who occupied the same reality distortion field as Adam. For several hours, Adam didn't share the news with Rebekah. He waited a day to call Berrent and Minson, to let them enjoy the holiday before sharing the disappointment. (Miguel, who was barely involved in the negotiations, was vacationing in New Zealand.) Adam was calm when he spoke to his deputies, and seemed to still believe he had a chance of winning his benefactor over. With Masa in Hawaii, everyone held out hope that maybe Adam could work his charm one last time.

On December 26, Adam flew to Maui for breakfast with Masa. SoftBank was already so deeply invested in WeWork that it made no sense for Masa to bail entirely on Adam. Both parties needed to save face. The $20 billion was off the table, but Masa agreed to invest an additional $2 billion. None of it would come from the Vision Fund.

Back in New York, Minson, Berrent, and several other executives interrupted their post-Christmas vacations to figure out what to do. They had never finished the S-1 document, which now had an urgency to it. WeWork's ten-year anniversary was coming up, and the company needed to file paperwork by the end of the year in order to maintain certain benefits the government gave to "young" companies. On December 28, WeWork confidentially sent a draft of its S-1 to the SEC. The moment Adam had hoped to avoid, and that his mentor had promised to help stave off, was approaching. "For Adam, to have this person who was like a father figure disappoint him like this—I can't emphasize how devastating that was," one of Neumann's top deputies said. "I don't think he ever really recovered. Almost all of his actions, from there to the end, tie back to that."

* * *

TWO WEEKS AFTER Fortitude fell apart, Adam sat for an interview on CNBC. He looked gaunt and haggard, his finger still in a brace after his surfing accident. He was seated next to Ashton Kutcher, who had made a 2010s pivot from playing stoners in movies and TV shows to playing the role of celebrity venture capitalist. Kutcher met Rebekah during her time in LA and had known Adam for a decade; Kutcher and his ex-wife, Demi Moore, had also been involved with the Kabbalah Centre. Kutcher had more or less given up acting since taking on the role of Steve Jobs in a 2013 biopic and was now running a venture capital firm called Sound Ventures along with Guy Oseary, the impresario best known for being Madonna's manager.

Kutcher wasn't invested in WeWork. CNBC's chyron listed him as a "WeWork strategic partner," and the company had brought Kutcher on to help reimagine the Creator Awards. (One idea was to judge a company's potential by mining WeWork visitor logs, to see which companies were getting visits from high-profile people.) Kutcher had struggled to understand how WeWork was a tech company like the ones that typically interested him, but said he had begun to change his mind. "When I actually got underneath the hood...I realized that it was a technology company," Kutcher said on CNBC. "I realized that through the technology that this company has, it has a greater capacity than any other company in the entire world to bring people together and to close that divide between the haves and the have-nots." Kutcher said that Fortitude's collapse was nothing to stress about. "It's the second-largest venture capital investment of all time!" Kutcher said of SoftBank's total investment in WeWork. "I'm an investor in Uber, so I know what the largest one was." Adam smiled and said that Kutcher would be receiving equity soon.

Neumann and Kutcher were in Los Angeles for WeWork Summit 2019, where the company was trying to spin the collapse of Fortitude as anything but a massive blow to its ever-loftier narrative. WeWork rented Universal Studios Hollywood again and had Diddy and Kutcher announce the winners of the Creator Awards. During his speech, Miguel wore a black T-shirt that read, simply, THE FUTURE IS AMAZING! Artie Minson walked onstage in a Hawaiian shirt, to the opening chords from Bob Marley's "Three Little Birds." He told WeWork's employees that he was there to ease their concerns. "How many of you have gotten emails, phone calls, texts about SoftBank pulling their investment?" Minson asked. "You can tell them your CFO walked out in a fucking Hawaiian shirt to tell you that every little thing is gonna be all right."

The line got a laugh, but WeWork's employees were nervous. The company had never been forced to tell its story from a chastened position. Adam got onstage and gave a roaming monologue explaining away the debacle, insisting that the news coming from outside the company was often "fake." He bragged about the new valuation that came with Masa's latest investment: $47 billion, pushing the company past SpaceX, Airbnb, and Juul to become the second most valuable private start-up in America, after Uber. There was some hesitation on the executive team about announcing the We Company rebrand without an appropriate amount of cash to back it up, but at a minimum, the change served as a distraction. Adam shared the original business plan he and Miguel had cooked up a decade earlier, with everything from WeSail to WeBank; the latter, he said, was on its way. The final component of the company's transformation was a new mission statement: "To elevate the world's consciousness."

The idea wasn't original to WeWork. In his book *Living Kabbalah: A Practical System for Making the Power Work for You*, Yehuda Berg, of the founding Kabbalah Centre family, described the center's goal as aiming to "elevate the consciousness of the entire world." The Neumanns had drifted away from Kabbalah, with Adam even reportedly referring to it as a cult. (In 2015, Berg and the Kabbalah Centre were forced to pay $177,500 to a former student at the Centre who claimed that Berg plied her with alcohol and prescription drugs with the intention of assaulting her.) But Rebekah had been taken enough with the idea, and with her recent interactions with Deepak Chopra, to propose the new mission statement. "The mission of WeGrow—and quite honestly the collective We that we're all living under—is elevating the world's consciousness," she had told an interviewer in the fall. The goal, Rebekah said, was for everyone to be "getting high on consciousness, instead of, you know, anything else."

For Rebekah, the assimilation of her personal belief system into WeWork presented a triumphant culmination of years spent figuring out how to mesh spirituality with business. Rebekah told her staff heading into Summit that she wanted to launch a podcast, and that the pilot would be an interview she conducted onstage at Summit with Anthony Kiedis, the lead singer of the Red Hot Chili Peppers.

The conversation quickly went off the rails. Rebekah asked Kiedis why his band had titled one of its albums *Mother's Milk*, then transitioned into a discussion of the importance of colostrum, the first breast milk that a mother produces after giving birth. Many employees squirmed in their seats. She asked Kiedis what it was like having an Israeli in his band — "I love Israelis — one in particular," Rebekah said, nodding to Adam in the audience — without noting the fact that the bandmate had died of a heroin overdose thirty years earlier.

The week in Los Angeles was a confusing one for many employees. Why, exactly, was Rebekah interviewing Anthony Kiedis? WeWork was worth more than ever, and the new investment would allow employees to cash out some of their shares, but it wasn't the windfall they had expected. Dividing up the company's business lines under the banner of the We Company made some sense, but the inscrutable mission statement was perplexing. They might have rolled their eyes when the company tossed around slogans like DO WHAT YOU LOVE and MAKE A LIFE, NOT A LIVING, but these were ideas that employees and members alike could get behind. In the wake of Ruby Anaya's lawsuit, and the company's ties to Saudi Arabia, and the struggles they were all having just keeping up with the pace of their jobs, it was more difficult to explain why they were all working so hard.

At Summit, Frances Frei, a Harvard Business School professor, gave a talk about her belief that companies often get in trouble when they began to "wobble" in one of three areas: authenticity, logic, and empathy. Wobbling was one way to describe how many WeWork employees felt a few weeks later, when they watched a new documentary on HBO about the rise and fall of Theranos. Both organizations depended on charismatic founders and stratified layers of information that left lower-level employees to hope that, somewhere, an adult was running the numbers. Theranos had no doctors on its board of directors; WeWork had no one from the world of real estate. WeWork employees took comfort in knowing that they provided a tangible service that customers liked, not blood tests that never really worked in the first place. But it gave them a creeping dread to watch their counterparts at another high-flying start-up find it increasingly hard to explain what exactly their company did.

One person at WeWork wasn't worried about the company's future. "Do you know how long it takes a diamond to be created?" Adam asked a reporter during Summit. "Half a million to four million years. I love that analogy—to make something very precious, you have to apply a lot of pressure."

CHAPTER TWENTY

The I in We

IN APRIL OF 2019, three months after the We Company began elevating the world's consciousness, I took a tour of the original WeWork, at 154 Grand Street in SoHo. It was a time capsule from another era, with Miguel's amateur wiring still lining the halls and WeWork's original stick-figure-smashing-a-computer logo pasted inside the painfully slow elevator. "We're never gonna be the best WeWork, but it's history now," Courtney Wallace, the building's community manager, told me as we squeezed through a narrow corridor lined with glass cubes. Wallace had been with the company since 2011 and couldn't believe how much We-Work had grown. He didn't think Adam was surprised. "Adam's ambition was limitless," Wallace said. "I would argue that Adam would say he's surprised it took so long."

Half a dozen tenants had kept offices at 154 Grand since it opened, nine years earlier, even though there were now many newer options nearby: one office at 154 Grand was being occupied by a WeWork employee who was managing the construction of a new location down the block. *New York* magazine had assigned me to write a feature story about WeWork, in part because Adam Neumann's empire seemed to be slowly closing in: there were suddenly a dozen WeWorks within a mile of the magazine's SoHo building, where Oscar Health, the health insurance provider founded by Josh Kushner, Jared's brother, had a brand new Powered by We office.

When I finished my tour of 154 Grand Street, I noticed that I had several missed calls from an unknown phone number. I stepped outside to call the number back. It belonged to a longtime WeWork executive who heard I was working on a story about the company. He was interested in sharing his experience, but hesitant to speak openly. He stood to benefit handsomely if WeWork successfully made it to an IPO; plus, he had seen how the company treated Joanna Strange and other employees who broke ranks. He believed the business was a good one, but found the ideas WeWork had been spinning up about being a tech company, or revolutionizing education, or improving corporate culture to be laughable. "WeWork has the worst corporate culture I've ever encountered in my life," he said. I heard a similar story from a former WeWork employee I met for an off-the-record conversation a few days later at a coffee shop in Dumbo, near the original Green Desk. "I've been involved in some of WeWork's previous puff pieces," he said when we sat down. He wanted to know if my article would be one of those.

As I spoke with more current and former WeWork employees, it was clear that many were indelibly marked by their time with the company. For some, WeWork had been among the most exhilarating experiences of their young lives, but also the most psychologically confusing. Many of those who left described their departure as if they had escaped Jonestown or Waco; those who remained were simply hopeful the company's IPO would arrive soon so they could cash out and move on.

The executive who called me while I was at 154 Grand had left a large corporation after WeWork made several attempts to recruit him. "Eventually I said, 'Fuck it. If half of what I'm hearing, and a fraction of what Adam says, is true, this is a rocket ship I want to be a part of," he said. Since then, the rocket ship had continued on its upward trajectory, and he understood all the reasons it could be a success, but he also believed a crash of some kind was imminent. The trouble for WeWork, he said, was that the company's greatest strengths, and its greatest flaws, came from the top. "Adam is a gifted sales-person," he said. "There's a cult of personality around him, and the cult factor is what keeps the machine going. It's what keeps everyone quiet." Adam's vision and the promises he made—to investors, to land-lords, to his employees—were WeWork's fuel. Even this executive was susceptible. When we met in person, at a hotel lobby bar, I couldn't help but notice that he still had a WeWork sticker on the back of his phone: DO WHAT YOU LOVE. What could he say? Adam was very convincing.

* * *

MANY OF NEUMANN'S colleagues in the real estate world were equally hesitant to speak up. They had seen plenty, and had all kinds of reasons to want to see Adam knocked back to earth. (One person connected me to a private investigator they had hired to dig up dirt on WeWork.) But practically every landlord had spent the past decade happily cashing WeWork's checks, and Adam's competitors were grate-ful that the flexible office space industry had such a capable prophet extolling a new way of managing corporate real estate. They couldn't explain WeWork's valuation, but they were all fearful that Adam might achieve his ambitions—nothing had stopped him thus far—and become even more powerful. No one wanted to be on his bad side. After I spoke to Preston Pesek, who ran Spacious, a small office-space provider in New York, he called me back to ask that certain critical statements be taken off the record in case Adam wanted to acquire his company. Three months later, Neumann paid $43 million to do just that.

As WeWork moved toward a potential IPO, those who had watched it defy the laws of business gravity for much of the past decade saw this as a moment of reckoning—not just for the company, but for the system. A few weeks after my visit to 154 Grand, I talked with Jake Schwartz, one of the cofounders of General Assembly, the Bezos-backed start-up that had ceded the coworking market to WeWork earlier in the decade. "What I didn't understand back then is that you could just take huge amounts of risk and be rewarded for it," Schwartz told me. "You see this a lot in real estate with people who aren't any smarter but are willing to put all their money on black 22—that was Trump's mode." General Assembly's education business was doing well, and Schwartz didn't have any regrets about abandoning coworking, especially after SoftBank entered the industry and warped its economics. He thought WeWork was a decent business, with a ton of revenue. He just didn't see how it could possibly be worth $47 billion.

But WeWork's rise didn't shock Schwartz, who had spent part of his career in finance. This was how the system worked. Adam had persuaded one investor after another to believe in his vision; each time he did, previous investors were able to mark up their stakes to escalating valuations, selling shares along the way and passing the risk on to the next fool. Even if WeWork went public and the IPO tanked, Adam owned roughly a fifth of the company, with preferred shares that would allow him to get out before most of his employees. "Let's say it trades down to a $5 billion valuation," Schwartz said, throwing out a number more in line with where the London Stock Exchange valued IWG. "Employees will suffer. Investors take a bath. But Adam's still worth a billion. So from an objective perspective, was it a mistake to play this long con and take on this hemorrhage-inducing risk? You could argue that was the rational mode."

What kept Schwartz up at night, at the end of a decade of unrestrained growth for the global economy, with enormous fortunes built out of nothing, was what WeWork's rise would signal to the next generation of entrepreneurs. "You get to a question of, is that what capitalism is supposed to do?" Schwartz asked. "There's so many little ways that a company like this tells the next generation of entrepreneurs what success looks like. One way to ask this question is, in the system we have set up, do the people who were successful reflect the values we want? Should we care, or not care, if someone makes a lot of money exploiting the system?" Schwartz didn't mind if Adam got rich; he wanted to get rich, too. "The reason I care is that if the most successful companies are the ones that just drive really hard, and play fast and loose with the truth," Schwartz said, "then maybe the whole idea that capitalism is great, or even useful, is really challenging to uphold."

* * *

"I THINK I'M GONNA CUT MY HAIR," Adam told me in his office at WeWork headquarters when we met in April of 2019. He had just shown me a black-and-white photograph from a decade earlier: he and Miguel, sitting next to each other, plotting the future of a company that didn't exist. Adam's hair was shorter back then, a cleaner look than the shoulder-length mane he had grown out since. With Fortitude dead, and a stock market debut on the horizon, Adam was thinking about going back to the way he looked when he and Miguel were still figuring everything out.

Adam told me he was enthusiastic about giving the public a look at WeWork's insides. "The numbers will speak for themselves," he said, repeating his long-standing trope about the company's future tracking with Amazon's. He was maintaining an air of privacy for now—"We have so many numbers we can't really share"—while insisting that he was ready to show his books to the world. "I think it's good to have a report card," Adam said.

But he was also in no rush. Earlier in the year, he told an executive he was trying to hire that WeWork would spend 2019 getting everything in order to go public in 2020. Adam was still dreaming big. I asked him about a poster conspicuously propped up against a couch in his office. It showed what seemed to be a futuristic WeCity with the date 2048 on it. "I should hide that," he said with a smile, telling me that he couldn't share any details except to say that it would actually be ready much sooner — by 2028.

Adam and Rebekah had spent the early months of the year on the West Coast, in their newest home: a $21 million house in Marin County previously owned by Bill Graham, the rock and roll promoter. It came with seven bedrooms, a pool with a waterslide, and a guitar-shaped room that had a small space where the headstock would be. The windows mapped out the opening chords to the Grateful Dead's "Friend of the Devil."

The Neumanns had several pieces of business to take care of on the West Coast. One day in early 2019, a member of WeWork's West Coast real estate team got a text from Adam, who was flying on Wildgoose I. For months, the team had been trying to find a space in Beverly Hills that would help WeWork break further into the entertainment business — and provide a home for Sound Ventures, Kutcher's investment firm. A potential location was 9830 Wilshire Boulevard, the former home of Creative Artists Agency, the Hollywood talent giant. The building was a monument to excess, designed by I. M. Pei with a giant Roy Lichtenstein mural in the atrium. WeWork's real estate team was skeptical that it made economic sense for the company, but from forty thousand feet, Adam gave simple instructions: close the deal.

In a matter of weeks, WeWork pushed through a lease that would typically have taken months, calling off the team responsible for conducting due diligence on new locations. The boss wanted the deal done. "It didn't make economic sense, but we did it anyway," an employee who worked on the project said.

Masa's war chest had become a double-edged sword when it came to negotiating with landlords, who knew that WeWork's real estate team was under enormous pressure to sign as many leases as it could. At 9830 Wilshire, WeWork was negotiating with Michael Ovitz, the CAA cofounder, who still co-owned the building. Ovitz was one of Hollywood's shrewdest dealmakers, and a young WeWork employee found himself reading Ovitz's memoir in a desperate attempt to find some negotiating angle. WeWork ultimately caved on various points to get the deal done, giving Ovitz veto authority over the type of wood they used and what the bathroom fixtures looked like, while agreeing to cover hundreds of thousands of dollars of mechanical work it never would have agreed to in more frugal days. On top of all the concessions, Sound Ventures was expected to occupy some of the space for two years without paying rent. By the time the lease was signed, the WeWork team realized the deal was so bad it would likely never make money.

WeWork was showing little sign of reining in its ambitions in advance of an IPO. WeLive still had only two locations—in 2014, the company had projected it would have sixty-nine by now—but the team was working on deals around the world, including one that would involve converting a Miami Beach hotel. Adam considered buying IWG, his longtime rival, and nearly paid $1.3 billion for BGIS, one of the largest building operation companies in the world. Several members of WeWork's West Coast team, already buckling under the pressure to meet its office-leasing goals, went to Montana to scout land to develop a Summer Camp for members, possibly with a Wavegarden surf pool as a central attraction. In March, Adam hired a Google executive, along with a friend who worked as a designer, to begin conceptualizing WeCities—2028 was just around the corner. In early 2019, Jared Kushner called Adam to ask for his help prepping a video to accompany a "Peace to Prosperity" summit in Bahrain in June, to promote economic growth in Palestine. WeWork's public affairs team balked at the idea, but Adam gave the job to Roni Bahar, one of his Israeli executives, who helped find an advertising firm to work on the clip. At the summit, Kushner screened the video—trees rise up from the rubble, blooms sprout in the desert—for the event's attendees. Masa was there, as was and Steve Mnuchin, America's treasury secretary, who compared Gaza to a "hot IPO."

Rebekah, meanwhile, spent the Neumann's time on the West Coast looking to expand WeGrow. The school's original location was being renovated to double its capacity for the fall, and Rebekah aspired to have a school in every city that had a WeWork, so that anyone with a "WeGrow Global Membership" could bring their kids with them around the world. WeWork's real estate team was sent looking for a Bay Area location that fit Rebekah's specifications. She wanted it to be close to nature, so they looked in Marin County, but she also wanted it to be close to the rest of the WeWork community, so they looked back in San Francisco. When they found a promising spot on the Embarcadero, Rebekah expressed concern that an earthquake would destroy the school.

The search felt like a distraction given the speed at which WeWork's real estate team was being asked to find new office space, but the line between WeWork's needs and the Neumanns' had become increasingly blurry. During their West Coast stint, the Neumanns pulled several WeGrow teachers out of the school to serve as private tutors for their children. Back in New York, one of WeGrow's teachers took Rebekah's absence as an opportunity to help another student. The Neumanns' eldest daughter was the lead singer and played piano in WeGrow's student rock band, and the family's sabbatical in Marin left the group without a frontwoman. The teacher approached an eight-year-old girl at the school who had been struggling, and asked if she might like to give singing a try. The girl didn't play an instrument, which was a requirement for joining the band, but the teacher thought they could make an exception. The girl agreed and almost instantly started thriving.

When Rebekah learned of the decision, she overruled it.. The change had broken protocol, she said. Rules were rules. The girl was removed from the band, and Rebekah's daughter returned to the microphone.

* * *

ONE AFTERNOON IN early May, while reporting my story for *New York* magazine, I visited the headquarters of Thrive Global, Arianna Huffington's company dedicated to "ending the stress and burnout epidemic." In 2018, Huffington hired WeWork to redesign Thrive's office as part of a new product line, Headquarters by WeWork—a sort of Powered by We lite. When Huffington greeted me, she also said hello to a member of WeWork's communications team who was tasked with following me around. Huffington had just been speaking with his boss, Jimmy Asci, WeWork's new head of communications. Asci had previously worked with Travis Kalanick from Uber, where Huffington was a board member. "I got to know Jimmy when he was representing Travis at Uber over a big crisis," Huffington said. "So a big bond was formed."

I spent the week leading up to the publication of my article battling WeWork's communications team. They insisted that Adam had never installed a vent allowing him to smoke pot in his office, that he had sold no more than $200 million of his WeWork stock, and that Rebekah had not tried to micromanage the WeGrow rock band. (They did say I could report that Laird Superfood was "killing it.") When I reported that Adam told another WeWork executive that his next start-up would likely be in the field of increasing human life spans, they said Adam had no such intention, because he did not plan to run another company. He expected to be CEO of WeWork for as long as he could.

WeWork employees told me that they read my story, which ran under the headline "The I in We," with a strange sense of relief. It was a comfort to know that the experiences they were having in one corner of the WeWork universe seemed to be symptoms of something broader. We chose the title because almost every story anyone told about their experience at WeWork came back to Adam, for good or otherwise. "Adam *is* WeWork," Francis Lobo, the former chief revenue officer, told me then. "He's one-quarter crazy, one-quarter brilliant, and the other half is a fight between his ego and genuinely caring for people. If Adam were hit by a bus tomorrow, I would look to sell my equity."

After "The I in We" was published, in June, WeWork's public relations team admitted to me that my interview with Adam had been unusually awkward. His charm had worked on many journalists over the years; for every reporter who pressed him to explain the company's financials, there was another eager to tell his story of technological disruption and the community-building effects of narrow hallways. A reporter for *Haaretz*, an Israeli newspaper, published a profile of Adam in 2017, then left a few months later to take a job at WeWork.

When I interviewed Adam, WeWork was launching a new investment fund called ARK, to replace WeWork Property Advisors. (Adam said the name stood for "Adam, Rebekah, and Kids," but when Bloomberg reported the acronym, a spokesman claimed it actually meant "Asset, Return, Kicker.") ARK would allow WeWork to buy more property, and its existence had reinvigorated interest in Adam's ownership of the IBM building and other WeWork properties. Adam dismissed concerns that this represented a conflict of interest; he had simply been putting his money where his mouth was to show other landlords that WeWork could be a worthy tenant. He was planning to sell the real estate back to ARK at cost, which he presented as a sacrifice. "I'm a great real estate buyer, so if bought for $100, it's probably worth $300," he told Bloomberg.

His personal interests were aligned with the company's, Adam said, repurposing the line he had delivered to Josh Simmons in the company's early days: "WeWork is me; I am WeWork." Despite cashing out hundreds of millions of dollars' worth of his stock, Adam was still WeWork's biggest shareholder. "My stock makes so much more money," he told me, relative to the rent he collected from his company. "I should buy more WeWork stock if I want to make money."

"I wish I had some," I joked.

"It's not too late," Adam said. "There's still a lot of upside."

CHAPTER TWENTY-ONE

Wingspan

A FEW DAYS after my interview with Adam, he and Rebekah boarded Wild-goose I with their five kids to begin a three-week-long globe-spanning trip in celebration of Adam's fortieth birthday. WeWork employees had report-edly spent three days downloading TV shows and movies for the Neumann children to watch on the plane, which had been retrofitted to add two bathrooms. (The Neumanns reimbursed the company for their personal travel.) The family flew to the Dominican Republic for a week of surfing before heading across the Atlantic at the end of April. Adam canceled a stop in Israel, where he was planning to show off his ancestral home to a *Fast Company* reporter as part of a forthcoming profile. Adam was nervous, but not about meeting yet another journalist. The Neumann's youngest child wasn't vaccinated, and a flight attendant on El Al, the Israeli airline, had just come down with measles, which had been spreading around the globe.

Instead, the Neumanns flew to the Maldives, an island nation five hundred miles south of India's southern tip, where they invited two dozen family and friends, including Michael Gross, to join them for Adam's birthday. The Neumanns rented out a chic beachfront resort with exclusive access to Pasta Point, a local surf break, and parked a yacht for themselves offshore. They requested that anyone who brought their children on the trip bring their nannies as well.

While Adam was in the Maldives, WeWork's executive team was figuring out the company's next move. Adam and Artie had fought over what to do as they moved toward a potential public offering. Artie argued it was wise to rein in the company's spending, shore up its finances, and prepare to go public. Managers were being asked to trim head counts and bring "discipline" to their spending. WeWork's board rejected Adam's attempt to buy Remote Year, a platform to help digital nomads find places to sleep and work around the world. The Creator Awards were shelved after one last show in Seoul, and Summer Camp 2019 was canceled. On April 1, WeWork got rid of the extravagant fees it had been paying to brokers; its battered rivals worried that the change might be an April Fools' joke.

Adam, however, said that WeWork should continue expanding. The company was becoming so large, he argued, that landlords would have to play ball if money got tight—the "too big to fail" argument. "If I say 'pencils down' to my people, the value of buildings will plunge," Adam reportedly said in one meeting. He was at least partly right. In mid-April, S&P Global Ratings declared that there was more than $3 billion in commercial mortgage debt securities at risk of default if the company collapsed.

The uncertainty made late April a complicated moment for Adam to go surfing halfway around the world. He remained in constant contact with executives back in New York, who were getting on calls with Adam in the middle of the night. But the nine-hour time difference between the Maldives and New York made things difficult. Adam went dark to observe Shabbat just as the team in New York woke up on Friday morning, and he eventually had one of his deputies fly to the Maldives to help him in person.

On the phone, Artie told Adam that he and WeWork's finance team were preparing to meet with investment banks in New York in early May to begin selecting one of them to manage WeWork's IPO process. Now was the time to go, Artie and others argued. WeWork would need a fresh infusion of capital sometime in the next year to fund its growth, and the markets were on the rise after the late-2018 dip that helped scuttle Fortitude. A bumper crop of other companies that had also spent the decade gulping from the venture capital fire hose—Uber, Lyft, Slack, Beyond Meat—were all going public. Zoom, the videoconferencing software provider, had just listed its shares, which shot up 72 percent on their first day of trading. WeWork didn't want to miss its moment, and Artie wanted to make sure to get ahead of any leaks, so WeWork could make the case that it was going public at a moment of strength, not desperation.

Adam remained uncertain, but there were few other options. On April 29, as Adam finished up his birthday celebration in the middle of the Indian Ocean, WeWork officially announced that it was preparing for an IPO.

* * *

THE NEWS WAS THRILLING for WeWork's employees. After years of accumulating stock options without knowing what they would add up to, and the brief tease of Fortitude, the chance to cash in was now at hand. Employees began talking about buying apartments, paying off debt, or leaving for a new job. Many who saw themselves as financially savvy advised their colleagues to buy their options now, as a way of reducing their capital gains tax when the time came to sell their shares. Some took out tens of thousands of dollars in loans to do just that. The "personal finance" channel on WeWork's Slack site, where employees typically chatted about credit scores and 401(k) plans, changed its name to cover the topic to which many employees were tying their financial futures: "IPO News."

When Adam returned to New York from the Maldives, his mood toward the IPO had shifted. He would prefer to stay private, but with the decision made, and the financial press alight with chatter about the offering, Adam seemed more at peace with it. WeWork executives wanted to take advantage of his change of heart and move quickly; the more time he had to reconsider, the more likely it was that he would change his mind. Artie was also worried that a summer spent hobnobbing with potential investors in the Hamptons would give Adam too many opportunities to say things he shouldn't. WeWork set a goal of going public by the end of July—the 18th felt like a lucky target date.

This was ambitious. A member of the IPO prep team grew concerned after chatting with a senior member of the team leading Slack's looming IPO, who said they had spent the previous six months doing almost nothing but preparing for this moment. Several members of WeWork's finance team, which was filled with recent arrivals from large public companies, were shocked the company thought it was ready to present its books for public scrutiny so quickly. They had just flown thousands of employees to California for a conference that featured a performance by the Red Hot Chili Peppers. Where was the fiscal responsibility the market would demand? "We all thought, We are not a company that is capable of doing this right now," one member of the finance team said.

Not long after the IPO announcement, a team from WeWork met with employees at Imagination, a marketing firm that helps companies prepare the front-facing parts of going public. When the WeWork team explained its timeline, the employees from Imagination laughed. Finishing everything that needed to be done, with the requisite approvals from the SEC, would be impossible to pull off that quickly. But it had never been WeWork's way to accept norms or restrictions. "It says everything about WeWork," an employee on the WeWork team said, "that the response from the top was, If you can't do this the WeWork way, we'll go somewhere else."

* * *

TWO WEEKS AFTER WeWork announced its IPO, an omen appeared. Adam had told me in his office that he would be watching Uber's stock market debut with particular interest; the companies shared not only investors, in both Benchmark and SoftBank, but a habit of burning cash. WeWork and Uber had both lost nearly $2 billion in 2018—a shocking deficit well beyond anything Amazon, the ultimate money-losing behemoth, had ever managed. Uber's debut would provide a gauge of the market's appetite for investing in unprofitable enterprises.

On May 10, Uber listed its shares on the New York Stock Exchange and promptly suffered one of the worst opening days of trading ever. The dip was troubling to everyone at WeWork, and at SoftBank. Masa had poured billions into WeWork and Uber at the peak of their private valuations. SoftBank's Uber shares were now underwater, just as Masa was pitching investors on joining a second $100 billion Vision Fund. He could scarcely afford a repeat.

Adam thought he knew how to avoid Uber's fate. When the ride-sharing company announced its first post-IPO earnings, at the end of May, it reported not only that its losses continued to mount but also that it had experienced its slowest growth in years. This was typical for companies leading up to an IPO, as they tried to showcase fiscal restraint. But Adam told others that he believed the diminishing growth had spooked investors. WeWork, he said, would double down. The company was opening two new locations a day, signing dozens of new leases each week, and onboarding a hundred employees every Monday. If things went according to Adam's plan, WeWork would wow investors with gobsmacking growth numbers in the second half of the year, spending freely along the way in order to expand faster than it ever had before.

* * *

THE FINANCIAL PRESS tends to treat IPOs as mini Super Bowls—a bonanza for investors, founders, and longtime employees, as well as a moment for casual stock traders at home to consider whether a new company might be the next Apple or Amazon that would pay for their children's college education. As a practical matter, an IPO is simply a way for a company to find money when doing so privately is no longer possible. WeWork was hoping to raise $3 billion from public investors to continue funding its growth; the company would need even more in commitments to make sure it hit that mark as investors bought and sold their shares. Doing so would require not only wooing the amateur traders watching CNBC for fun but more importantly the institutional investors capable of funding large chunks of an IPO. Unlike Benchmark or Masa, pension and mutual fund managers weren't going to risk their jobs on a gut feeling. They wanted to see the numbers.

The most important number to sort out was a fundamental one: How much was WeWork actually worth? A dirty secret of the start-up boom was the fact that private market valuations were all but meaningless, bearing little connection to how much money a company made or what economic value it created. They were hazy calculations backed as much by feelings as by math. In competitive situations, like WeWork's early fundraising rounds, venture capital firms were often willing to puff up valuations in order to entice founders to take their money instead of somebody else's. As the rounds went from Series A to B to C, bigger numbers begat even bigger ones.

Masa's arrival had pushed WeWork's valuation into even more inscrutable territory. No one could compete with SoftBank to invest billions into WeWork, which meant that the $47 billion valuation—three times what Hony Capital and others had invested at in 2016—was more or less an agreement between Adam and Masa alone. The details behind WeWork's latest valuation were even murkier. Of the $2 billion Masa had agreed to invest in Maui, half was marked at the $47 billion figure, while the other half went toward buying out existing shareholders at a much lower price: $23 billion, only a slight increase over the price SoftBank paid in 2017.

When the deal terms were finalized, some WeWork executives thought it would be prudent to publicize the lower figure, or perhaps a "blended valuation" between the two. The $47 billion number put a target on WeWork's back, and even some of the company's early supporters were skeptical. T. Rowe Price, which had grown frustrated with the SoftBank-fueled growth, tried to sell as much of its stock as it could at the beginning of the year, and priced the remainder of its shares at $25 billion. In April, Fidelity quietly marked its stake to a valuation of just $18 billion. When Adam met with a group of Fidelity portfolio managers in Boston over the summer, wearing his signature T-shirt and jeans, they told him Fidelity was on the fence about investing in WeWork's IPO at all.

But neither Masa nor Adam had much incentive to be modest. Masa was trying to raise money for his second Vision Fund, and a supersize valuation for one of his prized investments allowed SoftBank to boast about spectacular results, at least on paper. Adam, meanwhile, took particular pride in the fact that the new valuation, and Uber's IPO, made WeWork the most valuable private start-up in America. He pressed WeWork's communications team to push the $47 billion number, and Artie Minson told others that WeWork would go public above $50 billion. Adam told the *Wall Street Journal* that watching Masa do the math necessary to come up with WeWork's valuation had been "beautiful to see."

* * *

THEY HAD REASON TO FEEL BULLISH. The world's biggest banks had spent years cozying up to Adam and WeWork as the company moved toward an IPO. The most coveted role in such an offering is the "lead left" position, which goes to the bank with primary responsibility for telling WeWork how to sell itself and offering its stamp of approval to potential investors. The winning bank's name is printed in the left-most position among the banks involved in the offering, and it receives the bulk of the roughly $100 million in fees that would accompany an IPO of WeWork's size.

In May, WeWork held a "bake off" among three firms—JPMorgan, Goldman Sachs, and Morgan Stanley—for the lead left position. JPMorgan was the top candidate, given the bank's long history with WeWork. In addition to its 2014 investment, JPMorgan had assisted WeWork with various loans and other financing arrangements. The bank had also lent Adam $97 million in low-interest mortgages for the many homes that the Neumanns were buying, and helped facilitate a personal $500 million line of credit backed by Adam's WeWork stock. Adam had taken to calling Jamie Dimon his "personal banker." When it came time for JPMorgan to make its pitch for the lead left position, its bankers suggested that WeWork could go public at a valuation north of $46 billion and as high as $63 billion.

Morgan Stanley's pitch to WeWork was led by Michael Grimes, who had helped the firm land some of the biggest tech IPOs of the decade. (He won Uber's business after moonlighting as a driver.) A year earlier, a team from Morgan Stanley had advised WeWork on a possible private round of funding, before Fortitude, and said that investors could potentially be targeting a future IPO valuation of as much as $104 billion. But Grimes and his team gave a more sober presentation at the bake-off in May, suggesting a potential valuation between $18 billion and $52 billion, depending on how well WeWork could explain its path to profitability for skeptical investors.

In the second week of May, a few days before Uber listed its shares at a valuation above $70 billion, Goldman Sachs gave its presentation to WeWork with a huge top-end valuation: $96 billion. The bank had battled JPMorgan for Adam's affection over the years. Lloyd Blankfein, Goldman's recently departed chairman, introduced Adam at the charity dinner that he spoke at in December, and his successor, David Solomon—an eccentric by Wall Street standards, performing at nightclubs and music festivals under the name DJ D-Sol—visited WeWork headquarters in early 2019. (Adam told others that DJ D-Sol's music was played at a dinner that he and Michael Gross had with Solomon.) Its presentation to the company spared no hyperbole, comparing Adam's lofty ambitions to those shared by Steve Jobs, Mother Teresa, and Bob Marley, whom they quoted: "Love the life you live/live the life you love." At the time, Apple was the only company in the world that had been valued at more than a trillion dollars, but Goldman's presentation to WeWork had a slide laying out "Your path to $1 trillion." They compared the company favorably to Salesforce, Alibaba, Google, and Amazon with an ego-boosting modifier: "You are scaling faster."

The banks all knew that Adam remained hesitant about going public, and while Goldman was pitching WeWork on an IPO, it also offered one last chance to avoid doing so. While Adam was living in the Bay Area, he started talking with a senior Goldman executive about the possibility of a debt financing package similar in magnitude to Fortitude. The deal called for WeWork to open a credit line of up to $10 billion, using the cash flow from WeWork's buildings as collateral—an unusual financing arrangement of the kind in which Goldman specialized. "If you need brain surgery, you go to the best in the world," Adam told colleagues. WeWork wouldn't need to go public as part of the deal, but when it did, Goldman would likely get the lead left position.

Minson and other WeWork executives were skeptical. Even for Goldman, it was a significant amount to devote to a single investment. But Adam wanted to forge ahead, and into the summer, the Goldman bankers hashed out terms with WeWork. At the beginning of July, Stephen Scherr, Goldman's CFO, told WeWork that the firm was in. But as some of the final terms came together over the Fourth of July holiday, both sides got cold feet, and the deal fell apart.

Adam turned back to JPMorgan. In a meeting, Jamie Dimon told Adam he would put a team together to work on a similar debt deal on the condition that Adam didn't go back to Goldman. By the end of July, the two sides had sketched out a $6 billion loan package, backed by various banks, but with a catch; it would become available only if WeWork successfully went public and raised at least $3 billion. For JPMorgan, it would mean not only a $50 million fee but also the lead left slot. For Adam, it meant that successfully going public would give him access to $9 billion to fund his vision for the We Company.

* * *

DURING HIS WEST COAST SWING, earlier in the year, Adam had made another attempt at enmeshing WeWork into the ecosystem of tech giants he aspired to join. Elon Musk wasn't taking any more meetings with WeWork, but Adam and Michael Gross went fishing for potential partnerships. They talked about building an office-management app with Salesforce, and with Apple about ways to use iPhones as access devices to WeWork spaces. Adam and Bruce Dunlevie had dinner with Ruth Porat, the CFO of Alphabet, in the hope of enticing her to join WeWork's board.

But as each of the discussions grew closer to WeWork's impending IPO, Adam pushed the conversations in that direction. No one had raised private capital in the 2010s as successfully as Neumann, and he became less concerned about the specifics of what WeWork could offer potential partners and more focused on pushing his fellow CEOs to commit to investing in his IPO. Even a token commitment from Salesforce or Apple would go a long way toward building support for the story Adam was telling to investors.

In the spring, Adam secured a meeting with Tim Cook, Apple's CEO. Neumann and Gross worked with Adrian Perica, Apple's vice president of corporate development, and Luca Maestri, Apple's CFO, to develop a pitch to Cook on a collaboration that could lead Apple—which was already invested in WeWork through the Vision Fund—to invest in WeWork's IPO. When he visited Cupertino, Adam wore a T-shirt under a blazer and brought his dad. Cook and Neumann talked for ninety minutes. But the deal never happened. It was never clear to either side how they could collaborate.

On the last day of July, with word of the JPMorgan debt financing leaking out, WeWork held a three-hour "analyst day" at 85 Broad Street, the former Goldman Sachs tower where Adam had once hoped to open his penthouse club. The analysts would decide how much their firms might put into the IPO and what price they'd be willing to pay. Adam had been largely muzzled for two months by SEC rules that prohibited him from speaking publicly about the company's prospects in advance of an IPO, but he now had a chance to get back in front of a crowd, where he was most comfortable. Rebekah sat in the front row, having selected the backing track to accompany a two-minute sizzle reel kicking off the event: Macklemore's "Can't Hold Us," with the refrain "This is the moment / Tonight is the night / We'll fight 'til it's over."

More than a hundred investors packed the room. Adam repeated his assertion that the right analogy for WeWork was Amazon—and by that comparison, WeWork looked like a steal. It had become difficult for WeWork's executives to appraise the company's status since the blow from Fortitude's collapse, and they nervously scanned the room to gauge the reception to Adam's speech. They were relieved by the lack of tough questions and noticed that several analysts even came up to Adam afterward to ask for a selfie with him. The event was a success and gave everyone a jolt of confidence. After a hectic few months, it looked like this might actually work.

*　*　*

WEWORK WAS NOW IN A SPRINT to get ready to go public. July had come and gone, and now even August was unlikely. The company's internal projections had it running out of money before the end of the year, so the imperative to find more cash was high. Adam set a new goal of going public before Rosh Hashanah, at the end of September. They would shoot for the 18th.

The document at the heart of an IPO is the S-1, a typically dry financial report filed with the SEC. WeWork submitted a draft of its S-1 at the end of 2018, after Fortitude fell apart, but it needed to fine-tune the document to make sure that it presented the company's best side, while passing scrutiny from the SEC and acknowledging any risks that public investors should be made aware of. As one example: WeWork's S-1 mentioned that its business could be adversely affected by "natural disasters, public health crises, political crises or other unexpected events."

The code name for the S-1 was Wingspan—a bird taking flight and leaving its flock behind. Everything at the company now seemed to have a code name, including a marketing campaign called Stark, which was named after either the eccentric billionaire who had just died in the final Avengers movie or the doomed family from *Game of Thrones*. (Adam was a fan of both.) WeWork converted a quiet library space near Adam's office on the sixth floor of company headquarters into a "war room" for the team responsible for writing various parts of Wingspan. WeWork had waited until the last possible moment to hire JPMorgan, which had left Wingspan's development to proceed without the benefit of a banker leading the effort. A team of WeWork executives took turns crafting different sections of the document explaining WeWork's business, then tried to figure out how to make all the parts fit together. One person involved in the process referred to it as a "Frankenstein monster."

The encroachment of more outside advisers seemed to turn Adam toward the circle of people he trusted most—namely Rebekah. To this point, Rebekah had largely operated at the fringes of the company, managing projects like WeWork Studios or WeGrow that stood apart from WeWork's core business. But as Wingspan got off the ground, Rebekah was inserted into the middle of the process. As bankers and lawyers worked through the financial minutiae, Rebekah set about directing Wingspan's artistic presentation. Aesthetics are not typically given much thought in the production of an S-1; the process is hectic already, and there isn't much point to beautifying a document filled with hundreds of pages of charts and footnotes and financial disclosures written in tiny print.

But branding had been key to WeWork's rise, and both Adam and

Rebekah had internalized a belief that the company would only be successful if its backers understood that there was an energy coursing through WeWork that numbers couldn't convey. As Wingspan came together, Rebekah popped in and out of meetings to complain that the document was getting weighted down with numbers. "We've got to tell the story of 'We,'" she told one group of employees.

Rebekah devoted much of her attention over the summer to the creation of a photo spread that would appear in the middle of the S-1, squeezed between a section explaining WeWork's business and another listing "Quantitative and Qualitative Disclosures About Market Risks." Rebekah wanted to approve every photo, and there was no shortage of photographers the company could have tapped from the WeWork community they spoke so proudly about. But Rebekah thought they should think bigger: Could they get Steven Klein, who regularly shot for *Vogue*? (WeWork also hired a former director of photography from *Vanity Fair* magazine to send photographers to reshoot the company's locations around the world, because Adam Kimmel didn't like the way its existing photography looked; Alexei Hay, a high-end photographer who was Kimmel's stepbrother, also took new headshots for WeWork's executives.) The cost of the many shoots required to pull off the Wingspan spread quickly escalated: WeWork spent hundreds of thousands of dollars on the artwork alone. "Rebekah treated it like the September issue of *Vogue*," one WeWork executive said.

The resulting thirty-seven-page spread featured portraits of Ron Howard and Brian Grazer at a Los Angeles WeWork; the CEO of Zoom working on a laptop in San Jose; Arianna Huffington chatting casually with Adam Kimmel; and a community manager leaping off a couch in WeWork's new Johannesburg location. The final image showed Adam with his arms spread wide as confetti rained down all around him after announcing the winners of the most recent Creator Awards.

Rebekah's team went through drafts and drafts of the Wingspan art. She insisted that the document be printed on recycled paper, then rejected early versions as low quality with an unpleasant texture, setting the already harried process back again. So many visual tweaks were being made that an employee at the printer eventually yelled at their WeWork counterpart, "It's a financial document!" The SEC's filing system alerted it each time any tweak was made to the S-1, and they had called the printer to request that it push WeWork to cut back on its artistic changes.

On several occasions, WeWork executives pressed Adam on Rebekah's involvement in Wingspan. Adam understood some of their concerns; several executives said they overheard Adam and Rebekah get into a shouting match over Rebekah's ever-expanding list of roles, which had ballooned to include "co-founder, chief brand and impact officer, founder and CEO of WeGrow." But Adam ultimately said that Rebekah had his blessing to control her part of the Wingspan process. He and Rebekah went back and forth on what image should appear on Wingspan's final page, at the end of more than a hundred pages of appendixes. They wanted Wingspan to emphasize the company's commitment to sustainability; at one point, Rebekah told a group of employees that the only reason WeWork was going public was "to save the planet." She and Adam thought about closing the prospectus with an image of an ocean swell, but they worried about the symbolism of a crashing wave. Instead, they settled on a photograph of a forest in Belize that the Neumanns had recently purchased for the purpose of conservation. After all the back-and-forth, employees working on Wingspan began to worry that the energy being directed toward branding was a distraction. Some of them started to wonder if perhaps distraction was the point.

* * *

IN ADDITION TO explaining how a company makes money, a critical part of any S-1 is to offer an explanation for how a company operates, and what controls are in place to assure investors that a steady hand is at the wheel.

WeWork's lawyers at Skadden, Arps advised the company on the kinds of governance concerns that public investors had. In August, Neumann put the IBM building on the market, trying to belatedly eliminate one conflict of interest. And while some start-up founders were able to hold onto the supervoting shares they had received in early funding rounds, public investors tended to look with more caution at CEOs who exerted too much control.

Adam wanted to maintain as much as he could. He had begun working with attorneys at the law firm Paul, Weiss, including Bob Schumer, the younger brother of Senator Chuck Schumer, who helped him to press for greater control of the company. Adam wanted to boost his voting power from ten votes per share to twenty, to ensure he maintained control as a bevy of new shareholders bought in. The Neumanns pushed for a clause that would allow Rebekah to choose Adam's successor. Bruce Dunlevie and others pressed back on the idea, and an agreement was made that Rebekah would make the choice alongside two members of WeWork's board.

The succession plan brought to mind comments Adam had made to employees back in January, at WeWork's Summit in Los Angeles, when he told them not to worry about the company having to bend to the whims of the public markets. WeWork was a "controlled company," he said, by which he meant that "I, Adam, and my family control the company—100 percent." Adam said he intended to maintain that control long after his time at the company came to an end. WeWork was "not just controlled...we're generationally controlled." He didn't necessarily expect his children, or their children, to become the future CEOs of WeWork, but he wanted his descendants to keep their shares in the company and ensure that WeWork remained on the path he laid out for it. "It's important," Adam said, "that one day, maybe in one hundred years, maybe in three hundred years, a great-great-granddaughter of mine will walk into that room and say, 'Hey, you don't know me—I actually control the place. The way you're acting is not how we built it.'"

In mid-August, a few days before Wingspan's scheduled release, Noah Wintroub, the JPMorgan banker who had first begun wooing Neumann back in 2010, called Minson and Berrent to say that Jamie Dimon was planning to press Adam on the governance issues before the S-1 was finalized. "He's got to be firm," Artie said of the need for Dimon to push Neumann.

Adam met with Dimon at JPMorgan headquarters. Dimon recommended that Adam make several changes to the company's governance structure. Bankers at Goldman Sachs, which was assisting with the offering, had made a similar argument to Adam during an earlier meeting at the Neumanns' home in the Hamptons. Adam asked whether Dimon meant to say that he *couldn't* proceed like this, or *shouldn't*. Dimon told him that JPMorgan could get the deal into the market either way—it's what they did best. But he warned that Adam's level of control would likely depress its value. Adam considered the risk, and decided to stand his ground. He believed in himself and had succeeded in large part by ignoring conventional wisdom. Why start listening now?

* * *

EVEN BY WEWORK'S STANDARDS, prepping Wingspan had been chaotic. Each week brought a fresh emergency in need of an instant solution. WeWork's executive team sometimes struggled to get Adam to focus on the intricacies of going public—all the tiny details necessary to make sure the offering went off without a hitch—while he chased investors in Silicon Valley or tried to stave off the IPO with Goldman Sachs. The Neumanns spent part of the summer working with a branding consultant, Jonathan Mildenhall, who had Adam and Rebekah consider various "archetypes" by which they could think about their roles going forward. Mildenhall agreed with Rebekah's self-assessment: she was a "muse." One of the identities Adam considered was a "magician."

For a couple fast approaching the most critical financial moment of their lives, the Neumanns were strangely at ease. Rebekah spent much of the summer managing Wingspan's aesthetics from the Neumanns' home in Amagansett. Employees made the six-hour round-trip drive to and from Manhattan so many times that they came up with a euphemism that would explain to their colleagues where they were going for the day: "I'll be out East." When one executive went out East to meet with Adam in the Hamptons, Adam pushed the meeting back two hours because he wanted them to go surfing first.

Rebekah spent the days leading up to Wingspan's release tinkering with a pithy epigraph that would appear on the first page of the prospectus. This was a largely superfluous task to fill a page that analysts would glance at on their way to the numbers and models and disclosures necessary to sort out how much the company was worth. Uber's statement had been simple, if vague: "We ignite opportunity by setting the world in motion." Several members of the Wingspan team thought Slack's message offered an ideal mix of ambition and practicality: "Our mission is to make people's working lives simpler, more pleasant and more productive."

The task was complicated for WeWork by the fact that it had become increasingly difficult to define what exactly the company did. WeWork's communications team had struggled for much of 2019 to write a simple one-page company narrative. "We are captivated by the limitless potential of We," read one attempt. The We Company rebranding, under the banner of elevating the world's consciousness, had gone so poorly that some members of the Wingspan team wanted to leave the phrase out entirely; even Adam wasn't sure about it anymore. "Whenever WeWork had its voice right, and we were at our best, we sounded like we were trying to channel Barack Obama," a person who helped write parts of Wingspan said. "At our worst, we sounded like Marianne Williamson."

When Rebekah presented her final draft of the epigraph, several of the bankers, lawyers, and executives working on Wingspan balked. It didn't seem like the best way to begin a lengthy financial document. But when

Wingspan was unveiled to the public, just after 7:00 a.m. on August 14, 2019, potential investors were greeted by an otherwise empty off-white page with the following inscription in the center:

WE DEDICATE THIS
TO THE ENERGY OF WE—
GREATER THAN ANY ONE OF US
BUT INSIDE EACH OF US.

CHAPTER TWENTY-TWO

Always Half Full

ON AUGUST 22, eight days after Wingspan's release, Nicole Parlapiano, We-Work's head of US marketing, met with several sales representatives from Google to map out WeWork's advertising plan heading into 2020. Like every other fast-growing start-up with a hefty marketing budget, WeWork often paid to place advertisements atop relevant searches ("office space," "coworking") as well as queries for the names of its competitors. But the Google employees presented WeWork with a troubling report. "Google said this is the most alarming negative sentiment trend they have seen compared to prior companies in similar situations," Parlapiano wrote to her colleagues the next day.

Google was motivated to nudge companies toward buying their way out of difficult news cycles by burying bad press with paid ads. But the Google reps said the reaction to Wingspan had been so overwhelmingly critical that even SoftBank's largesse couldn't get WeWork out of this hole. Parlapiano told her coworkers that in this "very challenging" environment any attempt to redirect the company's narrative would require WeWork to "blow through our weekly paid search budget in a few hours." She offered a note of condolence to Jimmy Asci and the company's PR team.

Parlapiano sent her email to only a handful of people, but it spread around the company, backing up what everyone already knew: Wingspan was a flop. WeWork had largely avoided negative press over the years, with only occasional hiccups—the battle with the cleaners' union, Ruby Anaya's lawsuit—and nothing like the six-month public relations nightmare that overwhelmed Travis Kalanick and Uber in 2017. Bruce Dunlevie, from Benchmark, had lived through that experience and wasn't eager to do so again. "We haven't really had a torpedo below the waterline," Dunlevie told Katrina Brooker, a reporter at *Fast Company*, in April. While millions of people used Uber every day, WeWork still had only a few hundred thousand members, which meant that most of the public had never been inside one of its spaces. Many people had never even heard of the company.

Now, all at once, they were learning about WeWork's long-haired founder, who had been given the largest private valuation in America after spending money at never-before-seen rates to build an office-leasing company with an elementary school run by his wife and a mission to elevate the world's consciousness. Everything from Adam's personal ownership of WeWork buildings to Rebekah's role in choosing his successor made WeWork feel more like a family business than a public company. One of Wingspan's disclosures came in for particular derision: Adam had sold his personal ownership of several We-related trademarks to the company for $5.9 million. (A line explaining that Neumann was giving the money to charity had been deemed unnecessary, and was struck from Wingspan at the last moment.) The financial press torched the fact that WeWork had lost nearly $2 billion in 2018, and Rebekah's epigraph came in for instant mockery. Wingspan had so many obvious flaws that the very fact that it had been made public in this form felt disqualifying.

Once readers got past the kooky parts of Wingspan, what struck those who had been following the company for years were the numbers themselves. Wingspan didn't reveal a magic trick that somehow made WeWork's buildings exponentially more profitable than the offices everyone else was leasing out; it confirmed that Adam was playing the same game, just at a much bigger scale. The Dow dropped eight hundred points on the day Wingspan was released—its worst trading day of the year—on certain signals that the global economy was on shaky footing, and WeWork's arbitrage model suddenly looked just as risky as everyone suspected it to be. Some landlords began quietly reaching out to WeWork's competitors to ask whether they might be able to move in and operate WeWork's spaces in case the company collapsed.

Most of all, the public seemed to instantly recognize what Adam's charisma had persuaded investors to look past: the chasm between how the company presented itself and what it actually did. "We are a community company committed to maximum global impact," the S-1 began. "Our mission is to elevate the world's consciousness. We have built a worldwide platform that supports growth, shared experiences and true success." The word *community* appeared 150 times, outpaced by *platform* at 170. The phrase *office space*, meanwhile, received only nine mentions.

Two days after Wingspan's release, Adam tried to boost the spirits of his employees, many of whom were taken aback by the sudden mockery of the company to which they had devoted their lives and hitched their financial futures. On a call with senior employees, he told them not to worry: the haters were hating, Adam said, because WeWork was doing something different. He insisted that Wall Street's money managers were still eager to get in on the deal. Sebastian Gunningham, a former Amazon executive who joined WeWork in 2018, told another conference call of employees that potential investors bought into what WeWork was selling when Adam was doing the pitching.

This argument miffed many WeWork employees. They all knew how convincing Adam could be, but they also believed that they had built something of true value. Why did the pitch depend so heavily on Adam's salesmanship? Gunningham had spent more than a decade at Amazon, where Jeff Bezos had instituted a culture of succinct and thoughtful memo writing as a way of forcing his company to engage with ideas rather than personalities. At just shy of two hundred thousand words, WeWork's

S-1 was more than three times longer than Uber's and nearly as long as *Moby-Dick*. Yet it didn't seem to do a very good job explaining what WeWork actually did and why its business had potential. If anything, the document seemed to obscure it. The company had done away with "Community Adjusted EBITDA" only to replace it with "contribution margin," which concealed many of the same costs under the guise of a less laughable but equally obfuscating metric. A senior lecturer at Harvard Business School published a paper in response to Wingspan that was titled, simply, "Why WeWork Won't."

A week after Wingspan's release, Jen Berrent invited the bankers, lawyers, and WeWork employees who had worked most closely on the S-1 to gather one last time in the sixth-floor war room, where they had spent much of the summer. She relayed a quotation from Winston Churchill about how nothing good came from traveling the path of least resistance. She cited the many late Monday nights she and other executives had spent in meetings with Adam over the years, only to wake up the next day for early gatherings with Eitan Yardeni, Adam's Kabbalah rabbi. Life at WeWork could be difficult and all-consuming, she admitted, but it was worth it.

Berrent told the group in the war room that Yardeni had once relayed a novel interpretation of the story about a different Adam—the original one. In the traditional understanding of the Garden of Eden, the serpent's curse for contributing to humanity's fall from grace is to never walk upright. But Yardeni had told Berrent that the serpent's sorrow was not the loss of its legs, but the fact that it would never have to reach for anything ever again. It was a lazy creature, consuming only what fell in its path. True satisfaction, Yardeni argued, only came to those who strained to reach for things just beyond their grasp.

* * *

SHORTLY AFTER WINGSPAN'S RELEASE, I was texting with a real estate analyst at a large investment fund, who was preparing to meet Adam in WeWork's office at 85 Broad Street. "There could not be less excitement about this IPO," he said of the mood on Wall Street. A few months earlier, while I was working on "The I in We," the analyst had told me that he understood why the business had promise but couldn't comprehend the valuation. He'd taken tours and poked around WeWork's tech but came away thinking that nothing meaningfully differentiated WeWork from its competitors. Then again, maybe he was missing something. "It's either the biggest innovation in real estate ever," he said back in the spring, "or the biggest con."

The meeting at 85 Broad was part of a post-Wingspan tour Adam was making to gin up interest in the IPO. These were smaller gigs before Adam kicked off WeWork's official investor road show, which would begin a week or so before the actual listing. Having failed in his efforts to woo investment from potential partners in Silicon Valley, early commitments from a few major funds would be crucial to fulfilling WeWork's goal of raising $3 billion. When the small group of analysts arrived for the meeting, Adam told them that he hoped they had enjoyed reading Wingspan. WeWork, he said, had tried to make its S-1 more enjoyable than most.

For the next two hours, Adam talked, sending an assistant out for water when he needed to catch his breath. He continued to compare WeWork to Amazon and argued that no one had truly brought disruption to commercial real estate the way WeWork had. He flattered one of the analysts who asked a question—"You think like Warren Buffett"—but seemed to bristle at the light probing the group was able to conduct in the little time he left for Q&A.

The analysts' primary question was a simple one: *What is it, exactly, that you do?* Adam still struggled to articulate what made WeWork's business any different from that of IWG, which was then trading on the London Stock Exchange at a market capitalization of around $4 billion. The analysts noted that the branded cups WeWork put out in the meeting were printed with the tagline ALWAYS HALF FULL, which wasn't the most optimistic slogan for a company running a business in which 50 percent occupancy would mean insolvency.

As Adam continued his investor tours, he found that this kind of pitch was more difficult than dreaming on a three-hundred-year timeline with Masa. In August, he went to San Francisco to give several presentations, including one to Tiger Global Management, a large investment firm with a focus on tech. During the presentation, Adam repeated one of his favorite boasts: "We have never closed a building." One analyst jumped in to say that while this sounded like an achievement, it didn't make any sense. Was Adam suggesting that, of the more than five hundred locations the company had opened in the past decade, not a single one had been a mistake? The supposedly clean record made WeWork seem undisciplined.

During another presentation, Adam cued up a slide showing the profit and loss numbers for the WeWork location in which he was giving the speech—a favorite gimmick. The slide included the salaries of the employees who managed the building as a way of illustrating just how cheaply WeWork was able to operate its spaces. A woman listening to the presentation raised her hand. The salaries didn't amount to a livable wage in San Francisco, she said. Her concern was only partly ethical; practically speaking, how would WeWork keep its salaries low in the future, when it no longer had theoretically valuable stock options to offer employees? In a subsequent presentation, Adam removed the salary figures from the slide while making the same point.

Neumann's ability to put on a show and close a deal had been the key driver of WeWork's growth, but he was struggling to connect with small groups of investors suddenly primed for skepticism. "Adam was just off his game," an executive who sat in on several of the meetings said. He was meandering, dragging meetings on much longer than they needed to go and leaving no time for questions. He came off as desperate. The negative press surrounding Wingspan was so foreign to Adam that he seemed to be casting about for some kind of reassurance; he started calling investors after presentations to get a report card on his performance. JPMorgan's bankers had to convince him that doing so would only show a lack of confidence. Even Michael Gross, one of Adam's closest confidants, told another WeWork executive that it might be in the company's interest to pull Adam off the road. "Every meeting Adam has," one banker told Artie Minson, "you're losing a billion off your valuation."

* * *

AT THE END OF AUGUST, Masa summoned Adam to Tokyo. For WeWork's early investors, the response to Wingspan was embarrassing but not devastating. Benchmark stood to cash in around $1 billion at the higher-end projections on WeWork's IPO, but the firm had already sold more than $300 million worth of its shares to SoftBank—a twentyfold gain on its $16.5 million investment.

SoftBank, however, had invested more than $10 billion into WeWork and gotten nothing in return. The Vision Fund was down nearly $2 billion in the most recent quarter, during which Uber's stock had slipped. SoftBank shares were down 10 percent since Wingspan's release. Both WeWork and SoftBank executives were coming to grips with the realization that its IPO might be priced at a level far below its $47 billion valuation. While SoftBank's preferred shares gave it some protection— it could get its money out before the company's employees—a valuation below what SoftBank paid for its shares would mean that the firm's investment was underwater, much as it was with Uber.

To make matters worse, WeWork's trouble was emerging right as Masa was officially launching Vision Fund 2. In July, he announced nonbinding commitments from many of the original fund's limited partners, along with new investors such as Koch Industries and the National Bank of Kazakhstan. But the prospect of the original fund's two biggest bets suffering disappointing public debuts back-to-back threatened to impede Masa's hope that his second Vision Fund would be even bigger than the original.

Masa and Adam preferred to meet face-to-face when they could; they were both at their best when they were working a room. But it wasn't an encouraging sign for Neumann that his chief backer felt the need to summon him across the Pacific in the middle of the company's effort to shore up support for its IPO. Adam quietly made plans to fly to Japan, hopeful that Masa would step up and support him, either by committing to a sizable investment in the IPO or perhaps even by suggesting a reprise of something like Fortitude, which could keep the company private a bit longer.

Adam flew to Tokyo with Michael Gross and Noah Wintroub from JPMorgan, landing at Narita Airport in the afternoon, with plans to fly back out before the airport's 11 p.m. curfew that night. The group met Masa at his Tokyo mansion, where he was joined by Dan Dees, an executive from Goldman Sachs. It was an uncomfortable meeting. Masa thought WeWork should delay its IPO. The reaction to Wingspan had blown the company's momentum, and it would never go public at the valuation he and Adam had agreed to eight months before. It was time to save face, regroup, and try again later. Masa also wanted to renegotiate a portion of SoftBank's prior investment. It was committed to sending WeWork $1.5 billion in April 2020, at a price per share far above where it appeared WeWork's stock was heading. Adam was open to a potential compromise—taking a lower price on that tranche, perhaps, in exchange for a large commitment from SoftBank to WeWork's IPO.

As for the offering itself, Adam was torn. On the one hand, Masa had been the investor with whom he felt the closest kinship, the one in whom he had the most trust. But Masa had bailed on him once already. Adam pushed back, arguing that it was too late to drop out; now was the time to charge ahead. As mentor and mentee parted ways, Masa sent Neumann back across the Pacific with a warning. This path was unwise, he said—both for the company and for Neumann.

* * *

ADAM HAD PLENTY of time to consider what had just happened. He was in a rush to get back to New York and continue prepping for the IPO, but the WeWork team was sitting on Wildgoose I at Narita Airport when air traffic control informed them they had missed the curfew. A call was placed to Masa, hoping he might pull some strings, but nothing could be done. Adam would have to stay the night in Tokyo, thinking about what to do next.

After making it back to New York, Adam called an all-hands meeting at WeWork headquarters on the Wednesday after Labor Day. A rally in front of a friendly audience might offer a needed confidence boost. But the chatter on "IPO News" had taken a decidedly darker cast as it became clear that whatever spoils would emerge from WeWork's public offering would predominately accumulate at the top. Employees had already grumbled, the *Wall Street Journal* highlighted, that Adam had cashed out more than $700 million worth of his WeWork stock—far more than any other start-up CEO the *Journal* could find. Wingspan also revealed that WeWork had undergone a legal restructuring that lowered the tax rate on stock owned by Adam and other executives to a rate below what WeWork's rank-and-file employees would have to pay.

Some of WeWork's first employees were especially galled when they read a line in the S-1 about WeWork's commitment to sharing its prosperity. "Nine years ago, when we were just beginning our journey, we gave all employees equity because we were convinced that launching a successful company requires each and every person to take initiative, solve problems and think like an owner of the company," the S-1 read. But Lisa Skye, WeWork's second employee, received no equity, nor had Danny Orenstein, who worked at the company for three years. WeWork had not formally offered stock options to employees until 2013, three years after it was founded.

For the town hall, Adam had his staff clear out the couches and arcade machines from the sixth floor to set up a stage from which he could broadcast to WeWork employees around the world. Miguel got up to speak first. Fundraising efforts had never been his forte, and in the preceding weeks, he had largely been absent from the process, spending his summer at the edges of Wingspan's preparation. When the Goldman Sachs deal fell apart, over the Fourth of July holiday, Miguel was celebrating his forty-fifth birthday and musing about the past decade of his life. He hadn't had time to develop any hobbies since starting WeWork, but as the end of this particular road appeared, he wanted to start. "I've been dreaming of trying to make Neapolitan pizza," he wrote on Instagram, showing off his pizza oven. "I've learned so much already and it's so satisfying when a pizza turns out better than the last one. The dough is like a living thing—it has personality and it changes over time. The sauce is simple, but just the right amount makes a big difference. And of course the cheese...I'm vegan so I don't eat classic mozzarella, but I'm making it for my friends—and experimenting with various nut cheeses as well. So far so good!"

At the town hall, Miguel told WeWork's employees that there was a silver lining to the turmoil: think about how many more people know about the company now! He recognized that these were trying times but insisted that assertions that the company was greedy were off base. Miguel encouraged employees to stay connected to WeWork's original ethos: bringing people together, helping them do what they love. "Our intent was pure," McKelvey said. "Are we staying connected to that pure intent?" If they did, he believed they were still at the beginning of something exciting.

Miguel gave the microphone to Adam, who addressed all the negative attention. "Why is there noise?" he said. "Because we poked the bear." The real estate world had grown lazy and fat and was upset that WeWork had disrupted a comfortable system. They were happy to take WeWork's money when the company was riding high, but now that everyone smelled blood, they were on the attack, hoping things could go back to the way they were. He told his employees not to worry and said that he had learned several lessons. "Change your inner self," he said. "Change the world."

Adam turned his attention to some of the issues that had emerged in the wake of Wingspan's release. Among them was the fact that, while Adam had elevated his wife within WeWork, the company had few female executives and a board of directors made up of an Adam, a Bruce, a Ron, a Lew, a Steven, a Mark, and a John. All-male corporate boards had finally become problematic for public companies, and Adam had received warnings about the lack of diversity for more than two years. Over the summer, Jimmy Asci, the head of communications, presented Adam with a list of fifty female candidates for a seat on the board, but Adam seemed only halfheartedly committed to the idea. He didn't show up for a meeting with a former Cabinet member, while pining after executives who were unlikely to join WeWork's board, like Ruth Porat at Alphabet, and Elizabeth Pinkham, who ran real estate for Salesforce. When a WeWork executive pointed out that the CEOs of those companies were unlikely to allow their executives to serve on WeWork's board, Adam dismissed the concern. "No one says no to me," he said.

Adam claimed innocence on the issue during the town hall. "I don't see 'man' and 'woman,'" he said of his hiring practices. Nonetheless, he was announcing a new member of WeWork's board: Frances Frei, the Harvard Business School professor who had taught WeWork's employees about the dangers of wobbling. Frei had become a high-priced consultant to companies going through cultural and public relations crises, having served the same role at Uber. Adam then walked his employees through a version of the pitch he was giving to potential investors. The presentation went well, even when a glitch screwed up one of the slides, giving Adam the opportunity to joke that the SEC must have "infiltrated" WeWork. "Elon and I have our differences, but now that I'm dealing with the SEC, I agree with him," Adam said, referring to Musk's battle with the commission over his misleading tweets about Tesla's financial state.

Adam told the crowd that plenty of investors were still excited about

WeWork, including Eric Yuan, the CEO of Zoom. Adam had recently met with Yuan to talk about what the conference room of the future would look like, and the companies were in talks about Zoom investing in WeWork's IPO in exchange for WeWork pushing Zoom's videoconferencing service on its members. As Adam pitched it to Yuan: if you become WeWork's provider, you become the world's.

* * *

BY THE END of the town hall, many WeWork employees felt better—Adam had won them over again. He was at ease in front of a home crowd and wanted to schedule another event for the following week. But his employees weren't the ones who needed convincing. That day, John White, an attorney at Cravath, Swaine & Moore, responded on WeWork's behalf to a nine-page letter from the SEC listing various objections to Wingspan. Among them: Adam charging his own company $5.9 million for the We-related trademarks and the fact that WeWork's presentation of its business model was implausibly assuming full occupancy. ("Please explain to readers and tell us how your assumed workstation utilization rate of 100% is realistic," the SEC wrote.) The commission also asked WeWork to "clarify the relevance of imagery that does not appear to have a clear disclosure or investor protection purpose," by which it meant Rebekah's photo spread—specifically, a photograph of a participant in the 2017 New York City Pride Parade.

WeWork responded that it had unwound the payment to Adam for the trademarks, and removed the suggestion that its occupancy would be 100 percent. But the most contentious battle centered around "contribution margin"—the financial metric formerly known as Community Adjusted EBITDA. The gold standards for corporate financial metrics are those that conform to generally accepted accounting principles. Non-GAAP calculations like contribution margin had become increasingly common among start-ups, but WeWork's was especially aggressive, cutting out the sales and marketing costs that WeWork used to fill its spaces as well as the full costs of its leases. The SEC believed that the metric, which appeared more than a hundred times in the document, could be "misleading" to investors.

WeWork needed to make changes to Wingspan anyway. The company had omitted the fact that Neumann had been on WeWork's compensation committee in each of the past two years and had to adjust the number of desks WeWork built in the first half of the year. The original S-1 said 273,000 desks; the actual number was 106,000. They filed a revised prospectus dropping the projections that assumed full occupancy, but, at Adam's insistence, WeWork's lawyers pushed back on the contribution margin issue, sending forty-five pages of responses to the SEC, arguing that while the company would be willing to make changes to the metric, such as rectifying its exclusion of certain lease costs, it believed that this was a better way to understand the business than a straight measurement of how much money the company made or lost. Adam went so far as to make a trip to Washington, DC, to press the company's case.

While WeWork's lawyers did battle with the SEC, Adam got back on the road, driving to a private airport outside New York after his town hall for a midnight flight to London Stansted. He landed just before dawn for a meeting with Yasir Al-Rumayyan, the head of Saudi Arabia's sovereign-wealth fund. Saudi Arabia's skepticism of Adam and WeWork had only increased since its decision not to back Fortitude, and Al-Rumayyan declined to commit to buying a chunk of the IPO. Hat in hand, Neumann flew back to New York that night, then on to Boston and Toronto for meetings with more investors. When he met with Fidelity this time around, Adam wore a suit, and asked the firm's portfolio managers what it would take to get them to invest. Fidelity could easily pour a billion dollars into the IPO, but its real estate investors didn't think WeWork was worth the multiple of revenue it had been given, and nothing in the S-1 had given them confidence that the company had figured out a path toward becoming profitable.

By the time he returned to New York, in the second week of September,

WeWork's IPO was in serious danger. JPMorgan and Goldman Sachs told WeWork that the company might have to consider going public at a valuation close to $20 billion—or less. In the press, WeWork's valuation was falling: from $15 billion, to $12 billion, to $10 billion. On September 11, the shrinking number made it all the way to the US House of Representatives. During a meeting of a House Financial Services Committee's subcommittee, Representative Alexandria Ocasio-Cortez invoked WeWork's valuation as an example of how the ballooning private markets were screwing over public investors: "They had raised on a previous valuation of $47 billion, and now they just decided overnight, 'Just kidding, we're worth $20 billion,'" Ocasio-Cortez said, pointing out that if the company had gone public at SoftBank's valuation, everyday investors who put money in would be "getting fleeced."

Adam grew increasingly frustrated with WeWork's communications team, which was suddenly unable to control the news cycle. Someone was leaking information. Was SoftBank trying to scuttle the IPO? Was Benchmark hoping to stage another coup? Or maybe one of WeWork's newer executives, with less devotion to the cause and less to gain from the IPO bonanza, was leaking from the inside?

Adam became increasingly paranoid. He went back to Medina Bardhi, the former assistant he had pushed aside after she went on maternity leave, and asked her to help him navigate the situation. "I need a woman's touch," he said, according to Bardhi's complaint. Adam began holding meetings at the carriage house of the Neumann's Gramercy home, rather than at WeWork's headquarters. During one meeting, Arik Benzino, a WeWork executive who knew the Neumanns from Israel, went outside. When Adam noticed a man idly walking up and down the street, talking on a cell phone, he went out and barked at Benzino to come back inside, in case the man was surveilling them.

* * *

THE WORLD WAS SHOCKED by WeWork's losses and Wingspan's eccentricity, but much of the criticism centered on the Neumanns themselves. It was impossible to divorce WeWork from the Neumanns' influence over it. Slack's CEO, Stewart Butterfield, was mentioned forty-seven times in his company's S-1, and Lyft's two cofounders were cited fifty-five times combined. Adam's name alone appeared 169 times. (Rebekah was named twenty times, while Miguel got just six mentions.) The company had paid more than $20 million in rent on four buildings that Adam owned, and its leases on those buildings called for $236 million in future payments. His sister and brother-in-law were both on staff. Rebekah would have a hand in of choosing his successor. During the town hall, Adam had brushed many of the concerns aside. "I rarely give away my power, and when I do, it's to my wife," he said, adding that Rebekah was almost always "99 percent right."

Adam and Rebekah were taken aback by the public's reaction, having expected praise for their promise to give away $1 billion within ten years of WeWork's IPO. But next to everything else, the pledge barely registered. The Neumanns hired multiple high-powered publicists and consultants—Matthew Hiltzik, George Sard, the PR firm Edelman—to try to quickly reframe the image congealing around them and their company. Rebekah wondered if they might be able to get a pro-WeWork hashtag trending.

The governance issues that Adam had brushed off became a central critique of WeWork's IPO, and some of the attempts to address various concerns had backfired. The *Wall Street Journal* reported that Frances Frei was already working as a consultant for WeWork, charging the company $5 million, plus private jet travel from Boston to New York, which meant that she would not qualify as an independent member of WeWork's board.

On Thursday afternoon, September 12, Adam met at WeWork head-quarters with bankers from JPMorgan and Goldman Sachs, along with WeWork's lawyers, to discuss what changes might make the offering more palatable to investors. The bankers recommended getting rid of Adam's supervoting shares and Rebekah's say in choosing his successor. Adam pushed back. Peloton had just gone public, and its CEO was being granted twenty votes for each of his shares. But the bankers pointed out that Peloton's founders owned only a small chunk of their company. Adam still controlled more of WeWork than anyone else. Even if the company went public, he would still be its most influential figure by far—his power just wouldn't be absolute. They argued that Adam didn't need more control than he already had. If he didn't do something, WeWork's IPO might be in peril.

CHAPTER TWENTY-THREE

The Sun Never Sets on We

AFTER SEVERAL HOURS of back-and-forth, Adam made a number of concessions: he wouldn't ask for twenty votes on each of his shares, and Rebekah wouldn't get a say in naming his successor. That night, Miguel called an executive at Nasdaq to say that WeWork planned to go public in two weeks and would list its shares with Nasdaq rather than the New York Stock Exchange. Miguel's role over the summer had consisted largely of plotting out how to turn the day of WeWork's IPO into an event—specifically, a celebration of the company's commitment to sustainability. (WeWork printed T-shirts with a photo of the forest in Belize for employees to wear when the day came.) Both stock exchanges had made pitches to the company earlier in the summer at the Neumanns' house in Amagansett, and Nasdaq offered to create a new index of companies committed to sustainability: the We 50.

WeWork entered the second weekend of September bruised but hopeful. The company's road show was scheduled to begin the following Monday, when Adam and the bankers would make a whirlwind tour to woo prospective investors, leaving enough time to go public before Rosh Hashanah. Despite Masa's reservations, WeWork had reached a tentative agreement with SoftBank to buy another $1 billion of WeWork stock as part of the IPO. WeWork was also close to finalizing a smaller deal with

Zoom to buy $25 million worth of WeWork shares. The Zoom endorsement wasn't publicized—the company's imprimatur wasn't as valuable as it would be six months later—but the SoftBank deal became public, which some on the outside believed was an effort to show that investors remained confident. WeWork's stock would likely be priced at somewhere between $30 and $36 per share, which would value the company between $12 and $15 billion—a heavy markdown from $47 billion, but a number that would still richly reward Neumann, most of the company's investors, and other early employees and executives.

On Sunday, bankers from JPMorgan and Goldman Sachs met at WeWork headquarters in Chelsea to hash out the final price. Adam was expected to take part, but he was preoccupied. He still needed to film his portion of the company's road-show video, which would play for investors who gathered at each stop on the tour. Adam himself had come up with the initial theme and title for WeWork's video: *The Sun Never Sets on We*. It would feature executives at WeWorks around the world while showcasing the lives of fictional Jim DeCiccos in various countries using the company's spaces. (A production company posted an audition call for actors who had "an 'every day people' look," which meant "good looking, but not models" and "no outlandish tattoos or face piercings," although " 'normal' tattoos" were acceptable.)

But as the summer wore on, ambitions for the video had been cut back; some thought it should simply be a version of the talk Adam gave on analyst day. By mid-September, every other WeWork executive had filmed his or her portion of the video—Rebekah taped a clip in front of a sign promoting the "School of Life for Life"—but Adam had missed four separate tapings, which cost WeWork hundreds of thousands of dollars. (He also missed an appointment for his new headshot.) With the IPO imminent, there was some thought of moving ahead without Adam's segment at all.

Adam had never met a microphone he didn't want to grab, but this kind of performance wasn't the type at which he excelled. Adam was a man of the stage, feeding off the energy of a crowd. The red light of a camera didn't applaud. Adam's dyslexia also made it hard for him to read from a teleprompter, but this video, which needed to be reviewed by the SEC, wasn't the place to improvise. He wanted to wing it but gave in to advice to read from a script.

As his morning call time arrived, Adam was still in his office, working out exactly what he wanted to say. Jen Berrent, Artie Minson, Michael Gross, and several other executives frittered about the sixth floor, but Adam mostly ignored them. After a few hours, many of the senior executives and bankers left, leaving junior staffers to make sure Adam went through with the taping. A production team was waiting in a studio, ready to edit the footage as it came in so that it could be sent to the SEC first thing in the morning.

Around 5:00 p.m., Adam finally emerged from his office and arrived on the set near the bumper pool tables on the sixth floor of WeWork headquarters. He wore an unbuttoned suit jacket and asked an assistant to put on some music. Drake's "Started from the Bottom" began playing from a loudspeaker. As Adam began to speak, he tried to stick to what was scrolling past on the teleprompter, but he wasn't following the script precisely. Eventually, he arrived at a line pointing out that if WeWork's IPO successfully raised $3 billion, giving the company access to the $6 billion JPMorgan-arranged credit line on top of the $2 billion it had in the bank, WeWork would have $11 billion to fund its expansion.

Neumann paused. "Finally," he said. "Something good about this IPO."

Michael Gross was one of a handful of executives still around as the taping dragged into the night. No matter what price the bankers set for WeWork's IPO, Gross was among a group of employees and executives who had little to worry about, having already cashed out portions of his equity over the years. In July, Gross one-upped Adam's purchase of a $21 million home (the one with the guitar-shaped room) when he bought a $28 million house in Los Angeles that had once been owned by Lindsey Buckingham of Fleetwood Mac. As the night crawled on, and Adam kept working through his taping, Gross was in a jovial mood, and bumbled his way around the room, tossing his arm around the bankers, lawyers, and advisers who were growing increasingly frustrated that one of the simplest tasks facing the company's attempt to go public was taking so long.

By the time Adam finished taping his segment, it was nearly midnight. To cap it off, he told everyone to join him for one final tequila shot and thanked them all for sticking around. "This is a good example," he said, "of why you should never give up."

* * *

THE FOLLOWING MORNING, inside a Washington, DC, WeWork, the employees at a digital media company who rented a four-person WeWork office arrived to find their door jammed shut by an umbrella. It had fallen during the weekend and landed in just such a way that it prevented their glass office door from sliding open. There were no gaps in the wall, and the window to the outside world didn't open. Shoving the door and jiggling the handle did nothing. They found a magnet, but the umbrella wouldn't budge; one of the employees tried to snake several wire coat hangers between the glass and the aluminum, but that didn't work, either. It wasn't a big deal. There were more than a dozen WeWorks in DC and plenty of empty space. The employees simply took their laptops downstairs to another unoccupied office in the building while the WeWork team sat around figuring out what to do.

That morning, Artie Minson and Jen Berrent arrived at JPMorgan headquarters for a series of meetings. The taping had dragged on so long the night before that WeWork's bankers had to tell investors that the road show was being pushed back. Several people in the room at JPMorgan argued that they should forge ahead that week: the IPO had come this far, and backing out now would be embarrassing. But JPMorgan's bankers said they were uncertain that there was enough demand. Raising $1.5 billion might be possible, but that would cut the company off from the $6 billion debt deal that depended on WeWork's IPO bringing in $3 billion. The move to float SoftBank's backing of the IPO had backfired, emphasizing that only Adam and Masa seemed to truly believe in the most ambitious version of WeWork's future. Some investors weren't willing to commit to attending the company's road show at all.

A few blocks away from JPMorgan headquarters, Adam was huddling at a WeWork location in Midtown with David Ludwig and Kim Posnett, two senior bankers from Goldman Sachs. Now that JPMorgan was expressing doubts about the IPO, Adam had lost some faith in his "personal banker." Some wondered if JPMorgan was getting cold feet about the $6 billion loan, and didn't want the IPO to go forward at all.

That afternoon, Berrent called Adam and told him to come to JPMorgan. The biggest problem, the bankers insisted, was Adam himself. One junior Goldman Sachs banker had become so perturbed by Neumann's behavior during the road-show taping that he had called a colleague at JPMorgan to ask whether Adam was high while filming the video. Noah Wintroub had already told Neumann that he needed to stop smoking so much pot with WeWork's IPO on the horizon. After Adam arrived at JPMorgan headquarters, Artie took him into another room to ask whether he had been high; Adam insisted that he hadn't been.

But WeWork's PR team was already battling with Eliot Brown, a reporter at the *Wall Street Journal*, over a looming story detailing Adam's eccentric behavior. Among other details, Brown was preparing to report that Adam had smoked pot on a flight to Israel, after which the jet's staff had discovered a cereal box filled with marijuana for the ride home, prompting the jet's owner to order the plane to fly back to the United States without Neumann. Stories like this weren't news to anyone who had spent time with Adam, but WeWork's backers had been willing to excuse Adam's antics so long as his charm also continued to push the company's fortunes higher.

Now, the company's precarious position had turned Adam into WeWork's greatest liability. The bankers argued that it was crucial for him to give up even more of his control. Both Jamie Dimon and David Ludwig told Adam he needed to get rid of his extra votes entirely. At one point, Minson left the room to get a glass of water only to walk back in and find Adam flailing his arms and yelling at Mary Erdoes, the head of JPMorgan's asset management division, who had just told him that based on feedback the banks had received from investors, she didn't think the IPO could move forward with him in charge at all.

But Adam was still in control of the company. He was resistant to further changes and wanted to press ahead with the IPO. The bankers insisted that doing so would be an impossibility—there just wasn't enough interest. They suggested pushing the date deeper into the fall, when WeWork's third-quarter earnings would, they hoped, show the growth Neumann had been plotting out and reinvigorate the company's prospects.

By the afternoon, Adam had unhappily agreed to postpone the offering. He was frustrated. The IPO, which he had never wanted, was collapsing alongside his reputation. His grip on the company he founded a decade earlier was loosening. As they drove away from JPMorgan headquarters at the end of the day, he lashed out at Medina Bardhi, his assistant, who was in the car with him. "I hope you enjoyed your vacation," Adam said of Bardhi's maternity leave, according to her complaint. While bankers stayed behind to plot out a new strategy, Adam told WeWork's communications team to put out a statement saying the company was still planning to go public this year. He expected the IPO to happen by Halloween.

* * *

THE NEXT MORNING, WeWork held another all-hands meeting at headquarters. It was hard for anyone to muster the enthusiasm for another one of Adam's tent revivals, and instead of gathering in person, WeWork's employees were told to log in via videoconference. At 11:00 a.m., Miguel suddenly appeared on-screen, standing behind a clear Lucite podium decorated with WeWork's logo. He offered a few platitudes, noting how odd it felt to address everyone this way. He was somewhere in the building, but most WeWork employees weren't sure exactly where. Seeing one of their chastened leaders deliver a wartime address from a nondescript room made people feel as if they were living through *The Hunger Games*.

Miguel quickly gave the podium over to Adam, greeting his cofounder with an uncomfortable hug. Miguel was surprised to find Adam dressed up for the occasion.

"You're wearing a suit," Miguel said.

"This isn't a suit," Adam said. "It's a blazer."

As he settled in to address his employees, Adam's attire couldn't hide the fact that he seemed disheveled. He told WeWork's employees that he was "humbled" by the past month but grateful for the opportunity to embrace his superpower—the power to change. Adam said that although he and his company had "played the private market game to perfection," he admitted that they were still learning the realities of becoming a public company. He remained optimistic and believed that WeWork would be judged on a much longer timeline than one bad month.

During his travels to drum up interest in the IPO, Adam said, his spirits were buoyed by how much people still loved the company, especially abroad, where he said that the WeWork community was viewed less cynically than it was in the United States. "Everyone around the world believes in We," Neumann said. He began telling a story about a trip to Montreal—a funny coincidence, he said, because the last time he had visited the city, he got confused and kept telling people he was in Toronto.

A voice interrupted Adam from off-screen. His most recent trip had, in fact, been to Toronto.

Adam corrected himself and finished his speech, but the performance was concerning. He had always excelled at addressing his disciples, but he had never been forced to do so from anywhere but the next tallest peak, having risen on a decade's worth of momentum to ever-greater heights. The speech was the first time many employees had seen anxiety bubble up in Adam. The illusion that he was in control was now breached. Adam turned the microphone over to Artie, who looked at the camera and deadpanned, "Good morning, Montreal."

* * *

THE NEXT MORNING, Masa woke up in California to find a lengthy article about his protégé in the *Wall Street Journal.* WeWork's communications team had spent the week trying to fend off some of the anecdotes in the story, but while it had once been hard for reporters to coax Adam's critics to share stories about him, the preceding month of chaos had made even those close to him realize there might be a future without him. The king wasn't dead, but there was a lot less to be afraid of.

Masa was at a hotel in Pasadena, hosting the largest gathering yet of his Vision Fund companies. Adam was supposed to attend; Masa had even planned for him to sit at the head table. Despite his concerns about WeWork's IPO, Masa still shared a faith in Adam's vision. But with all the uncertainty around the offering, Adam stayed in New York.

Instead, Masa spent much of the event talking with investors and other Vision Fund CEOs about Adam; the consensus was that Masa had no choice but to get rid of him. Masa didn't mention WeWork in his speech at the conference, but he did remind the companies about the importance of profitability and corporate governance. Acting crazy was no longer enough.

Back in New York, Adam was attempting to move on. It was September 18, the day he hoped the company would go public. One employee looked on as Adam spent part of the day in his office, watching clips from the road-show video he had finally filmed a few days before, if weeks too late. He didn't seem as concerned about the *Journal* article as those around him were, even though he didn't have to look far to understand what could happen when things went south for the charismatic founder of a high-flying company. In January, Adam had personally invested more than $30 million into Faraday Grid, a Scottish firm trying to reinvent the delivery of renewable energy—another company in his mini Vision Fund. The investment valued Faraday Grid at $3.4 billion, thanks to supposedly revolutionary technology the company was loath to share many details about; whatever it was, Adam promised it would "fundamentally change the way we access and use energy in the future." Neumann had found an easy kinship with Faraday's founder, Andrew Scobie, an Australian with a big personality and lofty ambitions. In his office, Scobie prominently displayed a quotation that he attributed to Adam Smith: "All money is a matter of belief."

More or less since the announcement of Neumann's investment, things had gone awry for Faraday Grid. The company was burning through capital at an alarming rate, tripling its number of employees in a matter of months and occupying a large office in a Washington, DC, WeWork. Scobie, meanwhile, threw a fancy dinner party in Edinburgh for Adi Neumann, Adam's sister, who was looking after the investment on her brother's behalf. In June, Scobie was removed as Faraday's CEO. On August 14, the same day WeWork unveiled Wingspan, the *Wall Street Journal* reported that Faraday Grid had run out of money, having failed to prove it could fundamentally change the industry that it promised to disrupt.

* * *

ON FRIDAY, September 20, four days after Adam agreed to postpone WeWork's IPO, a group of students from WeGrow rode the elevators from their third-floor schoolhouse at WeWork headquarters up to the sixth floor, where they typically went once a week to sell produce. That day, around the world, children and adults alike were taking part in a daylong climate strike, skipping out on school and work to protest on the earth's behalf. The WeGrow students paraded around the floor, passing Neumann's office with signs displaying one of the growing protest movement's signature slogans: THERE'S NO PLANET B.

That afternoon, Neal DosSantos, a young architect who worked at a firm in Manhattan, was strolling back to his office after eating lunch in Gramercy Park when he spotted Adam heading briskly uptown on the sidewalk and talking animatedly into his phone. WeWork's CEO was walking past Pete's Tavern, one of New York's oldest bars, wearing a gray T-shirt, black pants—and no shoes.

DosSantos recognized Adam by sight. He had friends at WeWork and had considered applying for a job there over the years. Given all he had heard about the founder, the moment seemed to sum everything up: Neumann was moving quickly and talking fast, the only CEO who would casually walk the streets of New York barefoot during the most trying week of his life. (One of Adam's publicists at the time explained away the incident to me by arguing that this was simply who he was: "Adam grew up on a kibbutz and likes to walk barefoot. He is a kibbutznik. Should we ask him to stop?")

Adam had spent much of the week holed up in his Gramercy carriage house, around the corner from where DosSantos spotted him. He was in a jam that required careful maneuvering. The press continued to pillory him—reports of personal disputes with the contractors working on one of the Neumanns' homes had emerged that day—and critiques of the company were coming from near and far. Eric Rosengren, the president of the Boston branch of the Federal Reserve Bank, issued a statement expressing concern that in the event of an economic downturn, WeWork's collapse could precipitate huge losses for banks and commercial property owners.

The ground had been shifting beneath Adam all week as he suddenly found himself fighting to maintain control of the company he founded: a coup was fomenting on WeWork's board. The effort was being led in part by SoftBank, which held two of WeWork's seven board seats. Masa's deputies had long been frustrated by their boss's affection for Adam, and SoftBank executives had begun maneuvering to edge Neumann out of his job. Given how much of the poor reaction to Wingspan was tied to Adam, it was becoming an easier pitch to make.

The potential ouster remained sensitive for Benchmark. While Bill Gurley and the company's partners had long harbored doubts about Adam, it had been just two years since Benchmark pushed Travis Kalanick out of Uber, and the firm was still shaking off its new reputation as a place that let founders run wild only to oust them in the end. Benchmark also didn't have much love for SoftBank at this point; Gurley had recently gone on CNBC and declared that the Vision Fund was using "capital as a weapon," warping every industry it was entering. But the fact that WeWork's two biggest financial backers, SoftBank and JPMorgan, were both losing faith in the IPO, pushed many board members to believe a change was necessary. Bruce Dunlevie made plans to get to New York that weekend to meet with Adam.

*　*　*

ON SUNDAY, WeWork's official Twitter account tried to look on the bright side: "How do you plan to spend a moment relaxing today? #selfcaresunday." Adam had spent much of the weekend in the Hamptons, coming to the growing realization that he was losing his grip on the company. He still controlled WeWork and had the ability to fire the board of directors if they tried to oust him against his will—a dicey move, but the past decade had been one risk after another. If Adam had truly become toxic, however, he was putting his own net worth in jeopardy by sticking around and engaging in a public fight. On Saturday night, Adam was back in the city, and had dinner at his Gramercy home with Berrent, Minson, and Ilan Stern, who managed Adam's family investment office. They pointed out that Adam had already drawn $380 million of the $500 million credit line that was backed by the value of his WeWork stock. The company's collapse would make him insolvent. Both Jen and Artie argued this might be a moment where Adam needed to put aside his professional ego and focus on his family's financial future.

The next day, Adam met with Jamie Dimon on the forty-third floor of JPMorgan's headquarters. Adam told Dimon that he wasn't sure there was any way forward for him as CEO. Dimon agreed. No one scandal or decision had taken Neumann down, but it had been a year full of one blemish after another on the heels of a decade in which he could do no wrong. "How could this happen?" Adam told Dimon, according to a person familiar with the conversation. "I did everything you told me to do."

"Adam," Dimon said. "You did nothing that I told you to."

This wasn't strictly true. JPMorgan, SoftBank, and WeWork's other investors had enabled and encouraged Adam for years. It was only when his erratic behavior threatened their own reputations that they turned on him. That night, Adam ate dinner in a private room at a Midtown restaurant with Bruce Dunlevie, Michael Eisenberg, who flew in from Israel, and Steven Langman, the investors who had backed WeWork in 2012. The group had been among the first members of the business elite to give Adam their stamp of approval and welcome him into their club. Dinner was tense but cordial. They told Adam the choice was his; he still controlled his company. But all three men believed that he should step down. When WeWork's board met on Tuesday morning, Neumann's fate was sealed.

CHAPTER TWENTY-FOUR

Brave New World

AFTER ADAM'S RESIGNATION, Artie Minson and Sebastian Gunningham held a company town hall as the new co-CEOs of WeWork. They had decided to postpone the IPO indefinitely. Four thousand printed copies of Rebekah's Wingspan artwork would remain shrink-wrapped. At the town hall, Artie told WeWork's employees not to worry. "Everyone loves a comeback, and this is going to be one of the all-time amazing comebacks," he said. There would be layoffs and cuts, Minson said, but he promised to handle them humanely. He opened the floor to questions.

"Hi," one employee said. "This is my second week here at WeWork." Everyone laughed.

The IPO postponement left WeWork without a clear path forward. The company no longer had the $3 billion it had hoped to raise from its IPO, not to mention the $6 billion loan package that was to come with it. Distracted by the rush up to the IPO, no one had been keeping a clear eye on the company's finances. JPMorgan brought in a restructuring firm to conduct a deep dive into WeWork's books. External projections estimated that the company had enough money to keep growing through the spring of 2020, but the accountants discovered a much more dire situation. It was October, and without new funding, WeWork would run out of money before Thanksgiving.

This was a far cry from the "four to five years" Adam had projected in his CNBC interview with Ashton Kutcher just nine months earlier. Adam's plan to juice WeWork's 2019 numbers had been risky to begin with, but without the $9 billion the company had expected to raise, the decision verged on catastrophic. WeWork was spending money so rapidly that its cash reserves, which sat at $2.5 billion in June, were fast approaching the $500 million threshold at which the terms of its $702 million bond would put it in default.

By one estimate, the company needed to quickly cut $500 million in costs to survive. Minson and Guningham began slashing away at Neumann's empire. Twenty or so of Adam's friends and relatives were removed from or left the company, including Michael Gross, Chris Hill, Adam Kimmel, and Rebekah. WeGrow announced that it would close after the school year. At Salesforce Tower, Adam's spa in the sky was taken apart; in Chelsea, the pink couches in Rebekah's office were removed and workers converted Adam's office into a conference room. The company planned to put Wildgoose I up for sale, but not before a WeWork employee posted his own listing on an internal classifieds page: "Selling a Gulfstream G650 for a friend. $60 million OBO."

WeWork shut down Spacious, the company Adam had acquired for $43 million over the summer, and put several other acquisitions on the market, selling one for 11 percent of what WeWork had paid for it in April. The company all but stopped leasing new spaces and backed out of several that weren't yet under construction. WeWork's West Coast team found itself struggling to explain to their new bosses how the deal for the CAA building had made sense, or ever would. A ground-up development in Seattle that was meant to contain the third WeLive was scrapped, and a team from SoftBank approached a competitor about taking over WeLive altogether. Adam's ambition to become the next Amazon had been dashed: WeWork sold the Lord & Taylor building, the site of Adam's next castle, to Amazon itself.

Minson and Gunningham worked through various plans for the most painful cut: laying off many of WeWork's fifteen thousand employees. Managers were asked to come up with plans that could trim 20, or 40, or even 60 percent of their teams. WeWork's headquarters had largely emptied out, with employees choosing to work from home or managers too ashamed to confront their teams. One day, the in-house barista started sobbing at the thought of all her colleagues who were going to lose their jobs. The only good news was that the company quickly realized it would have to delay the layoffs: by mid-October, it was a few weeks from running out of money and couldn't afford to fund severance payments.

*　*　*

YET AGAIN, WeWork needed more cash. The board appointed Bruce Dunlevie and Lew Frankfort to consider potential rescue-financing packages. Some of WeWork's shareholders argued that the company should head toward bankruptcy, and figure out how to pick up the pieces after that. Minson and Berrent began working with JPMorgan on a deal to save the company without giving up control. The bank was willing to offer WeWork $5 billion worth of debt, backed by all of WeWork's assets.

The only other interested party was SoftBank itself, which was in a precarious position. The firm had already sunk more than $10 billion into WeWork. Aside from his initial twelve-minute visit with Neumann, in 2016, Masa had spent hardly any time in the company's spaces, and he made a show of spending four days visiting a WeWork in Japan, promising to use his expertise to analyze the business and figure out a path forward. Like Adam, Masa believed that he knew best.

But even he was no longer so certain of his judgment. On a call with investors from the Vision Fund, Masa admitted that he had put too much faith in Adam. "We created a monster," he said. He had begun telling the CEOs of the Vision Fund's other portfolio companies to "know your limit." Toward the end of October, SoftBank executives were heading to Saudi Arabia for the country's annual financial conference, where they hoped to secure commitments to Vision Fund 2. One way or another, the WeWork situation needed a resolution, and on October 22, SoftBank came to the table with an offer that matched JPMorgan's $5 billion debt deal—with an additional offer that served as both carrot and stick. If WeWork agreed to the deal, SoftBank would move up the existing $1.5 billion commitment that wasn't due to be paid until April of 2020. If WeWork chose JPMorgan's package, SoftBank would pull the $1.5 billion altogether.

The deal had one additional component: SoftBank wanted Adam out of WeWork altogether. The board had already blocked Adam's access to WeWork headquarters. His public reputation had been torn so rabidly apart that there seemed to be no chance of redeeming it in the near term. The longer he stayed connected to the company, the more his growing infamy would tarnish whatever comeback WeWork might make.

Adam made it clear to SoftBank that it would have to make him feel comfortable stepping away. Marcelo Claure, one of Masa's top SoftBank deputies, led the negotiations with WeWork. Claure said that in addition to offering $5 billion in debt financing, SoftBank was willing to buy $3 billion worth of WeWork stock from existing shareholders, an amount that would give the firm near-total control. The deal valued WeWork at $8 billion, roughly a sixth of what Masa and Adam had declared the company to be worth nine months earlier.

As part of the deal, Adam could potentially sell as much as $970 million worth of his shares—a third of his remaining stake. SoftBank would also loan him $500 million to pay back his credit line, forgive $1.75 million in unreimbursed personal expenses, and pay him a $185 million consulting fee. In return, Adam would lose his supervoting shares, vacate his role as chairman, and leave WeWork with an agreement to not start an office-space competitor for four years. "Adam, we trusted you," Claure said. "Now it's your turn to turn around and basically pay back that trust." Adam took the deal.

With the financing secured, WeWork could now fund the severance that would come with its layoffs. The era of unrestrained growth was over, even if certain things remained the same. Everything still had a code name, and the layoff plan was no different. It went by Huxley. WeWork had entered a brave new world.

In the coming months, the company that Adam built slowly came apart, and the people inside it drifted away. Minson and Gunningham stepped aside as co-CEOs, replaced by Sandeep Mathrani, an experienced real estate executive. Several WeWork employees had left to join smaller coworking companies elsewhere, or to start one of their own. Rebekah eventually bought the rights to WeGrow's curriculum, so that she could start her own school, which she intended to do under the name SOLFL. As a cost-cutting measure, WeWork decided to end its lease at 154 Grand Street, where everything had started.

A few months after Adam's departure, Miguel stopped cold while walking past a neon sign on the wall at 222 Broadway, WeWork's old Gordon Gekko headquarters. The sign read, DON'T QUIT YOUR DAYDREAM. Miguel had stayed at WeWork after his cofounder's ouster, but it was even less clear what role he could play now. There was some thought given to Miguel taking over as chief product officer, getting his hands back into the physical design of WeWork's spaces, but Miguel didn't want to go back to his old job.

In June of 2020, Miguel announced that he was leaving WeWork. He had become especially moved by the Black Lives Matter movement that had reached a new fervor that spring. "I am complicit in and benefit from structural racism," he wrote on Instagram. He promised to do more to fight broader injustice. WeWork, however, was giving up on pushing cultural transformation. Miguel's chief culture officer position would not be filled. The company was now a humble landlord.

* * *

STRIPPED OF THE JOB he poured himself into for more than a decade, Adam didn't know what to do. He holed up in Gramercy, where *Vanity Fair* reported that he kept a card on his desk to remind himself of three lessons he hoped to take away from his experience: *Listen. Be on time. Be a good partner.* He thought about flying to Tokyo to see Masa and writing a letter to his employees, but WeWork's new management asked him not to.

When Travis Kalanick was pushed out of Uber, in 2017, his ouster was met with protest from employees who couldn't imagine the company without him. But Adam had managed to upset practically every person at WeWork, from his executive team down to the new community manager in Johannesburg he never got to meet. In a matter of six weeks, Adam's bluster, antics, and delusions of grandeur had been revealed as both the reason why he was able to persuade investors and employees that, just maybe, this office-space company could change the world—and the primary reason why things fell apart. Employees and WeWork share-holders alike blanched at the fact that SoftBank was giving Neumann a billion-dollar exit package just to get him out the door.

And yet as WeWork employees surveyed the wreckage, they couldn't help feeling that Neumann wasn't the only one to blame. They had been assured that there were adults in the room; sometimes the adults in the room *told* them they were the adults in the room. When the *Wall Street Journal* reported that Mark Schwartz, one of SoftBank's representatives on the board, had finally grown angry enough in one recent meeting to stand up and declare, "I've stayed silent too long," the sentiment felt as if it was coming far too late to be taken seriously. Everyone around Adam had been too afraid to challenge him, or had chosen to enable his ambitions so long as the company and the value of their stake in it went up and up. Whatever adults were in the room were no more to be trusted than the kids. "They're trying to make this about Adam being a lunatic," one real estate executive told me a few days after Neumann resigned. "These people invested, they knew the terms, they knew about the governance issues, and they told this guy, 'Be you, but be ten times you.' What did they expect?"

At the end of 2019, Adam, Rebekah, and their kids boarded a commercial flight from San Francisco to Israel. Nearly two decades after arriving in New York with a dream of getting rich and then going back home, Adam was doing just that. The Neumanns settled into an affluent neighborhood of Tel Aviv before moving to a larger house on the beach north of the city, not far from where Arie Eigenfeld, Adam's driving instructor, made his prediction about Adam's future. He had become a laughingstock in New York, but in Israel, strangers embraced Adam and restaurant owners bought his meals—the local boy made good. If Adam went back to Nir Am, the kibbutz where he grew up, he would have seen the fruits of his labor sprouting: the dining hall where he once ate meals had been converted into a coworking space.

A few months later, in late February of 2020, Asher Gold, the latest in a series of spokespeople to take on the job of representing the most infamous man in business, reached out to ask if I would be interested in talking with Adam. No one expected Adam to leave New York forever, having gotten a taste of the success his skills could bring, and Gold wanted to set up an off-the-record call in advance of a possible meeting in the city.

But the call never happened, and Adam's return to New York was delayed. If Adam's billion-dollar parachute represented the climax to a decade of excess and growth, Covid-19, which had just begun its rampage around the world, brought an end to that era for good. Everything had changed for WeWork all over again. With the world mired in lockdown and uncertainty, SoftBank reneged on its deal. It was now refusing to buy the $3 billion worth of shares that would fund Adam's exit package, citing various issues—including investigations into WeWork's IPO that had been launched by the SEC, the Justice Department, and several state attorneys general. Adam promptly sued his old benefactor. As of this writing, the fate of his billion-dollar package was up to the courts.

A few weeks after pulling the deal, Masa gave his fiscal year report to SoftBank's shareholders. There were no tickets being handed out to events like this one anymore, and it was no longer clear that people would have wanted to attend even if they could. SoftBank had posted an operating loss of more than $12 billion—its first loss of any kind in fifteen years. Masa's second Vision Fund was teetering, but he asked for patience: on a conference call with investors, Masa said that he may be underappreciated in his time, much like Jesus Christ.

During his presentation, Masa came to a slide showing several unicorns running up a hill. Halfway to the top, several of them fell into an unforeseen ditch: the Valley of Coronavirus. The good news was that he remained hopeful that some of his Vision Fund bets were well positioned for the future, and when he clicked to the next slide, it showed one of the unicorns sprouting wings. WeWork did not seem likely to take flight. SoftBank was marking down its investment to a new low—$2.9 billion, or just 6 percent of its valuation a year earlier. After all that, WeWork was worth roughly as much as IWG.

Neumann had built the perfect business for the 2010s: filling acres of vacated real estate with armies of newly minted freelancers, then convincing big companies that they wanted in on this communitarian spirit while embracing the glut of global capital that allowed anyone with a dream and some guts to make a go at building a behemoth. But after a decade of success, a force more powerful than Adam's personality had emerged, revealing the paradox at the company's heart all along. "The time when community is measured is actually times of trouble," Adam said back in 2015. But Adam had never built the networked community he had promised. The business as it actually was depended on squeezing people into smaller and smaller spaces— a pandemic nightmare. In the spring, as cities shut down, WeWork was forcing its members to continue paying for offices they couldn't use while pressing its own landlords to lower the rent it was paying. David Zar, who had rented Neumann his second building over a bottle of Johnnie Walker Black, politely told the company that he would hold

WeWork to its word, just as Adam had once done with him. Capitalism had been unable to save the kibbutz, and the community spirit of the company dissolved—the physical social network having been ripped apart by a virus.

* * *

WHAT WOULD HAVE happened if Adam had never met Masa? WeWork would likely be a public company, having run out of private money sometime in 2017 and listed its shares at a valuation somewhere in the teens. Its growth would have slowed, and the buildings that were reaching maturity would have been kicking off significant revenue. There would have been little time, money, or freedom to launch a school and a gym, or to make multiple investments in coffee creamers. Whether Adam would have stuck around is another question. WeWork's shareholders might have pushed to replace him with a steadier hand, or he might have come to the realization that the company was no longer the place for him. He was a visionary and a salesman, not an operator. In the end, he may have just gotten bored.

It was hard to figure out what lesson Adam, or the entrepreneurs of the future, should learn from his rise and fall. (When I met up with Stella Templo for Chinese food, her fortune cookie read: "Forget things that aren't worth remembering.") There were warnings about the kinds of behavior that modern capitalism rewards—the excess and myopia of the venture capital ecosystem—as well as age-old reminders about the dangers of hubris. But there was also a blueprint for a certain kind of success. As a test, one prominent Silicon Valley venture capitalist began asking start-up founders what they thought of Adam; the correct answer was to recognize his faults while acknowledging the unbelievable thing he had done.

Back in 2010, when Adam and Miguel started WeWork and Masa presented his three-hundred-year vision, the SoftBank founder pointed out that the planet had gone through five great extinctions. The rapidly cooling earth had eliminated 70 percent of life 440 million years ago, at the end of the Ordovician period, and changes in the ocean did similar damage eighty million years later. Meteors and volcanic activity made another dent in the population 250 million years ago, while an event 65 million years ago wiped out even more. By the time Masa announced his Vision Fund, 99.9 percent of every species that had ever lived on the planet had gone extinct.

Masa's point was that companies went through similar extinction periods. True visionaries didn't let disasters derail their ambitions. They survived and evolved. For now, Adam was stuck at home, his skills temporarily neutralized in a world where getting into a room and charming an audience was no longer possible. No one knew what the post-Neumannian period would look like, but unless the ironclad forces of capitalism had truly been broken, it seemed likely that someone, somewhere, would be willing to take a chance on a charismatic man with a vision. If Adam could take one final lesson from his former mentor, sooner rather than later, he'd be back.

AUTHOR'S NOTE

This book is the culmination of eighteen months of reporting that began in early 2019, when I started working on an article for *New York* magazine that was eventually titled "The I in We." This account is based on more than two hundred interviews with many of WeWork's most senior executives; employees at all levels and in every department; the landlords and investors who bolstered the company's rise; the bankers, lawyers, and advisers who worked on its failed IPO; and Adam Neumann's friends, critics, admirers, and rivals. I've drawn from these interviews, as we all interviews given to other journalists, as well as various documents, legal complaints, internal emails and recordings, contemporaneous news reports, and other materials in recreating events.

Many WeWork employees were eager to share their stories. When I set up a meeting with one former employee, after the company's IPO collapsed, he suggested that we go ahead and meet at a WeWork. What was there to be afraid of anymore? He wanted to show me that the password that he used to get free printing on the company's printers hadn't changed in the four years since he left WeWork. He also wanted to make sure the fullest possible account of this saga was told. Many others would only speak to me on the condition of anonymity, fearing reprisal, or embarrassment, or simply wishing to move on to a new chapter of their lives. The stories they all told encapsulate not only a company but an era—the venture-capital-funded start-up boom of the 2010s. At the time of this writing, that moment has come to a close. Adam Neumann, WeWork, and SoftBank remain mired in a legal dispute over its spoils, and a new era much like the recession that launched WeWork is just beginning.

ACKNOWLEDGMENTS

Thank you first to the WeWork employees who lived this book and were willing to share their experiences with me. Many of them did so for hours on end, over multiple interviews, and with little to gain other than—as many of them put it—the opportunity to use our conversation as a free therapy session. This book would not have been possible without you.

This account would also be incomplete without the work of my many journalistic colleagues, especially: Eliot Brown, Maureen Farrell, and my college roommate, David Benoit, at the *Wall Street Journal*; Ellen Huet at *Bloomberg*; Katrina Brooker and Sarah Kessler at *Fast Company*; the staffs of *The Real Deal, Business Insider,* and *The Information*; Moe Tkacik at *Bustle*; David Gelles and Amy Chozick at the *New York Times*; Brendan O'Connor for *The Awl*; Eric Platt at the *Financial Times*; Thomas Hobbs of *Property Week*; the producers of the podcast *WeCrashed*; and many others. Gideon Lewis-Krauss, Ariel Levy, Marisa Meltzer, Gabriel Sherman, and Andrew Rice were particularly generous fellow travelers on the WeWork beat.

Thank you to Savannah Lewis, Ramsey Khabbaz, and Timmy Facciola for their help researching this book, and Mairav Zonszein for swift work in Israel. Bridget Read, my colleague at *New York* magazine, conducted deft reporting on the early life of Rebekah Neumann. Brendan Lowe tracked down Miguel McKelvey's college basketball coach. Peter Lachman helped me understand the world of finance. I'm deeply grateful to Jake Bittle, who did remarkable work under considerable pressure to make sure this book is as accurate as it can be.

Many people have helped me along the way in my journalism career. An incomplete list includes Kevin Armstrong, Don Troop, Brad Wolverton, Eric Nusbaum, Mike Hofman, David Owen, Peter Canby, Blake Eskin, Amy Davidson, Susan Morrison, Ben McGrath, Nick Paumgarten, David Remnick, Willing Davidson, and many others. I'm especially grateful to everyone at *New York* magazine, which has been my professional home for half a decade. Noreen Malone brought me into the fold and shepherded "The I in We" into existence. Max Read edited its sequel from start to finish in a matter of days. Nick Tabor, Liz Boyd, and the magazine's fact-checking department have saved me countless times. And for their good humor and support: James Walsh, Allison Davis, Molly Fischer, Ruth Spencer, Lisa Miller, and the members of the *New York* magazine editorial union's bargaining committee. Thank you to Adam Moss for allowing me to write for his magazine and to David Haskell for taking it to new heights. Thank you to Ann Clarke for giving me the time that I needed to write this book. I'm grateful to Pam Wasserstein for her family's stewardship, and to Jim Bankoff and Vox Media for continuing the magazine's proud tradition.

Chris Parris-Lamb leaped at the chance to make this book happen, and Vanessa Mobley believed in my ability to do it, despite various obstacles along the way. Thank you to Barbara Clark for her copy editing and to Ben Allen and Tom Louie for making sure everything got done. I'm grateful to Elizabeth Gassman and Sarah Bolling for all manner of things, and to Lena Little and Ira Boudah for getting the book into the world. Thank you to Rebecca Gardner, Caspian Dennis, and Huw Armstrong for bringing it to the UK.

For guidance in work and life, I'm grateful to the Thursday Crew— Rob Fischer, Jessica Weisberg, and especially Katia Bachko, who braved quarantine and a toddler to read an early version of this book. Housing and moral support in trying times were provided by Nick Salter and Anthony Mercurio; Kylee Sunderlin and Lara Finkbeiner; and Luke and Jenna Oehlerking. Carolyn Wiedeman took care of my cat. KK Apple and Casey Pugh took care of so many things that I lost count. Thank you to all of my friends and family in Kansas City, New York, and beyond.

Throughout the writing of this book, I thought often of my mother, Fifi Wiedeman, who showed me what a real community looks like and how much work has to go into building one. I miss you every day. Dad, Sam, and Katie—I love you all so much. And thank you most of all to Lauren Green, whose heart and intellect can be found in every word of this book.

INDEX

ABOUT THE AUTHOR

Reeves Wiedeman is a contributing editor at *New York* magazine. He has written for *The New Yorker,* the *New York Times Magazine, Rolling Stone, Harper's,* and other publications. This is his first book.